Martin Wegenau

Englische Übungsgrammatik

ademo

Englische Übungsgrammatik

ISBN 978-3-86715-350-8

Genehmigte Ausgabe für ademo.

Vorwort

Die **Englische Übungsgrammatik** ist ein lehrbuchunabhängiges Übungsbuch mit mehr als 4.500 Übungssätzen. Die Übungsgrammatik eignet sich für Schüler ab dem 2. oder 3. Lernjahr, fortgeschrittene Volkshochschüler, Studenten und Selbstlerner, da sich der Schwierigkeitsgrad der Übungssätze von einfachen Übungssätzen am Anfang bis zu schwierigen Übungssätzen am Schluss einer Übung steigert. Somit haben Sie die Möglichkeit die Ihrem Kenntnisstand entsprechenden Sätze zu lösen.

Besonderer Wert wurde auf einen *übersichtlichen* Aufbau gelegt, denn Übersichtlichkeit erleichtert entscheidend das Lernen und beugt Verständnisschwierigkeiten vor.
So wurde stets darauf geachtet, dass die Einsparung von ein paar wenigen Seiten im Endeffekt, nicht auf Kosten der Übersichtlichkeit ging.

Hierzu tragen auch die klaren Arbeitshinweise am Anfang jeder Übung bei sowie - am Ende jedes Kapitels - die Verweise auf die Seite, auf der die entsprechenden Lösungen im Anhang zu finden sind.
Im Lösungsteil im Anhang dieses Buches finden Sie die richtige Lösung *zu jedem einzelnen* Übungssatz und nicht nur zu den ersten Übungssätzen der ersten Übungen. Im Lösungsteil befinden sich zusätzlich zur Auflösung jedes einzelnen Übungssatzes auch die entsprechenden *Erklärungen* zu *jeder* Übung. Dies hilft Ihnen zu verstehen, warum Ihre Lösung falsch war.

Jede Übung ist so gestaltet, dass das Wesentliche eines grammatischen Themas deutlich wird. Daher wurde nicht nur eine Übungsart, wie zum Beispiel Einsetzübungen, gewählt. Zusätzlich macht die unterschiedliche Gestaltung der Übungen das Lernen abwechslungsreich.

Ferner sind die grammatischen Kapitel in einzelne Lernschritte, die in den einzelnen Übungen verarbeitet wurden, unterteilt. Dies bietet Ihnen zum einen zahlreiche Übungsmöglichkeiten und zum anderen die Möglichkeit Ihre Schwächen genau zu lokalisieren, um diese dann ganz gezielt auszumerzen.

Die Kennzeichnung schwieriger Übungssätze und solcher die typische Fehler bergen mit einem Ausrufezeichen sind weitere entscheidende Vorteile, denn dies hilft Ihnen typische Fehlerquellen in Zukunft zu erkennen und solche Fehler somit zu vermeiden.

Verfasser und Verlag

Inhaltsverzeichnis

Inhaltsverzeichnis

Inhaltsverzeichnis

Abkürzungen und Symbole

Angespro.	Angesprochener
Conditional Perf.	conditional perfect
Cont. Form	continuous form
Dir. Rede	direkte Rede
Indir. Rede	indirekte Rede
Past Perf. Simple	past perfect simple
Past T. Simple	past tense simple
Pres. Perf. Simp.	present perfect simple
Pres. T. Simp.	present tense simple
s.o.	someone
s.th.	something
	das Ausrufezeichen kennzeichnet Sätze, die typische Fehler bergen, es soll dazu beitragen, dass solch typische Fehlerquellen erkannt werden und solche Fehler damit vermieden werden

DAS VERB

Die Konjugation (The Conjugation)

Die Konjugation der Verben

1 Fill in the missing verb forms using the personal pronoun that is indicated.

Infinitive	Pres. T. Simp.	Past T. Simple	Pres. Perf. Simp.	Past Perf. Simple
1.				
2.				
3.	it happens			
4.				
5.	you fight			
6.				
7.				
8.	she hates			
9.				
10.				
11.				
12.				
13.				
14.				
15.				
16.	he stands			
17.				
18.	she prefers			

Future Tense	Future Perfect	Conditional	Conditional Perf.	Cont. Form
		she would stay		
		he would plan		
		you would listen		
he will wash				
she will mix				
you will permit				
you will regret				
she will visit				
		they would like		
he will teach				
		she would play		
she will miss				
		she would tell		

Infinitive	Pres. T. Simp.	Past T. Simple	Pres. Perf. Simp.	Past Perf. Simple
19.				
20.				
21.	I refer			
22.				
23.	he suffers			
24.				
25.				
26.				
27.		he watched		
28.	we get			
29.				
30.				
31.	you spring			
32.				
33.				
34.				
35.				
36.	we make			
37.				
38.	you leave			
39.	I believe			
40.				

Future Tense	Future Perfect	Conditional	Conditional Perf.	Cont. Form
you will answer				
		they would cover		
I will remember				
		she would read		
		I would change		
		I would promise		
		he would lie		
		he would lay		
he will continue				
		I would ring		
		he would arrive		
		she would reply		
they will behave				
		I would feel		

DAS VERB

Infinitive	Pres. T. Simp.	Past T. Simple	Pres. Perf. Simp.	Past Perf. Simple
41.	he bursts			
42.	I smile			
43.				
44.				
45.	I live			
46.	we grow			
47.				
48.				
49.	they send			
50.				
51.				
52.	he sets			
53.	we draw			
54.				
55.				
56.				
57.				
58.				
59.				
60.				
61.				
62.				

Future Tense	Future Perfect	Conditional	Conditional Perf.	Cont. Form
		she would touch		
		she would carry		
she will advise				
you will build				
		he would do		
		she would catch		
he will pass				
		we would be		
I will be				
		you would be		
he will be				
he will sing				
		he would destroy		
		he would control		
		I would quarrel		

DAS VERB

Infinitive	Pres. T. Simp.	Past T. Simple	Pres. Perf. Simp.	Past Perf. Simple
63.				
64.				
65.				
66.				
67.				
68.				
69.				
70.				
71.				
72.			she has guessed	
73.				
74.				
75.				
76.	they sit			
77.	we think			
78.				
79.				
80.				
81.				
82.				
83.				
84.	you run			

Future Tense	Future Perfect	Conditional	Conditional Perf.	Cont. Form
		they would travel		
		they would use		
we will move				
I will recognise				
		they would mean		
		he would bring		
you will love				
they will know				
I will imagine				
you will describe				
		she would keep		
you will notice				
		she would try		
		she would enjoy		
he will push				
		I would meet		
		he would reach		
he will buy				

DAS VERB

Infinitive	Pres. T. Simp.	Past T. Simple	Pres. Perf. Simp.	Past Perf. Simple
85.				
86.				
87.	we begin			
88.				
89.		I was born		
90.		she bore		
91.				
92.				
93.				
94.				
95.				
96.				
97.	she supposes			
98.				
99.	you throw			
100.				
101.	we swim			
102.				
103.				
104.				
105.	he hurts			
106.				

Future Tense	Future Perfect	Conditional	Conditional Perf.	Cont. Form
		she would see		
		we would lend		
we will wake				
he will find				
he will die				
you will shake				
we will give				
he will hurry				
		we would decide		
		she would cry		
		I would learn		
he will hold				
		he would have		
I will have				
		she would lose		

DAS VERB

Infinitive	Pres. T. Simp.	Past T. Simple	Pres. Perf. Simp.	Past Perf. Simple
107.				
108.				
109.				
110.				
111.	it costs			
112.	she develops			
113.	she stops			
114.			she has wished	
115.	you hear			
116.	you eat			
117.				
118.	I agree			
119.	I hope			
120.				
121.	you break			
122.				
123.				
124.				
125.				
126.	he cuts			
127.				
128.				

Future Tense	Future Perfect	Conditional	Conditional Perf.	Cont. Form
		she would wear		
she will finish				
he will satisfy				
		I would drive		
		I would show		
		I would speak		
we will realize				
he will fall				
they will drink				
		she would come		
he will beat				
he will steal				

DAS VERB

Infinitive	Pres. T. Simp.	Past T. Simple	Pres. Perf. Simp.	Past Perf. Simple
129.				
130.	we dream			
131.				
132.				
133.				
134.	she lets			
135.	he puts			
136.				
137.				
138.				
139.				
140.	he shuts			
141.	she hits			
142.	we forbid			
143.				
144.				

☞ Die entsprechenden Lösungen befinden sich im Lösungsheft auf Seite 8ff.

Future Tense	Future Perfect	Conditional	Conditional Perf.	Cont. Form
		he would go		
they will take				
he will worry				
he will say				
I will spend				
he will choose				
I will sleep				
they will write				
they will forget				
		she would fly		

Kurzformen (Contractions)

1 Put the following verbs into the corresponding short forms.

Bejahte Kurzform	have	had	be	will/ shall	would/ should
I					
you					
he, she, it					
we					
you					
they					

2 Put the following verbs into the corresponding short forms.

Verneinte Kurzform	have	had	be	was	will/ shall	would/ should	do	did
I								
you								
he, she, it								
we								
you								
they								

☞ Die entsprechenden Lösungen befinden sich im Lösungsheft auf Seite 16.

Das Hilfsverb to do (The Auxiliary Verb to do)

To do im verneinten Satz

1 Make the following sentences negative with the verbs in the present tense simple.

1. They **(show)** their feelings so easily.
2. Many people **(like)** Peggy, but she can be very charming to her friends.
3. You **(seem)** to like my idea.
4. Barbara **(like)** grapefruits.
5. Southern Ireland, which is called Eire, **(belong)** to the U. K.
6. It **(make)** sense.
7. I told you. It **(help)** at all.
8. He **(do)** anything.
9. I **(have)** time for these games.
10. **(Say)** that!
11. We can't do any skiing here because we **(get)** enough snow.
12. Everyone says that the English are so reserved and cold, but I **(find)** them so at all.
13. My mother **(go)** to work as she is kept very busy in the house.
14. Mr Barton **(wish)** to be disturbed.
15. The Queen reigns, but she **(rule).**
16. He **(take)** any interest in reading.
17. The passing motorist **(have)** time to read more than six words on a poster.
18. **(Do)** that!
19. If you **(play)** fair in life, people will say that you are a bad sport.
20. **(Keep)** asking me!

21. The computer **(compare)** with the human brain in handling data that haven't yet jelled.

2 Make the following sentences negative with the verbs in the past tense simple.

1. They **(send)** us a postcard.
2. Richard **(listen)**.
3. She **(write)** because I hadn't told her my new address.
4. Mike **(wait)** for the others because he **(feel)** well.
5. I **(sleep)** that night.
6. She **(leave)** a letter of any kind.
7. Jack **(obey)** his father.
8. Ben was frightened he would miss his plane if he **(find)** his ticket soon.
9. He **(have)** a chance to say any more. Doctor Richardson interrupted him.
10. I certainly **(do)** so.
11. In her hurry to escape, she **(notice)** a fallen branch that lay across the path.
12. I **(hear)** any more, as I went away.
13. The landing was worse than the take-off, but it **(last)** long.
14. We ran as fast as we could. But we **(catch)** the train.
15. The driver **(stop)** at the crossing. He went on at full speed.
16. If she **(quiet)** herself, she would certainly faint.
17. I **(explain)** why I thought Harry's idea all wrong.
18. I am quite sure Smith **(do)** the murder.
19. What a pity I **(have)** time to meet Bill and Claire.

3 Make the following sentences - containing an auxiliary verb - negative.

1. I **(have decided)** yet.

2. Andrew **(had told)** anybody where he was living.
3. He **(had left)** a message to tell his father where he had gone.
4. He **(has forgotten)** to ring me up.
5. He **(has had)** time.
6. I **(am)** fond of walking.
7. I**('m allowed)** to tell you.
8. I'm sorry I **(was)** at home when you called yesterday.
9. Let's walk home from here. It **(is)** far.
10. Thank you very much for your last letter, I'm so sorry that I **(have replied)** for so long.
11. The driver **(had waited)** for them.
12. You **(are allowed)** to smoke here.
13. You **(were)** very careful.
14. You must admit you **(have been)** there.
15. A number of people were interviewed by the police, but it **(has been found)** out how the accident happened.
16. We**('re doing)** very well.
17. This problem **(has been solved)** satisfactorily.
18. Meals **(are served)** on short distance flights.
19. I hope my English **(is)** too difficult to understand.
20. They **(were)** guilty of the crimes they were charged with.
21. I **(am)** likely to fail in my duty.
22. It **(is)** what he's done, but what he's likely to do.
23. If it **(were)** for the people who have encouraged me already, I don't think I would ever make it.

4 Make the following sentences - containing a modal auxiliary verb - negative.

1. It's too bad that I **(can read)** that French letter.
2. She **(could remember)** my name.
3. You **(may be)** sure, but I am.
4. I think I'll ring him up first: he **(might be)** at home.
5. The man at the gate said he **(could let)** Mike through without a ticket.
6. We **(must get)** impatient.
7. We **(shall know)** until next year.
8. I **(can come)** to the playground because I must repair my bike.
9. We **(can do)** anything more, but we **(must give up).**
10. You **(ought to smoke)** here.
11. I'm afraid there **(will be)** time for that.
12. The town was building a new sewer system so that rains **(should flood)** the roads.
13. Mother **(will mind)** if I give you something to eat afterwards.
14. My Dad said that he **(would like)** to drive such a huge lorry, he prefers his taxi.
15. Their expectations **(may have been)** realistic enough.
16. If the driver had watched the traffic more carefully, the accident **(might have happened)**.
17. You **(should have given)** the flowers so much water.
18. You **(would believe)** me when I said that she poisoned her husband.
19. You must put a coat on, but you **(need take)** an umbrella along.
20. I told Benjamin to make sure that we **(should be interrupted)**.
21. She **(ought to have said)** that.
22. We **(shall always expect)** to find them supporting our view.

23. You **(need have troubled)** yourself.

5 Make the following sentences negative with the verbs in the present tense simple and use **to do** where necessary.

1. I **(have)** any needles.
2. I **(can tell)** you where he was.
3. Anyway my husband **(must find)** you here.
4. You **(should talk)** about Mrs Collins.
5. The boy believes that he **(do)** anything wrong.
6. John and Jack **(could hear)** what else the people were saying.
7. At twelve o'clock you **(might be)** here.
8. I **(shall go)** to the office until noon.
9. So far I **(have had)** any car to drive.
10. Even the rich **(have got)** everything they need.
11. Sheila Winters **(will be able)** to come to school today.
12. She **(ought to lie)** in the sun nowadays.
13. Do you know the old proverb: Barking dogs **(bite)?**
14. I **(get)** the impression that you were rich.
15. The working housewife **(need)** to spend too long in the kitchen when she returns home.
16. You may well do one thing and **(need leave)** the other.
17. You **(need worry)** about me.
18. We just **(need)** this.
19. One way to see a film is to go to a 'drive-in movie', where you **(need)** to leave your car.
20. Nothing seems to have been disarranged, and the drawers **(have been interfered)** with.

21. To be ordered about **(was)** his idea of a free life.

22. His memories **(were)** continuous.

23. He **(would sit)** here for an hour thinking.

24. He threw remarks at the silent Philip - remarks that **(need)** an answer.

25. Boys and girls of 16 **(need be looked after)** all the time.

To do im Fragesatz

1 Make the following sentences interrogative with the verbs in the present tense simple.

1. Harry knows what you're doing.
2. Buses run on Sundays.
3. German people eat a lot of potatoes.
4. Mrs Summers teaches music.
5. She wants to go out this evening.
6. This little bag has to be weighed too.
7. You have a job for me.
8. You know William.
9. You like dogs.
10. You really expect me to do a stupid thing like that.
11. You think I did it.
12. You want the porter to carry your bags upstairs.
13. Your brother likes dancing.
14. Your friend knows my uncle.
15. You think people like having their secrets screwed out of them.
16. He regrets having studied so hard.

17. Drivers have to have a licence.
18. Drivers have to give way to ambulances.
19. A scientist has to think about possible consequences of his work.
20. Your tyre wants blowing up.
21. The translation does justice to the meaning of the original.

2 Make the following sentences interrogative with the verbs in the past tense simple.

1. You caught many fish.
2. You got many birthday presents.
3. You bought your groceries at the supermarket.
4. You fed monkeys at the zoo.
5. You slept in a tent.
6. You saw lions at the zoo.
7. Peggy found the right articles.
8. You went to school in Boston.
9. He really said that.
10. You got hurt.
11. It hurt.
12. You read the paper yesterday.
13. You tried to analyse it.
14. You sent Tom a postcard.
15. You had a good time.
16. Your aunt died and left you a fortune.
17. He really had all the good qualities he thought he had.

18. They received the benefits to which they were entitled.

19. You knew that American and English people often use different words to mean the same thing.

20. He did it to her.

3 Make the following sentences - containing an auxiliary verb - interrogative.

1. He was seasick.
2. Linda had gone.
3. You are afraid of mice.
4. Your uncle has got a car.
5. It is necessary to copy all this material.
6. You were able to see him before he left.
7. You are getting on well at school.
8. It has stopped raining yet.
9. She is hurt.
10. You have spent your holidays in a castle.
11. They were friends of yours.
12. He had been drinking.
13. He was wanted for a serious crime.
14. It was likely she would be dismissed for disturbing some papers.
15. You have got some cigarettes with you.
16. The fellow had stopped when I commanded him to do so.
17. You have heard of someone so stupid.
18. The new rocket has sufficiently been tested.
19. I am not right.

20. I am supposed to stand here for good.

4 Make the following sentences - containing a modal auxiliary verb - interrogative.

1. We can go now.
2. You could shut the window.
3. I may borrow your umbrella.
4. I might use your phone.
5. You must get up early tomorrow.
6. We should go in there.
7. You will take me to the station.
8. You would do it.
9. I may come along with you.
10. You must smoke.
11. That would be wise.
12. We shall have lunch here.
13. You can lend me a hand.
14. I could have another drink.
15. We shall do the dishes now.
16. The flow of newcomers should be diminished.
17. You will do what I order.
18. You will stop interfering.
19. I shall make some coffee.

5 Make the following sentences interrogative and use **to do** where necessary.

1. You have asked Dr Miller to be present.

2. Columbus discovered America.
3. He has been here for some time.
4. Henry could see the man's face properly.
5. I shall post this letter for you.
6. Mike's business was a success.
7. The pigeons you see in front of St Paul's Cathedral are not afraid of people.
8. They serve a meal on the plane.
9. We had switched the radio off.
10. Your mother writes with her left hand.
11. Your sister talks in her sleep.
12. The gang of eight or nine boys, aged around 18, have been caught.
13. The present owner hasn't got enough money to keep the place up.
14. Things have been going well with you.
15. I wonder why Ken hasn't turned up yet. He may have had an accident.
16. It doesn't mean anything to you.
17. She hadn't been invited.
18. The matter hasn't yet been put to the test.
19. He doesn't tell us anything.
20. You didn't pay any attention to it.
21. The private TV stations, mainly supported by the viewers' fees, broadcast nearly any advertising.

6 Make the following sentences interrogative with the verbs in brackets in the present tense simple.

1. Whom you **(believe)**?

2. What your mother usually **(drink)** for breakfast: tea or coffee?
3. When you usually **(get up)**?
4. When the plane **(leave)**?
5. Where your mother usually **(buy)** her groceries?
6. Why **(have)** giraffes such long necks?
7. What an architect **(do)**?
8. Who **(belong to)** this black bag?
9. Which bus I **(have to)** take to Big Ben, please?
10. What else you **(do)**?
11. What you **(want)** to be?
12. When you usually **(have)** breakfast?
13. Where he **(want)** me to put the bag?
14. Which rules he **(not obey)**?
15. What your breakfast usually **(consist of)**?
16. What the National Health Service **(do)**?
17. Which of the mass media you **(consider)** the most entertaining?
18. Who you **(think)** is to be blamed for Miller's failure to get the job?
19. Who you **(take)** me for?
20. Which condition he **(add)** to his choice?
21. What reasons a trainer **(give)** for active sportsmen disregarding the rules of fair play?

7 Make the following sentences interrogative with the verbs in brackets in the past tense simple.

1. Who she **(marry)**?
2. What the burglar **(do)** after he'd slipped into the house?

3. What he **(mean)** by this?
4. What she **(look like)**?
5. What he **(wish)** to do?
6. What you **(say)**?
7. When you **(come)** home yesterday?
8. Who you **(send)** it to?
9. What she **(die of)**?
10. What he **(have to)** do that evening?
11. Why the children **(keep standing)** in the shadows?
12. Why the Americans **(make)** Washington their first President?
13. What the knights **(live on)**?
14. Why Linda Adams **(ask)** Dr Robins for news of Philip Doyle?
15. Whom Mr Brown **(suspect of)** being the thief?
16. What you **(see)** him do after that?
17. What Mr Adams **(tell)** Linda and the officer to do?
18. What the captain **(make)** Humphrey say?
19. Where the girl **(ask)** him to come?
20. How you **(do)** your washing on board?
21. What the judge **(find)** Jack Smith guilty of?

8 Make the following sentences interrogative using the interrogative pronouns that are indicated.

1. He gave her that lovely ring. - Who .....?
2. The boy in the blue jacket broke the window? - Which of the boys .....?
3. He goes there. - Who .....?

4. The Anglo-Saxons invaded England after the Romans. - Who .....?
5. Susan invited Mike and Walter to tea. - Who .....?
6. The policeman knows the way to the station. - Who .....?
7. Mr Clarke left the house first. - Who .....?
8. Peter married her. - Who .....?
9. My sister read English books. - Who .....?
10. Peter reads aloud. - Who .....?
11. Columbus discovered America. - Who .....?
12. My father rode the old bicycle. - Who .....?
13. I sent you a postcard. - Who .....?
14. My mother taught him that. - Who .....?
15. Something strange happened when John, his father, and Mr Robins were chatting in the office. What .....?
16. His strange behaviour irritated her about him. - What .....?
17. His strange voice made her notice Dr Williams. - What .....?
18. Changing situations in life move people to change their habitual ideas and attitudes? What .....?
19. The director general gives her the list of names as a binding suggestion. – Who .....?
20. Having won the race gives him a sense of satisfaction. - What .....?
21. Their fantasy made people think that there may be intelligent beings on Mars? What .....?

9 Make the following sentences - containing an auxiliary verb - interrogative using the interrogative pronouns that are indicated.

1. Your wife is in the garden. - Where .....?
2. I'm leaving at six o'clock. - When .....?

3. She was born in 1900? - When .....?
4. You were doing your homework there. - What .....?
5. He has come back to get his glasses. - Why .....?
6. You have been doing my homework. - What .....?
7. You have often been to the pictures since last Sunday. - How often .....?
8. Mr Green had spent the previous evening reading. - How .....?
9. The city of London has impressed me most during my stay in England. - What .....?
10. He was promising to come back early. - What .....?
11. I will go to the cinema next Sunday. - Where .....?
12. I would like to spend my next holidays in Spain. - Where .....?
13. These are my socks. - Whose socks .....?
14. I was supposed to go in one hour. - When .....?
15. It is your bad behaviour he is accusing you of. - What .....?
16. I will be having a sandwich for lunch. - What .....?
17. It is an architects job to make plans for houses. - Whose job .....?
18. The weather was terrible. - How .....?
19. He had been arrested for having stolen my car. - What .....?

10 Make the following sentences - containing a modal auxiliary verb - interrogative using the interrogative pronouns that are indicated.

1. You can get the book in the library. - Where .....?
2. You could do that by hand. - How .....?
3. He may want your camera. - What .....?
4. You should know that by trial and error. - How .....?
5. A doctor must be sent for when somebody is ill. - Who .....?

6. In 10 years' time we shall be back in America. - When .....?

7. The advance of urbanization could be slowed down or stopped by improving the living conditions of the rural areas? - How .....?

8. Husbands might prefer staying at the plant to being at home because they don't like housework. - Why .....?

11 Make the following sentences interrogative using the interrogative pronouns that are indicated. Use **to do** where necessary.

1. He helps you with your homework. - Who .....?

2. He needs to ask her.- Who .....?

3. His strange behaviour makes her realize the situation. - What .....?

4. He could have a new cheque book. - What .....?

5. The young man with the very dark hair and eyes is Peter. - Who .....?

6. You have the rings. - Who .....?

7. Your mother needs a dishwasher. - What .....?

8. They need these apples for making cakes. - What .....?

9. I do my homework in the afternoon. - When .....?

10. People have to have their photograph in their passports. - What .....?

11. That suits you? - What .....?

12. The public has the right to hear about all the details in connection with a murder case. - Who .....?

13. She could have acted otherwise. - How .....?

14. A lot of advances have been made in the last few years in computer technology. - What .....?

15. Her forgetfulness makes her believe that she is becoming absurd and middle-aged. What .....?

16. Someone has got the books. - Who .....?

17. I have to be blamed for that? - Who .....?

18. It was always going to be like that? - How .....?

19. We can do better with all the resources of a mechanical age? - How .....?

☞ Die entsprechenden Lösungen befinden sich im Lösungsheft auf Seite 17ff.

Die Modalverben (Modal Auxiliary Verbs)

Can, could und ihre Ersatzverben

1 Put in **can, could** or their substitute **to be able to.**

1. As you ..... see, the whole place needs doing up.
2. Sheila and Susan ..... not hear what the people were saying.
3. John ..... not hold the string any more, and the kite flew away over the sea.
4. ..... you hear me?
5. I hope I will ..... write to you in German, although I don't think my German will be as good as your English.
6. I want to ..... express my opinion freely.
7. It doesn't look as if we ..... please anybody this morning.
8. Shall I help you carry the deck-chairs? No, thanks, I ..... manage.
9. Suddenly the fever rose and the boy ..... not breathe properly.
10. You must ..... move about freely.
11. Anything of value missing? Not that I ..... discover.
12. He'd just wanted me to believe he ..... not drive.
13. I ..... arrange for some money to be paid to you, if you wish.
14. I think I ..... do it if I put my mind to it.
15. I was the only person who ..... have caught him if I'd wanted to.
16. I wished I ..... swim as well as you can.
17. It hurt terribly and I ..... not walk.
18. It hurts terribly and I ..... not walk.
19. Peter ..... win a reward if he wanted to.
20. You won't ..... speak this language fluently unless you go to this country.

21. If ever I came to know that you told me a lie, I would never again ..... trust you.

22. I had the feeling that my dining there displeased her, but I ..... not imagine why.

23. No new facts came out, and the police said little as they ..... so far ..... (past perfect) to make no arrest.

24. He earns less than enough to ..... (infinitive) keep his family at an accepted standard.

25. Don't use colloquialisms without ..... (gerund) pronounce them properly.

Can, could und may, might und ihre Ersatzverben

1 Put in **can, could,** their substitute **to be able to**, or **may, might.**

1. If it goes on raining like this, we ..... not have our picnic.
2. The doctor asked Gerald to open his mouth so that he ..... have a good look at his teeth.
3. I'll move the rock and you will ..... pull your foot out.
4. Buy a lottery ticket: you ..... win £ 1,000!
5. Why didn't you drink your tea? Did you think it was too strong? No, I thought it ..... be too weak.
6. A hundred years ago, there was no problem of what working people ..... do with their spare time.
7. Since Mr Harrison has no money, he ..... not buy a new van.
8. What makes scientists believe that there ..... be life on Mars?
9. If I had a camera I ..... take a picture of your sad face.
10. I haven't decided yet. I ..... go for a bicycle ride.
11. Had the fellow stopped when I commanded him to do so, all this ..... have been avoided.
12. ..... you get Sunday afternoon off?
13. The sound I had heard ..... not have been that of a window being shut.

14. A good sport often means a man who plays games well, but it **.....** also mean a man of good character.

15. If only I **.....** do something useful.

16. Shall we **.....** reach you here for the next few days, in case there are any more questions?

17. It occurred to me that he **.....** have been listening.

18. The affluent may **.....** get out at the weekends but the poor are condemned to live within a relatively small area.

19. In order to **.....** vote in the U.S.A., you have to have your name entered in a list called the electoral register.

20. The purposes to which the laser **.....** be put are so many and so varied as to suggest magic.

21. If you were to ask her advice, she **.....** give you one.

2 Put in **can, could, may, might** or their substitutes **to be allowed to, to be permitted to.**

1. I **.....** not let you through without a ticket.
2. When the clock strikes ten, you **.....** open the envelope.
3. We **.....** take as many sweets as we liked.
4. You **.....** not have any more money this month.
5. In some states of the U.S.A. boys and girls **.....** drive a car at the age of sixteen.
6. The patient **.....** only eat meat if the doctor approves.
7. He said that he **.....** not let you do it on your own.
8. The Town Clerk suggested that Bob **.....** listen to their discussion.
9. The fact that they **.....** not **.....** do it will in no way stop them.
10. You **.....** be for whom you like.
11. The prisoner **.....** speak on his behalf.

12. He just called me up three days ago and said I **.....** use his room if I cared to.

13. The boss will have to read this before I **.....** let you put it in the shop window.

14. He said I **.....** use his hotel room for a few days, because mine happens to be so badly heated.

15. If a player is carrying the ball he **.....** be tackled and made to fall down.

16. So long as they **.....** not**.....** have standards of comparison, they never even become aware that they are oppressed.

17. Some states even passed laws that no person was **.....** (present infinitive passive) vote if his grandfather had been a slave.

Can, could und may, might und will, would

1 Put in **can, could, may, might, will, would.**

1. **.....** you give short answers to all the questions?
2. **.....** you show me how I get to Piccadilly Circus, please?
3. It's so loud. **.....** you make it quieter?
4. **.....** I use your phone?
5. Daddy, **.....** we go to the zoo?
6. **.....** you tell us where you live and what you do?
7. **.....** I have another drink?
8. **.....** you stop interfering?
9. **.....** I have a look at it?
10. **.....** you stand by me and do just as I order you?
11. **.....** you mind coming downstairs?
12. **.....** you render me a service?

13. **.....** you like me to help you?

14. **.....** you lend me a hand?

15. **.....** n't you be serious for once?

16. **.....** I express the hope, sir, that you will honour Mrs Burton and myself by a visit to our apartment?

17. **.....** you be making coffee for me?

18. **.....** you have him come up, please?

19. ..... I invite you for a drink at the hotel before you go up to your house?

Must, need und ihre Ersatzverben

1 Put in **must, need** or their substitute **have to.**

1. There isn't much bread left. Someone **.....** go to the baker's.

2. You ..... not think that I am too stupid to do that.

3. He will, of course, know what **.....** be done.

4. You **.....** not worry about me.

5. He told them that they **.....** change trains.

6. We **.....** (negative) tell him why.

7. We **.....** find a means of solving our problem.

8. ..... drivers **.....** give way to ambulances?

9. She **.....** not have told him that.

10. You **.....** see for yourself.

11. The press **.....** not invade private rights or feelings.

12. There is no escaping the fact that the exercises **.....** be done.

13. You **.....** no longer consider yourself obligated to me in any way.

14. **.....** you ever **.....** (present perfect) get up at 4.a.m.?

15. He ..... (past perfect) choose blindly between life and death.

Should, ought to und ihre Ersatzverben

1 Put in **should, ought to** or their substitute **to be supposed to.**

1. You ..... have told me the truth.
2. You've kicked the cat. You ..... be ashamed of yourself.
3. All the members of the Music Club ..... come to last week's meeting.
4. You ..... stand to attention.
5. Children ..... be listened to.
6. He ..... be pardoned this time.
7. Charles is a delicate boy whom one ..... not laugh at all the time.
8. The United States Congress consists of two houses, which ..... be equal in importance.
9. Such things ..... not be spoken about in public.
10. You ..... have known better than believe all those lies.
11. She ..... not have said that.
12. ..... I stand here for good?

2 Put in **should** or its substitutes **to be to, to want s.o. to do s.th., to be supposed to.**

1. How often have I told you that you ..... never pick up stamps with your fingers.
2. When ..... you ..... go?
3. They always said I ..... be careful.
4. You ..... not have given the flowers so much water.
5. He ..... us ..... leave the room slowly and quietly.
6. The sign said that everybody ..... go slow because there is a school ahead.

7. Where do you **.....** me **.....** put the bag with the books?

8. Do you **.....** me **.....** give the wounded men some water?

9. In the eyes of the law one **.....** not make a distinction between one person and another.

10. Councillors **.....** concentrate on policy, leaving details to the officials.

11. I certainly don't **.....** you **.....** be late.

12. Parliament alone **.....** decide which taxes **.....** be imposed.

13. It **.....** not be thought that the House of Lords is unimportant.

14. You **.....** (future tense, negative) correct your pen-friend's letters.

15. He **.....** be addressed as captain.

16. I know she would **.....** me **.....** find the criminal who drove him to death.

17. I **.....** like you to ask them for me.

18. He said that they **.....** do.

19. I **.....** have met her at the station.

20. Professional drivers **.....** not **.....** drink gin, though in practice they could get hold of it easily enough.

☞ Die entsprechenden Lösungen befinden sich im Lösungsheft auf Seite 25ff.

Die reflexiven Verben (Reflexive Verbs)

Die Formen des Reflexivpronomens

1 Put in the corresponding reflexive pronoun.

1. A selfish person thinks: first I must care for **.....** , let the others care for **.....** .
2. Aren't you ashamed of **.....** ?
3. Billy is a little too proud of **.....** .
4. When Peggy looks in the mirror, she sees **.....** .
5. We wrapped **.....** in blankets and huddled together to keep warm.
6. After a look at **.....** in the mirror he decided to shave first, and he went to the room to get his electric razor.
7. Look, some animal must have helped **.....** to the berries we picked yesterday.
8. England is only a part of the United Kingdom, which **.....** is a part of a big group of countries called the Commonwealth.
9. There's a self-service shop in our town. Customers help **.....** to things they want.
10. Do not excite **.....** .
11. Someone who wants everything for **.....** is selfish.
12. Everybody had made **.....** comfortable, only Sheila remained standing.
13. To buy a house, a person does not usually need to have all the money **.....** to pay for it.
14. It was dreadful to find **.....** alone in such a place.
15. Seating **....** on the bed, he adjusted his spectacles, and in a suffused voice began to read.
16. It is worth trying for a moment to put **.....** in the position of a foreign observer.
17. One knew that it was all rubbish so why let **.....** be worried by it?
18. Propelling ..... safely through the environment is a skill that we learn in infancy.

19. Don't let ..... be trapped in there.

Reflexive und nicht reflexive Verben

1 Put in the reflexive pronoun or the expression given in brackets.

1. You can't please **(ourselves; everybody).**
2. Next time, we'll just please **(ourselves; everybody).**

3. He often talks of **(himself; Ray Williams).**
4. Did I hear you gentlemen talk of **(himself; Ray Williams)**?

5. John is only two years old. He can't wash **(himself; your face).**
6. You must wash **(himself; your face).**

7. Why do you defend **(themselves; this criminal).**
8. The Indians tried to defend **(themselves; this criminal)** against the white enemy.

9. Luckily, the keepers were able to calm **(yourself; the tigers).**
10. Calm **(yourself; the tigers)**, madam.

11. You must hide **(yourself; messages).**
12. There aren't many places to hide **(yourself; messages).**

13. He told me to show **(themselves; her)** my passport.
14. They dare not show **(themselves; her)** by day.

2 Put in the reflexive pronoun or the expression given in brackets.

1. I will punish you if you don't behave **(yourself; -)** properly.
2. Behave **(yourself; -)**!

3. He lay back on the bed and tried to compose **(himself; his next letter).**
4. Tom began to compose **(himself; his next letter)** to them.

5. We hope you will enjoy **(yourselves; the dish).**
6. You boys enjoy **(yourselves; the dish)**!

7. Who helps **(myself; you)** with your homework?
8. He'd told me to help **(myself; you)** to his ties and jackets.

9. Tell me freely. Can we serve **(ourselves; you)**?
10. We can serve **(ourselves; you)**.

3 Translate the verbs in brackets and decide whether to use a reflexive pronoun or not. Use the present tense simple if no other tense is indicated.

1. The motorist stopped and *(sich nähern;* past tense simple) the man.
2. I can't *(sich vorstellen)* that he would ever agree to such a proposition.
3. I've got a few friends who *(sich kümmern um)* my safety.
4. She could not *(sich erinnern an)* my name.
5. He *(sich fragen;* past tense simple*)* if he would find Sheila.
6. Many people slept in the streets while homes stood empty because nobody could *(sich leisten)* the rent.
7. Mr Winters was no longer young when he *(sich verlieben in;* past tense simple*)* Shirley Adams.
8. America *(sich verändern;* present perfect simple*)* quite a lot since the first settlers arrived in the New World.
9. The receipts from a football game may *(sich belaufen auf)* $ 100,000 or more.
10. He *(sich beklagen über)* having too much to do.
11. Would you please fill up this form and then *(sich anschließen)* the queue by the door?
12. All you *(sich kümmern um)* is yourself.
13. We are *(sich freuen auf)* to seeing you.
14. You can *(sich verlassen auf)* me to stand by you if you are in trouble.

☞ Die entsprechenden Lösungen befinden sich im Lösungsheft auf Seite 30ff.

Das Verb und seine Ergänzungen (The Verb and its Complements)

1 Put in **to** where necessary.

1. Can you give short answers **.....** all the questions?
2. Do you remember **.....** me?
3. Tom gave some milk **.....** the cat.
4. Tom gave ... the cat some milk.
5. He followed **.....** the man towards an empty table at the back of the little room.
6. I asked you to come here so that we can all thank **.....** the courageous girl.
7. It is necessary that we should help **.....** the poverty-stricken areas of the world.
8. Let me see, shall I send a messenger **.....** you with the dictionary?
9. Let me see, shall I send ... you a messenger with the dictionary?
10. Mrs Miller wrote a postcard **.....** the Barton family.
11. Susan Anderson told her story **.....** her friends.
12. On Christmas Day, 1066, William, now known as 'the Conqueror', was crowned **.....** King of England in Westminster Abbey.
13. She handed the teapot **.....** her mother.
14. She handed ... her mother the teapot.
15. The prisoner refused to answer **.....** the judge's question.
16. Before introducing the teachers **.....** them, he showed them a list of the staff printed at the back of the school magazine.
17. By a new law, immigrants were allowed to enter **.....** Britain only if they had certificates to show that they had jobs waiting for them.
18. He just waved his hand **.....** me.
19. I don't believe **.....** those forgeries for one minute.

20. I heard footsteps outside, so I went up to my room just as Atkinson opened the door ..... you.

21. I see you do not trust ..... me as Linda trusts ..... me.

22. She asked me not to come at that time because her boss would be dictating a letter ..... her.

23. Some states allow ..... local communities to impose their own speed limits.

24. Technical and business colleges offer further education ..... the young workers in industry and commerce.

25. That's why I spoke ..... you the other day; I thought you might pass the message ..... him.

26. The law does not permit ..... any person or group to control more than 7 television stations for commercial use.

27. When all witnesses for the prosecution have been examined the counsel for the defence explains his case ..... the jury and calls his witnesses.

28. You can't serve ..... two masters and be at two places at the same time.

29. Generally, people readily accept the fact that obeying ..... the law is necessary for the smooth running of national and neighbourhood affairs.

30. He resented the courtesy ..... her.

31. How did Mrs Robinson come to make this confession ..... you.

32. If he fails ..... a course, he must repeat only that course.

33. I'll give the document ..... the next person to speak.

34. It was once assumed that no Catholic could hope to be elected ..... President, and when John F. Kennedy was hoping to be adopted as Democratic candidate in 1960 the fact that he was a Catholic was regarded as a disadvantage.

35. People who find that they share interests with others tend to join ..... groups and organisations which try to influence political decisions.

36. That is precisely why they seem an irrelevancy ..... us.

☞ Die entsprechenden Lösungen befinden sich im Lösungsheft auf Seite 32.

Die Zeiten (The Tenses)

Die Bildung der Zeiten

1 Put the verbs in brackets into the present tense simple.

1. What is Linda doing there? **(cry)** Peter.
2. Sport **(play)** a big part in English school life.
3. The United States **(lie)** across the Pole to the North.
4. When a forest **(catch)** fire, the air is soon polluted.
5. My children never **(wash)** behind their ears.
6. The British Museum is the biggest museum in London. It **(possess)** the finest collection of Greek and Roman art in the world.
7. Rowing, in fours or eights, **(occupy)** a leading place in the sporting life of schools.
8. If M.P.s **(die)** or **(resign)** their seat a by-election is held to replace them.
9. The concentration of newspapers **(reach)** its most extreme form in Britain.
10. The Department of Education and Science **(establish)** standards to which schools ought to conform.
11. I am certain, however, that they **(miss)** what is gone.
12. Who **(marry)** does well, who doesn't marry does better.
13. The English legal system **(enjoy)** a good reputation for fairness.
14. The origins of America's colour problem today **(lie)** in a great crime against humanity, committed long ago.
15. I cannot deny that I value in some degree the status which **(attach)** to the rank of a Consul.
16. What mostly **(distinguish)** them is their dress.

2 Put the verbs in brackets into the past tense simple.

1. Tom's mother **(try)** hard to be a good mother to him.

2. The animals Sheila **(enjoy)** most of all were the elephants.

3. Mrs Miller **(hate)** the thought of listening to her aunt's gibberish.

4. They took only one suitcase of Jack's between them, because they **(plan)** to be away only three nights.

5. Julia **(burst)** into the room.

6. I **(send)** Tom to buy some stamps.

7. He **(choose)** a hotel called the Casa Grande, very near the Rialto bridge.

8. She **(bury)** her face in her hands, then jumped up and ran from the room.

9. Tom turned the radio on to a station that **(play)** dance music.

10. I found four large pieces of board and **(tie)** them together to make a boat.

11. The United States and the western countries of Europe **(agree)** to co-operate in international affairs.

12. Mr Miller **(prefer)** his children to walk from Piccadilly Circus to St Paul's instead of taking a bus.

13. His mother, one of those massive working-class matriarchs with eight children, **(suffer)** from rheumatism.

14. This short story bears resemblances to a story I **(read)** some weeks ago.

15. We **(bend)** down and looked through the keyhole.

16. Families **(lend)** and borrowed puzzles from each other like books.

17. They **(sit)** in a café and **(drink)** a couple of Jim Beams.

18. Subjects **(teach)** in commercial classes include typing, shorthand, book-keeping, business arithmetic.

19. I **(think)** that night would never end.

20. I **(study)** him quietly without appearing to do so.

21. He **(obey)** an instinct that he did not know he possessed.

22. He **(die)** in hospital from acute alcoholic poisoning and exposure.

23. She wisely **(change)** her tactics.

24. By a tremendous effort, he **(control)** himself.

25. On account of his getting something to drink he **(recover)** fast.

26. He **(set)** himself to making some necessary things.

27. They **(lay)** the foundations of the Welfare State.

28. He **(wear)** a dark grey suit and a light blue tie.

3 Put the verbs in brackets into the present perfect simple.

1. Most college graduates **(study)** away from home.
2. New England **(play)** a very important part in the history of the United States.
3. Can either of you tell me if the Burtons **(receive)** any strangers during this past week or so?
4. He **(drop)** a vase.
5. Dad **(hit)** his head about twenty times on the doorway of the cabin.
6. Australia **(build)** one atomic reactor and is building another.
7. Machines **(become)** part of our everyday life.
8. All rulers in all ages **(try)** to impose a false view of the world upon their followers.
9. Since the second world war Australia **(enjoy)** its greatest period of economic growth.
10. The injured **(die)** from their wounds.
11. He **(have)** time.
12. Industrialization, urbanization and population growth **(cause)** environmental ills.
13. His name **(slip)** my memory for the moment.
14. The American way of speaking **(develop)** independently of England.
15. Many great industrialists **(put)** large amounts of money into foundations which sponsor all kinds of projects.

16. Only Consul Cramer **(send)** his children to private schools in search of superior education.

17. Bistros, barbecues, espresso cafés, salami-bars and smorgasbord tables **(spring)** up in the cities.

4 Put the verbs in brackets into the past perfect simple.

1. After little Billy **(try)** the ice-cream, he threw it on Ray's right shoe.
2. The first time I met her we **(play)** bridge together.
3. The patient **(die)** when he came.
4. He was a happy-go-lucky fellow and everyone **(like)** him.
5. Later he could not remember well why he **(stop)** swimming and taken in so much water.
6. This was the first time he **(travel)** so far west, and already he regretted it.
7. When Bob and his father came home, Mrs Miller wanted to know what **(happen)** at the customs office.
8. Ralph cried out as though he **(hurt)** himself.
9. Adam told Tom about Rome and the week he **(spend)** there.
10. He remembered the way he **(feel)** when he had been fired from the warehouse job.
11. I wondered whether he **(have)** friends with him.
12. Before the men could see them, the children **(hurry off)** to tell the others what they **(see).**
13. Ronald had a house in Rome, and Adam **(stay)** with him several weeks before he came to Paris.
14. They **(continue)** to stroll slowly down the corridor, but now Tom halted.
15. When he suggested it to Betty she **(agree)** with unexpected readiness.
16. She **(let)** her cigarette go out and was listening intently.
17. Cortez defeated the Aztecs who **(build)** up a civilized and wealthy state.

18. She was looking at herself proudly in the mirror when she saw that she **(forget)** her brooch.

19. His father opened the door after he **(get)** his stick ready.

20. When Charles woke up the hands of the clock **(creep)** round to nearly nine.

21. Her husband told her that Jack **(mow)** the lawn.

22. He stood up, reaching for money to pay the little tabs that the waiter **(stick)** under their coffee cups.

23. When midnight **(strike)** I couldn't stay quiet any longer and went down into the street.

5 Put the verbs in brackets into the future tense simple.

1. You're supposed to write in German, and the German pen-friends **(reply)** in English.

2. You **(receive)** orders and you **(obey)** them, without knowing why.

3. This time I **(teach)** you a lesson.

4. London **(continue)** to be a world centre of finance.

5. It is time to adopt strategies for action that **(produce)** quick and visible progress.

6. I feel sure that she **(let)** me know.

7. I **(put)** it more precisely.

8. I **(give)** you the money on condition that you spend it sensibly.

9. A drowning man **(catch)** at a straw.

10. He **(live)** to be ninety, he is so strong.

11. We made the final arrangements for what it is hoped **(prove)** a successful demonstration.

12. Some universities are very selective in their admission, while others **(admit)** any students provided that they have passed through all of the high school courses.

13. He is not obliged to give way, but his reputation **(suffer)** if he obstinately refuses to do so.

14. Sooner or later they **(see)** you for what you are, and then they will tear you to pieces.

6 Put the verbs in brackets into the future perfect simple.

1. I **(finish)** by 10 o'clock.
2. By 2050 earlier, probably all real knowledge of this language **(disappear).**
3. Women are fickle, and in twelve months she **(forget)** all about me.
4. If a state is choosing a senator in November the two parties in that state **(choose)** their candidates at a primary election some months before.
5. If you have listened carefully to the announcer at the beginning of the film, you **(hear)** that the programme is sponsored by ICC LOGISTIC.

Die Verwendung der Zeiten

1 Put the following expressions of time into the corresponding sentence.

1. **.....** he stayed under water for almost a minute.	**yesterday**
2. They stayed only **..... .....** went back to England.	**that night**
3. It's six weeks now **.....** we moved in.	**once**
4. He arrived at the inn **.....** morning and he's still there.	**for a year and then**
5. They boarded a train for Munich, and arrived around eleven o'clock **.....** .	**since**
6. **.....** about 1930 **.....** very recent times the cinema enjoyed an immense popularity in Britain.	**this morning**
7. **.....** I received a legacy - enough to allow me to realize a dream.	**after 1945**
8. I rose **.....** while it was still dark and walked twelve kilometres to catch these fish for you.	**from ... until**
9. The first migrants who made their homes in Australia **.....** were refugees and displaced persons.	**a year ago**
10. **.....** the school-leaving age was, after some postponement, raised from 15 to 16 years.	**last summer**

11. ..... I decided to go on a crash diet guaranteed to make me lose 20 pounds in a month.	**at the beginning of the 20th century**
12. ..... most town-dwellers lived as tenants in terrace houses built in the nineteenth century.	**in 1972**
13. John Kennedy owed his success ..... to his personal appeal, and in 1976 Carter used similar tactics.	**for two years**
14. Brian has studied English ..... he wants to take up Spanish.	**in 1960**
15. We have known each other ..... 1984.	**this week**
16. Every day ..... we've discovered dead fish in the river.	**since**
17. Mr Spencer has played a lot of tennis	**yet**
18. London has changed a good deal ..... - in architecture, street scenes, the attitude to the Queen.	**today**
19. I wonder why John hasn't turned up ..... . Perhaps he has forgotten about our trip.	**these last three months**
20. Travelling ..... has become much easier and faster than it used to be in the past.	**in the past few years**
21. ..... they have received most of their financial needs from the state.	**meanwhile**
22. ..... 1960 big towns have enjoyed excessive representation, to the disadvantage of rural areas.	**in recent years**
23. ..... it has become less easy than in the past to guess a person's status from his car.	**since**

2 Put the verbs in brackets into the past tense simple or the present perfect simple.

1. I **(know)** him all his life.
2. In twenty years I never **(change)** my mind about this.
3. Mary wants to know where they **(spend)** their last holidays.

4. Nearly all of the early settlers **(leave)** Europe for the New World to enjoy a free life.
5. Thank you very much for your last letter, I'm so sorry that I **(not, reply)** for so long.
6. The King of Spain **(prepare)** a huge fleet, called the Armada, for the invasion of England.
7. These pictures show how much North America **(change)** since the Pilgrim Fathers **(arrive)** there.
8. We **(live)** there till my wife **(die).**
9. During the twentieth century the English police forces **(become)** well-known throughout the world.
10. For more than two hundred years, the need for cheap labour in the South **(make)** slave trading profitable to European and American traders.
11. I **(marry;** passive voice**)** for almost 25 years and have two children.
12. The founders of the Constitution **(think)** of the President as a replacement for the English king.
13. The Northerners **(try)** to prevent the new states in the West from becoming slave states.
14. When the judge in wig and robes **(take)** his seat on the bench the prisoner is brought in.
15. William the Conqueror, and the feudal lords who **(rule)** England for a long time never **(learn)** to speak the language of the people.
16. Fifty years of headlong industrial development **(leave)** the Soviet Union with a gigantic cleanup problem.
17. From his earliest days he **(live)** out of doors.
18. Not many blacks **(enjoy)** extensive spontaneous personal relations with white people outside their work.
19. Thatcher **(make)** up for the revenue shortfalls by raising value-added taxes.
20. The recent increase of criminal violence **(leave)** Britain less violent than many similar countries.
21. The rest of the United States **(go)** so far in material development that it is no longer satisfied with being a cultural desert.
22. You know the burden I **(bear)** since your mother **(leave)** us.

3 Put the verbs in brackets into the past tense simple or the past perfect simple.

1. The burglar **(come)** in through a window which someone **(leave)** open.
2. He **(meet)** her once or twice when he **(be)** in London.
3. She **(name)** a place where they **(can)** meet after work.
4. The children **(burst)** into laughter because Bob **(tell)** a funny story.
5. I **(give)** him an account of all that **(happen)** that evening.
6. Gipsy **(be)** a stray dog Susan **(acquire)** a few days ago.
7. He **(put)** on the pair of brown leather gloves he **(stick)** into his overcoat pocket.
8. He **(not know)** what **(make)** him pour out this stream of rubbish.
9. I (just, **finish)** trying on my new costume when I **(find)** that I **(forget)** my brooch.
10. He **(move)** a little to one side, so that he **(have)** a better view of the thing on the table.
11. I also **(hear)** that Philip **(have)** a conversation with a girl that afternoon.
12. During the Industrial Revolution, England **(become)** the only country that **(have)** the machines to make cotton cloth at a low price.
13. Tom **(wonder)** if Richard **(have)** friends with him at his hotel.
14. An American **(inform)** Tom that the young man and the girl who **(invite)** him were going to be married.
15. It **(strike)** him at once that she **(change)** in some ill-defined way.

4 Put the verbs in brackets into the future tense, the present tense simple, or the present tense continuous, or use **to be going to**.

1. You **(come)** back in a few minutes?
2. Father says I can't buy a motor-cycle until I **(be)** 18.
3. He **(play)** tennis this afternoon.
4. I **(fly)** to Paris this evening.
5. I expect we **(make)** a lot of mistakes when we write our first letters in English.

6. I hope you **(enjoy)** the rest of your stay in England.
7. I'm sure you **(like)** it.
8. The day **(come)** when you **(believe)** me.
9. The train **(leave)** at 8 a.m. From which platform?
10. Well, I **(not, travel)** all over the country. I can't afford it.
11. We **(move)** to our new house in January.
12. Who **(come)** in at this moment?
13. Long before the ship **(enter)** Dover harbour, the passengers have their first sight of the English coast.
14. She is afraid that he **(take)** revenge.
15. The passenger cannot claim his seat unless he takes possession of it by the time the train **(leave)** the station.
16. You **(not, tell)** us?
17. The police **(come)** over in about an hour and I'm supposed to be here.
18. The ship **(take)** a whole day at least to reach the British coast.
19. I **(go)** to Rome the day after tomorrow to meet Adam's father.
20. I **(have)** new curtains in my room.
21. All increases in a salary **(date)** from tomorrow.
22. It seems likely that the formerly under-developed areas now **(continue)** to grow fast.
23. I **(not, pretend**) that at that moment I knew what would happen in the next weeks.
24. I believe that right **(**ultimately, **conquer)** wrong.
25. I feared he **(annoy;** passive voice**)** at my telling the news of the gold ring.
26. Today, and in the years to come, American labour **(face)** a difficult task of adjustment.

☞ Die entsprechenden Lösungen befinden sich im Lösungsheft auf Seite 33ff.

Simple (Ordinary) und Continuous (Progressive) Form

Die Bildung der continuous form in den einzelnen Zeiten

1 Put the verbs in brackets into the present tense continuous.

1. He **(carry)** two bags and the carpet.
2. We **(fly)** north now across the broad Pacific.
3. Philip and Tom **(lie)** in the sand.
4. No one **(blame)** you, my child.
5. He **(leave)** the house by the back door.
6. I **(see)** a film tonight.
7. A burglar **(slip)** into the house.
8. What **(happen)** to us all?
9. What you **(say)** may be English, but it sounds like Double Dutch.
10. How can you be sure that he **(obey)** you.
11. He **(live)** beyond his means.
12. Time **(get)** short, and we ought to start back soon.
13. Time **(run)** out for the old man?
14. The problem of what is to be done with the ever increasing amount of leisure **(occupy)** American sociologists a great deal.
15. I noticed one of the yellow road signs the police put up on sites of recent accidents when they **(try)** to trace a runaway driver.
16. The manager **(enclose)** the card with his signature for your permanent record as you requested.
17. Local authorities also provide technical and commercial colleges, which are remarkably active and many-sided institutions, whose work **(develop)** very rapidly.

2 Put the verbs in brackets into the past tense continuous.

1. I told Mr Robinson that Philip **(stay)** at the inn.
2. The sick and wounded **(die)** like flies.
3. Mary **(lie)** in the sun too long. Of course she got sunburnt.
4. Can't you see the sign 'No smoking' over there? the conductor said to a man who **(smoke)** a pipe.
5. All the people **(dance)** in the street to celebrate Thanksgiving Day.
6. McDonald had turned himself a little in his chair so that he **(face)** Gerald.
7. It **(get)** dark, so we pushed the van off the road and decided to stay there for the night.
8. I wondered why Burton **(listen)** at the door when you came out.
9. The donkey, the peasant, and his wife **(ride)** on was rather old.
10. He **(hurry)** along with frozen hands and watering eyes when he saw her not ten metres away.
11. I **(try)** to decide whether to go to the chemist's.
12. A cold fear **(run)** over Tom's body.
13. I wondered whether she had been out, for she **(breathe)** hard as though she had been running.
14. The tennis player **(play)** safely, depending upon his opponent to make a fault.
15. Donald **(prove)** even more useful than he had hoped.
16. The two **(argue)** about the town's race-course and what official rating it deserved.
17. The facts **(fit)** into place.
18. The newspapers **(run)** out of sensational things to say about the Atkinson case.
19. Simon's disappearance **(stir up)** a great deal of excitement in the press.

3 Put the verbs in brackets into the present perfect continuous.

1. This is the ball I **(play)** with all the time.
2. He **(write)** all the morning.
3. Tremendous changes **(take place)** particularly since 1945.
4. In the past few years prices **(rise)** sharply.
5. To these of us who **(try)** to solve this problem for the past 14 years, it seems like a miracle.
6. David's mother **(run)** a one-woman campaign to wipe out hazing.
7. Self-destruction begins only when the plastic **(lie)** for some time under the more energetic ultra-violet of direct sunlight.
8. Despite all difficulties, scientists **(try)** to devise ways of evaluating animal intelligence.
9. For many years the federal government **(promote)** industrial development in the south by building up the economic infrastructure.
10. For the last decision the judge is helped by two Justices of the Peace who **(sit)** beside him throughout the proceedings.

4 Put the verbs in brackets into the past perfect continuous.

1. In a moment the two men who **(lie)** on their beds had disappeared.
2. For the last two and half weeks Bob **(live)** with Adam Collins, a young man he hardly knew.
3. I didn't know where Daniel **(go)**.
4. After a short discussion at the club-house, David and Mary went to the police station to report what **(happen)**.
5. She had sent the white sweater with the red stripes that she **(knit)** for Simon.
6. On and off he **(worry)** about it all day.
7. The shops she passed every day in the bus along Regent Street and Oxford Street **(celebrate)** Christmas for some time.

8. For more than three hours he **(tap)** a message out into the storm and darkness: S...O...S.

9. Bob wondered if Richard had had friends with him at his hotel, or wherever he **(stay)**?

10. One afternoon, half-way through the summer, they **(bathe)** in the river under the hanging oak-trees.

Die Verwendung der continuous form

1 Put the following expressions into the corresponding sentence.

1. **.....** we are flying over the endless prairies and wheat farms of central Canada.	**as**
2. Traffic is getting **.....** and **.....** dangerous.	**while**
3. That process is continuing **.....** and **......**	**when**
4. I came in **.....** you were watching the film.	**denser and denser** **more and more**
5. **.....** he came in, Linda was making the beds, whistling a gay tune.	**day by day** **minute by minute**
6. **.....** I was leaving the house it started to rain.	**at the same time**
7. **.....** he saw a boy who was crying.	**worse and worse**
8. **.....**, the Interstate Commission on the Potomac River Basin is developing a monitoring program to determine what happens to the estuary's water.	**suddenly**
9. Things are getting **.....**	**at present**
10. She had been waiting for the traffic lights to change, **.....** instead of turning green they had gone out.	**as**
11. We are loading and disgorging more than 600 passengers **.....** every day?	**when**
12. He should be ashamed of himself, just walking along and whistling, **.....** his brother is working himself to death.	**increasingly**

13. Who did Sean watch, what did he see and hear **.....** he was standing on Jack's shoulders?	**as**
14. An old man asked him for money **.....** Bob was leaving the cathedral square.	**while**
15. The state universities are becoming **.....** important.	**while**
16. I am having my car washed **.....** I am doing my shopping.	**suddenly**
17. **.....** he began writing in sheer panic, only imperfectly aware of what he was setting down.	**when**
18. We were sitting there having a nice quiet pause in the conversation **.....** Dad turned up.	**while**

2 Put the verbs in brackets into the simple or continuous form of the past tense.

1. The water **(rise)** fast, and the passengers **(get)** very nervous.
2. Quickly he **(jump)** to the side and **(try)** to grab his son.
3. For several months they **(work)** on the van every evening and every weekend.
4. Bob wrote to Mr Atkinson that he **(stay)** with Simon for a few days.
5. He **(stay)** at the hotel all the time.
6. Some **(play)** cards, others **(sit)** around talking, others **(drink)** at the bar.
7. David Mitchell **(ask)** the visitors to sit down round the table and then **(try)** to answer some of their questions.
8. Mr Jackson **(lead)** him to the living-room where Billy **(play)** cards with his mother.
9. Mr Johnson **(leave)** the house at eight o'clock every morning and **(return)** at six o'clock every evening.
10. Will you have the goodness to explain what on earth you **(talk;** present tense**)** about?
11. Everyone **(wait)** for the winner of the Marathon to run in through the gates.
12. When she **(hear)** that she **(change)** colour.

13. They **(have)** a geography lesson and Mrs Summers, the geography mistress, **(talk)** about all the things England gets from the Commonwealth countries.

14. He **(feel)** himself beginning to sweat, and he **(try)** to relax.

15. He **(reach)** out for the book, which **(lie)** on the floor, and **(sit up)** against the bedhead.

16. Look, the two gentlemen **(talk;** present tense**)** of taking lessons in knife-throwing.

17. He **(continue)** to apply the battery current to the carbon lamp filament from time to time.

18. It was gin that **(sink)** him into stupor every night and gin that **(revive)** him every morning.

19. In the hotel the lamps **(light;** passive voice**).**

20. I **(steer)**, and instead of watching where we **(go)**, I **(look)** at the big factories along the road.

21. Bob **(go)** rigid and cold, but he **(try)** not to move a muscle.

22. He **(sweat)** so heavily, he **(take off)** his jacket so as not to soil it.

23. For some inscrutable reason, people **(**always, **ask)** me the way.

24. He **(**always, **pick)** on me.

3 Put the verbs in brackets into the simple or continuous form. Mind the tense.

1. Look, John **(repair)** his bicycle.

2. I **(fly)** to New York this afternoon.

3. One evening Jack **(walk)** along the shore all by himself.

4. Mary is still in bed. She **(sleep)** long enough, it's time to wake her up.

5. This is the book she **(speak)** of all the time.

6. He **(not know)** how long she **(look)** at him.

7. He **(love)** me as a child **(love)** his father.

8. At the age of twenty-three Robert **(marry)** and **(start)** his own business as a butcher in Huntsville.

9. The world population **(grow)** at a rate that will double by the year 2000.

10. Lucky for me, I got a job and was made a spot welder and that's what I **(do)** ever since.

11. The police **(come)** over in about an hour and I'm supposed to be here.

12. We **(stay)** out a few hours and back we **(come).**

☞ Die entsprechenden Lösungen befinden sich im Lösungsheft auf Seite 39ff.

Das Passiv (The Passive Voice)

Die Bildung des Passivs in den einzelnen Zeiten

1 Put the verbs in brackets into the passive voice in the present tense simple.

1. Entrance requirements **(set)** by the individual colleges.
2. More and more houses **(build)** nowadays with central heating.
3. We know that your time **(occupy)** by affairs of the highest importance.
4. In the Washington metropolitan area a highly efficient sewage-treatment plant **(plan).**
5. The city **(lay out)** rectangularly in twelve long avenues running north and south.
6. The automobile alone **(estimate)** to cause 60 % of America's total air pollution.
7. The arrangement of the business of the House of Representatives **(control)** by a committee called Rules Committee.
8. Once the Government has decided to introduce a bill, one minister **(put)** in charge of it.
9. At the age of 11 all Primary School pupils, instead of being graded, **(send)** to the same Comprehensive School.
10. The Queen's consent and approval **(require)** before a minister can take up office.
11. Indians **(bear)** with an instinct for riding, rowing, hunting, fishing and swimming.
12. The most interesting innovation is the Open University, whose costs **(bear)** mainly by state funds.
13. A man **(judge)** by the make of his car.
14. By the Hippocratic oath doctors **(bind)** to preserve life at all costs.
15. Everything around us **(tie)** together in a system of mutual interdependence.

2 Put the verbs in brackets into the passive voice in the past tense simple.

1. The harvests **(destroy)** by floods.

2. A reward **(promise)** to anyone who would write a good article for the school magazine.
3. Hawaii became the 50th state when it **(admit)** to the Union in 1959.
4. The man **(hit)** by Mr Green's car outside a zebra crossing. He **(knock over)** over.
5. A few days after the end of the war, Abraham Lincoln **(shoot)** by a fanatic Southerner while attending a theatre in Washington.
6. The man who **(hurt)** died soon after.
7. He **(leave)** standing by himself.
8. Where she **(take)**? I think she **(take)** to the hospital.
9. Growing trade between East and West **(accompany)** by an increase in trading at home.
10. The plan (thoroughly and carefully; **work out)**, but within a year it **(judge)** to have been a failure.
11. The question **(raise)** whether to leave or to stay.
12. The women in Australia **(permit)** to vote before their English sisters had even begun their long battle for emancipation.
13. The end of the rope **(tie)** to the metal ring at the prow.
14. The news **(receive)** in a silence of incomprehension and disbelief.
15. In a statement by a Yard spokesman three similar art thefts **(refer to)**.

3 Put the verbs in brackets into the passive voice in the present perfect simple.

1. Several reforms **(carry)** through in recent years.
2. About ten million new immigrants **(admit)** in the past fifty years.
3. Millions of pounds **(spend)** on the preparation of middle-term and long-term plans.
4. Enough **(say)** on that question.
5. Since 1958 the financial position of students **(improve)** by the provision of loans by the Federal government.
6. England **(divide)** into counties for more than 1,000 years.

7. In Europe scientific and economic advance and rising material prosperity **(accompany)** by a decline in religious observance.

8. New schools **(build)** as part of the efforts to raise the standard of education throughout the country.

9. Central government funds **(use)** to contribute to local transport subsidies.

10. Most of what he **(tell)** is lies.

4 Put the verbs in brackets into the passive voice in the past perfect simple.

1. Two places **(lay)** in the large dining-room.
2. Two men sat in the dining-room, where coffee **(serve)** to them.
3. Every evening the teacher asked if the duties **(do)**.
4. After the steam-engine **(invent)** and a lot of factories **(build)** our air became more and more polluted.
5. The present buildings of the Palace were erected between 1840 and 1852, to replace older buildings which **(destroy)** by fire in 1834.
6. The paper said that no forgeries **(commit)** against him.
7. For a long time Nixon denied that he **(involve)** in the cover-up.
8. The doctor **(send)** for before he was taken to hospital.
9. Nothing **(see)** of him for nearly six months.
10. All the drawers were pulled out, the floor was strewn with scattered garments and the wardrobe **(empty)** of his best suits.
11. By 1978 the House of Lords included about 300 life peers, 40 of them women; most of these life peerages **(confer)** on the advice of labour Prime Ministers.
12. Thinking she **(take)** ill, I hurried to see her.

5 Put the verbs in brackets into the passive voice in the future tense simple.

1. Much of the programme **(carry)** out.

2. At the convention some candidates **(propose).**
3. The next economic summit **(hold)** in Japan in the summer next year.
4. I only hope that nobody **(hurt)**.
5. Extensive alterations **(require).**
6. As a general reporter she **(send)** on a large number of jobs.
7. Each of you **(give)** a brochure.
8. There you **(meet)** by a friend.
9. In a space suit you **(cut off)** in your own environment.
10. You **(make)** royally welcome.

6 Put the following verbs in brackets into the passive voice in the present tense continuous.

1. Today, cinemas and theatres **(change)** into bingo halls, wrestling arenas, dance-halls, and bowling centres.
2. More and more newspapers **(control)** by fewer and fewer people.
3. The New York - Washington railway **(develop)**, but rather gradually.
4. Mr Summers has just left home and **(drive)** to his office.
5. A new airport **(build)** outside the town.
6. English **(teach)** in the library this morning.
7. English **(speak)** all over the world.
8. In the US, land **(urbanize)** at the rate of 3,000 acres a day.
9. Much **(do)** to educate people in the nature of the problems they have to solve.
10. For a few intercity links of between 200 and 800 kilometres the railway **(revive).**

7 Put the verbs in brackets into the passive voice in the past tense continuous.

1. A terrible hurricane was raging and the ship **(toss)** about.

2. I could scarcely understand what **(say)**.

3. While the bags **(bring)** he stood aside.

4. He **(wait for)** in the garden.

5. The strange thing is that I didn't know I **(look for)**.

6. There was of course no way of knowing whether you **(watch)** at any given moment.

Die Umwandlung aktiver Sätze in passive Sätze

1 Put the following sentences containing one object into the passive voice.

1. All the team obeyed the trainer's orders without any protest.

2. By the next afternoon some people had invited him to a party.

3. He delivered the parcel next door by mistake.

4. Several first-class orchestras regularly give orchestral concerts in London.

5. The afternoon train will take him there on Wednesday.

6. Their Clerks advise the Justices of the Peace on points of law.

7. They planned new industrial estates around the city.

8. They will help them on and off every bus and across every street.

9. We told Susan to come too, and she was the first to arrive.

10. We will do everything to make your flight comfortable.

11. They had set the table on the terrace for three.

12. We will find radioactive pollutants on the earth's surface for generations.

13. Her sister will join her.

14. We are making great efforts to ensure that poor people are helped.

15. We consider only 16.7 million out of Kenya's 140 million acres good enough for high potential farming.

16. Do not enter the studio, we are filming a play for today's programme.

17. Bob had the feeling that somebody was following him.

18. They put the growth in average earnings at 7 3/4 %, a fraction higher than last summer.

19. If I hadn't fled and changed my name, they should have put me into prison.

20. There a friend will meet you.

21. As soon as they discovered the crime search parties combed the whole forest.

22. In 1968 new laws enable courts to take away the driving licence of a driver whom they found to have more than 80 ml of alcohol.

23. The Justices of the Peace are ordinary but worthy citizens whom the Lord Chancellor has appointed to their positions.

2 Put the following sentences with two objects into the passive voice using the correct object as the subject of the passive sentence.

1. He realized too late that someone addressed the letter to Mr Harrison.

2. He recommended me another doctor.

3. Here they offer vagabonds warm food and dry beds.

4. In the antechapel, next the hall where we were, they presented petitions to the queen.

5. On Christmas Day, 1066, they crowned William the Conqueror King of England in Westminster Abbey.

6. There they will give you all the instructions you need.

7. They allow him five marks pocket money a week.

8. They announced the event to everybody.

9. They considered him a prudent man.

10. They granted her a small pension.

11. They made George Washington the first President of the United States of America.

12. They promised a reward to anyone who would write a good article for the school magazine.

13. They saved him a lot of trouble.

14. They shall ask us several questions.

15. They showed him all the books.

16. They will appoint him director general.

17. A top-level expert explained the computer to us.

18. At the airport passengers can buy duty-free cigarettes, spirits and perfume and during the flight they may serve them dinner or a snack, depending on the time of day.

19. At today's press conference at the Yard they handed the journalists photographs of the stolen paintings.

20. I hope they may spare him this ordeal.

21. In general they give the Bachelor's degree to students who pass examinations at the end of three or four years of study.

22. Should we give them the chance?

23. They offered this assistance to anyone who cared to take it.

24. They pay most full-time directors of large companies salaries between £ 20,000 and £ 30,000 a year.

25. We should make all things possible reality.

26. At the cocktail party people took no notice of the famous professor, but they made a fuss of his lovely young wife from the moment they introduced her to the guests.

27. He was so stupid that they made him the laughing stack.

28. They gave the beggar an alms.

29. They will have to offer workers who lose their jobs through labour-saving techniques another job of similar status and pay.

30. You must hand every question to the officials of the house in writing at least 48 hours before they are to give the answer.

3 Put the following sentences into the passive voice.

1. An expert has dealt with this question.
2. We have never heard of him since.
3. They have always laughed at him.
4. They listened to him with pleasure.
5. When Mrs Douglas came home from hospital, she found that they had looked after the cat.
6. They looked upon him as a sportive man.
7. They arrived at the solution by chance.
8. People have often discriminated against people because of race, religion, or colour.
9. Have they come to any decision?
10. You can rely on it that we will attend to your orders without delay.
11. Charles hardly knew Parker, and had no idea what work they employed on him.
12. Nothing seems to have been disarranged and nobody has interfered with the drawers.
13. Somebody has sat on my hat.
14. Somebody has slept in the bed.
15. They forgot their quarrels on seeing that somebody infringed upon their right.
16. In among all this terrible poverty there were just a few great big beautiful houses in which rich men lived who had as many as thirty servants to look after them.
17. Oxford, like Rome, abounds in beauty, but it is a hidden beauty that you must sought for.

Die Umwandlung passiver Sätze in aktive Sätze

1 Put the following sentences in the passive voice into the active voice.

1. English is spoken by more than 800 million people in many different countries all over the world.

2. Bob checked in at the hotel Miramare which had been recommended to him by some Americans.

3. That pat of the road was closed for resurfacing.

4. Several reforms have been carried through in recent years.

5. He had run away at seventeen but had been brought back.

6. My business will be finished in a few seconds.

7. He was given another 1,500 dollars.

8. The matter had long been dealt with.

9. Boys and girls of 16 needn't be looked after all the time.

10. The total loss resulting from all thefts is estimated at $ 6 million.

11. Disposable dishware is used for everyday occasions.

12. The court is presided over by a judge, but the decision on guilt or innocence is made by a jury.

13. The public were warned of the dangers of drinking.

14. We are being followed.

15. Something was being done.

16. Some women with small children would like to work, if the children could be cared for during mothers' working hours.

17. It was hoped that the Health Service would improve health in general.

18. It is a shame that he should have been treated like that.

19. The trivial tasks are being turned over to the machines.

20. A person in a middle-class salaried job may well be paid his full salary for long periods of absence through sickness.

21. What advances have been made in the last few years in computer technology?

22. In 1961 they decided that a third new airport for London would be needed by the early 1970s.

23. First, every bill has been approved by the Cabinet that was brought in by the Government.

24. What is being done about the situation?

25. I don't want to be seen off.

☞ Die entsprechenden Lösungen befinden sich im Lösungsheft auf Seite 44ff.

Die indirekte Rede (Reported, Indirect Speech)

Die Umwandlung von Aussagesätzen

1 Change the verbs in the present tense into the correct tense in reported speech.

1. He muttered: <<My name **is** Roger.>>

   He muttered that his name **.....** Roger.

2. Mother remarked: <<We **need** a new car.>>

   Mother remarked that they **.....** a new car.

3. They said: The army **doesn't need** any female nurses.

   They said that the army **.....** any female nurses.

4. David's friends thought: <<The apple-tarts his mother **makes are** the best.>>

   David's friends thought that the apple-tarts his mother **.....** the best.

5. The announcer said: <<Most of the audience **is going** to the bar for a drink.>>

   The announcer said that most of the audience **.....** to the bar for a drink.

6. Simon said: <<In summer I **do not use** the room, because I **like** to save it as a change of scene for the winter.>>

   Simon said that in summer he **.....** the room, because he **.....** to save it as a change of scene for the winter.

7. One evening my wife reported: <<My hairdresser **swears** that fresh lobster or shrimp or crabmeat **is** non-fattening.>>

   One evening my wife reported that her hairdresser **.....** that fresh lobster or shrimp or crabmeat **.....** non-fattening.

8. The Supreme Court ordered: <<The southern educational authorities **are to integrate** their schools with all deliberate speed.>>

   The Supreme Court ordered that the southern educational authorities **.....** their schools with all deliberate speed.

9. He said: <<They **are to do**.>>

   He said that they **.....**

10. He said: <<If anything **happens** to me I **want** you to have these documents.>>

    He said that if anything **.....** to him he **.....** me to have these documents.

2 Change the verbs in the past tense into the correct tense in reported speech.

1. The boy said: <<I **didn't do** anything wrong.>>

   The boy said that he **.....** anything wrong.

2. He claimed: <<I **was** an expert.>>

   He claimed that he **.....** an expert.

3. Some people complained: <<There **was not** enough hard learning in the schools.>>

   Some people complained that there **.....** enough hard learning in the schools.

4. He protested: <<I **was** still quite wide awake.>>

   He protested that he **.....** quite wide awake.

5. He said: <<Miles apparently **had** a few drinks.>>

   He said that Miles apparently **.....** a few drinks.

6. I said: <<Mr Stevens **died** of a disease of the stomach, made worse by the habit of overdrinking strong spirits.>>

   I said that Mr Stevens **.....** of a disease of the stomach, made worse by the habit of overdrinking strong spirits.

7. I found: <<After all I still have the desire for the old busy days and the old work which I **thought** I **was** so glad to leave.>>

   I found that after all I still have the desire for the old busy days and the old work which I **.....** I **.....** so glad to leave.

8. Our teacher said: <<While Isaac Newton **was** in his orchard he **saw** an apple fall to the ground, and this **gave** him the idea that the Earth must have been pulling at the apple.>>

   Our teacher said that while Isaac Newton **.....** in his orchard he **.....** an apple fall to the ground, and this **.....** him the idea that the Earth must have been pulling at the apple.

9. He said: <<Prior to the IMF meeting I **had** discussions with colleagues of the EEC in Venice and with Commonwealth colleagues in Guyana.>>

   He said that prior to the IMF meeting he **.....** discussions with his colleagues of the EEC in Venice and with his Commonwealth colleagues in Guyana.

10. He said: <<It **took** 96 weeks to build a factory in Britain; the next slowest countries, West Germany and France, **had** an average construction period of only 56 weeks.>>

    He said that it **.....** 96 weeks to build a factory in Britain; the next slowest countries, West Germany and France, **.....** an average construction period of only 56 weeks.

3 Change the verbs in the present perfect into the correct tense in reported speech.

1. You said: <<He **has** just **left** the city.>>

   You said that he **.....** just **.....** the city.

2. She exclaimed: <<I **have torn** my coat.>>

   She exclaimed that she **.....** her coat.

3. He confessed: <<For years I **have been** a member of an underground organization.>>

   He confessed that for years he **.....** a member of an underground organization.

4. I said: <<The Mayor **hasn't found** any of our ideas good enough yet.>>

   I said that the Mayor **.....** any of our ideas good enough yet.

5. People said: <<Mr Witherspoon **has been** a very cautious man all his life.>>

   People said that Mr Witherspoon **.....** a very cautious man all his life.

6. He admitted: <<This year's crop in Russia **has been** even worse than in previous years.

   He admitted that this year's crop in Russia ..... even worse than in previous years.

7. The computer explained: <<I **have been given** the wrong licence number by one of my human operators.>>

   The computer explained that it ..... the wrong licence number by one of its human operators.

8. He said: <<Nigeria, an OPEC member **has had** particular trouble selling oil recently.>>

   He said that Nigeria, an OPEC member ..... particular trouble selling oil recently.

9. The papers said: <<Atkinson **has** just **been requested** by the Rome police to answer questions concerning the disappearance of Gerald Winterbottom.

   The papers said that Atkinson ..... just ..... by the Rome police to answer questions concerning the disappearance of Gerald Winterbottom.

10. Some people said: <<We **have lost** the artistic sense and feeling for the highest aesthetic values.>>

    Some people said that we ..... the artistic sense and feeling for the highest aesthetic values.

4 Change the verbs in the past perfect into the correct tense in reported speech.

1. The document said: <<The fingerprints really **had guaranteed** his innocence.>>

   The document said that the fingerprints really ..... his innocence.

2. He said: <<$ 50,000 **had been collected** as a present for her.>>

   He said that $ 50,000 ..... as a present for her.

3. He said: <<The last communication from William Atkinson **had been** his letter to the Bank of Paris.>>

   He said that the last communication from William Atkinson ..... his letter to the Bank of Paris.

4. He confessed: <<I **had been** a spy in the pay of an Eastasian government.>>

   He confessed that he ..... a spy in the pay of an Eastasian government.

5. The Indians said: <<Our people **had been** killed, our lands settled on, our game wantonly destroyed, and our young men made drunk.>>

   The Indians said that their people ..... killed, their lands settled on, their game wantonly destroyed, and their young men made drunk.

6. She meant: <<It was extraordinary that I **had failed** to find out.>>

   She meant that it had been extraordinary that she ..... to find out.

7. He pretended: <<I **had seen** a piece of paper which proved them innocent.>>

   He pretended that he ..... a piece of paper which had proved them innocent.

8. The Party claimed: <<The infant mortality **had been** 300 per thousand before the Revolution.>>

   The Party claimed that the infant mortality ..... 300 per thousand before the Revolution.

9. He said: <<Only two of the boys were bad, the others **had been led away** by them.>>

   He said that only two of the boys had been bad, the others ..... by them.

10. She said: <<My sufferings **had been** more than anyone should be asked to bear.>>

    She said that her sufferings ..... more than anyone should be asked to bear.

5 Change the following verbs in the future tense, future perfect tense or in the conditional I into the correct tense in reported speech.

1. He remarked: I **will be** absent tomorrow.>>

   He remarked that he ..... absent the next day.

2. She replied: <<I **will make** preparations at once.>>

   She replied that she ..... preparations at once.

3. I said: <<I **won't drink** any wine with my dinner.>>

   I said that I **.....** any wine with my dinner.

4. I thought: <<That night **will** never **end**.>>

   I thought that that night **.....** never **......**

5. She thought: <<I **will have been** back by then.

   She thought that she **.....** back by then.

6. My Dad said: <<I **wouldn't like** to drive such a huge lorry, I prefer my taxi.>>

   My Dad said that he **.....** to drive such a huge lorry, he preferred his taxi.

7. The inspector said: <<I **would like** to examine the study.>>

   The inspector said that he **.....** to examine the study.

8. His father exclaimed: <<This **will be** a good way in which one could spend the holidays.>>

   His father exclaimed that this **.....** a good way in which one could spend the holidays.

9. He swore: <<I **will have** my revenge.>>

   He swore that he **.....** his revenge.

10. He said: <<The supervisory board **will have** his full approval.>>

    He said that the supervisory board **.....** his full approval.

11. I think: <<Gloria and I **will have left** right then.>>

    I think that Gloria and I **.....** right then.

12. I believed: <<Right **will** ultimately **conquer** wrong, virtue conquer vice, harmony take the place of discords.>>

    I believed that right **.....** ultimately **.....** wrong, virtue conquer vice, harmony take the place of discords.

6 Put the following modal auxiliary verbs into reported speech.

1. My wife complained: <<I **can't** find my passport anywhere.>>

   My wife complained that she ..... find her passport anywhere.

2. He said: <<I **couldn't** do it.>>

   He said that he ..... do it.

3. People said: <<There **may** be intelligent beings on Mars.>>

   People said that there ..... be intelligent beings on Mars.

4. She supposed: <<You **might** have flunked.>>

   She supposed that you ..... have flunked.

5. He suggested: <<We **ought to** go.

   He suggested that they ..... go.

6. I explained: <<I **might** be called away to attend a patient.

   I explained that I ..... be called away to attend a patient.

7. He said: <<All of us **must** be educated to fit us for life.>>

   He said that all of us ..... be educated to fit us for life.

8. The Constitution said: <<No person **shall** be deprived of his life, liberty or property.>>

   The Constitution said that no person ..... be deprived of his life, liberty or property.

9. After I had been on the island about ten or twelve days I thought: <<I **should** need some way of making the days.>>

   After I had been on the island about ten or twelve days I thought that I ..... need some way of making the days.

10. She said: <<The money **ought to** be left to me.>>

    She said that the money **.....** be left to her.

11. He said: <<You **have to** make a report within twenty-four hours.>>

    He said that I **.....** make a report within twenty-four hours.

12. The Chancellor said: <<If the nation **is to** work harder and increase output, wage increases will be fully justified.>>

    The Chancellor said that if the nation **.....** work harder and increase output, wage increases would be fully justified.

7 Put the following personal pronouns into reported speech and insert them into the table on the right hand.

1. **I** said: <<**I/we** don't like that guy.>>

   I said that **.....** didn't like that guy.

2. **I** said: <<**He/they** has/have one of those new electric cleaners.>>

   I said that **.....** had one of those new electric cleaners.

3. **I** said: <<**You** were driving carefully.>>

   I said that **.....** had been driving carefully.

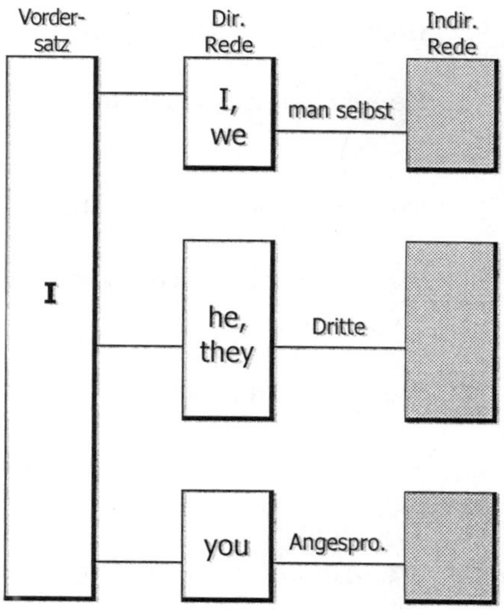

4. **You** said: <<**I/we** don't advise you to try that.>>

   You said that **.....** didn't advise me/us to try that.

5. **You** said: <<**He/they** lives/live in an ivory tower.>>

   You said that **.....** lived in an ivory tower.

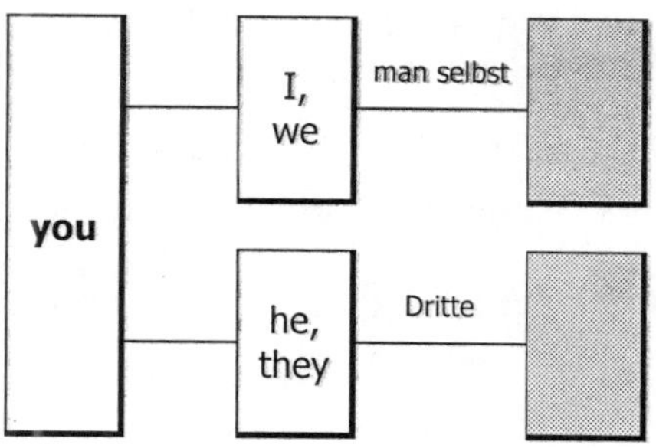

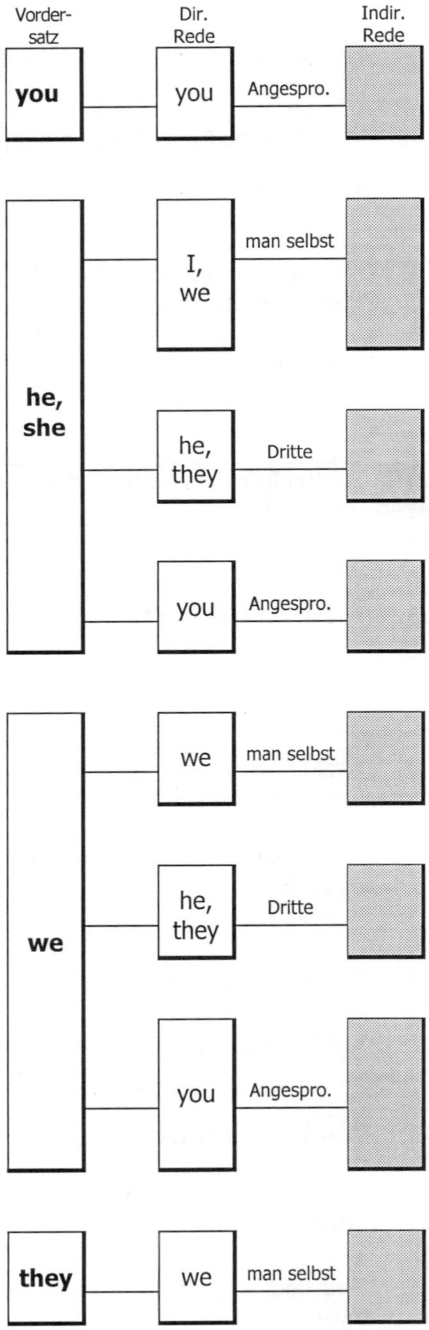

6. **You** said: «**You** have to set the table.»

   You said that **.....** had to set the table.

7. **He** said: «**I/we** will receive the Blairs out of doors and give them tea in the garden.

   He said that **.....** would receive the Blairs out of doors and give them tea in the garden.

8. **He** said: «**He/they** spoke the truth.

   He said that **.....** had spoken the truth.

9. **He** said: «**You** should go.»

   He said that **.....** should go.

10. **We** said: «**We** are too highly specialised.»

    We said that **.....** were too highly specialised.

11. **We** said: «**He/they** will find a solution.»

    We said that **.....** would find a solution.

12. **We** said: «**You** will develop a better computer system.»

    We said that **.....** would develop a better computer system.

13. **They** said: «**We** will see her soon.»

    They said that **.....** would see her soon.»

14. **They** said: <<**They/he** will solve the crime problem.>>

    They said that **.....** would solve the crime problem.>>

15. **They** said: <<**You** waste your money on idle luxury.>>

    They said that **.....** wasted your money on idle luxury.>>

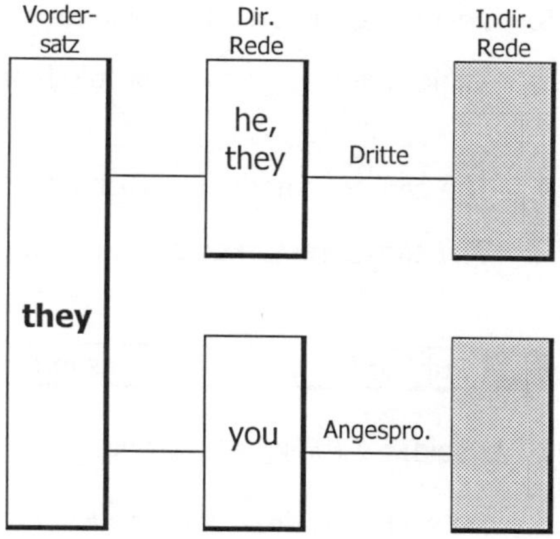

8 Put the following expressions of time and location into reported speech.

1. I said: <<I have seen her **today**.>>

   I said that I had seen her **......**

2. I said: <<He visited him at some time **yesterday**.>>

   I said that he had visited him at some time **......**

3. I said: <<He visited him at some time **the day before yesterday**.>>

   I said that he had visited him at some time **......**

4. He remarked: <<I will be absent **tomorrow**.>>

   He remarked that he would be absent **......**

5. Peter regretted: <<I cannot come to your party **next week**.>>

   Peter regretted that he could not come to my party **......**

6. Peter regretted: <<I could not come to your party **last week**.>>

   Peter regretted that he could not come to my party **......**

7. He said: I took my examination two years **ago**.

   He said that he had taken his examination two years **......**

8. I said: <<George and I would leave **now**.>>

   I said that George and I would have left **......**

9. The carrier remarked: <<**Here** is a letter with seals from Madrid.>>

   The carrier remarked that **.....** was a letter with seals from Madrid.

9 Put the following sentences into reported speech.

1. I said: <<I think he is wrong.>>
2. He said: <<Andrew Johnson is innocent.>>
3. You said: <<She doesn't admit anything.>>
4. They said: <<This will have only negative consequences.>>
5. The Speaker said: <<It is time to go on to the next question.>>
6. The doctors said: <<He had been dead at least twelve hours.>>
7. We said: <<The burglar entered the garden from the back.>>
8. He said: <<There has been no risk of an accident.>>
9. The captain said: <<It was no use arguing with the angry crew.>>
10. They said: <<We will disarm and arrange to have a conference to settle the matter.>>
11. He told us: <<He will receive the Burtons on Sunday out of doors and give them tea in the garden.>>
12. He said: <<These two moves between them will lay a basis for future cooperation.>>
13. They said: <<Man's lot can no more be improved by violent and doctrinaire assaults.>>
14. She said: <<There should be redistribution of the male and female roles in society.>>
15. I said: <<He set out with the idea of calling upon Clayton.>>
16. I said: <<He sets out with the idea of calling upon Clayton.>>
17. He said: <<Before taking a decision on some bill it ought to make thorough enquiries into the background and the desirability of the new proposals.>>

18. They said: <<Marriages should hold all kinds of work combinations, without society attaching any stigma to the man who stays at home or the mother who opts for a full-time career. >>

Die Umwandlung von Fragesätzen

1 Put the following interrogative sentences without an interrogative pronoun into reported speech.

1. I wanted to ask you: <<Have you got any razor blades? >>
2. He asked: <<Could you bring Carol over for a drink around five o'clock?>>
3. Our teacher asked us: <<Would you like to form a pen-club?>>
4. I wondered: <<Is that sweet little cat still sitting on the roof?>>
5. I wondered: <<Will he make it?>>
6. I wondered: <<Shall I ever have time to see London?>>
7. I wondered: <<Have any strangers been seen round here?>>
8. I wondered: Would you like to come to our house and see the President from our balcony?>>
9. The Clerk read the indictment and asked the prisoner: <<Are you guilty or not guilty?>>
10. He wondered: <<Would they necessarily inform him if any radio messages had come about him?>>
11. She wondered: <<Would I ever get married?>>
12. He wondered: <<Is there a microphone hidden somewhere near?>>
13. Bob wondered: <<Had Daniel had friends with him at his hotel or wherever he had been staying?>>
14. He wondered: <<Has Daniel people waiting for him anywhere?>>
15. I hesitated with my hand on the door handle, looking back and wondering: <<Is there anything I had left undone?>>
16. My wife asked me: <<Did you happen to see my passport lying about?>>

17. I wondered: <<If we regard the machine not as an adjunct to our powers but as something to extend our powers, can we keep it controlled?>>

18. At the end of every debate the Speaker put the question: <<Will you accept the motion that has been debated?>>

19. The Government decided to put to the people the question: <<Should Britain remain within the E.E.C. or not?>>

20. He wondered: <<Does she take in washing for a living, or was she merely the slave of her grandchildren?>>

2 Put the following interrogative sentences with an interrogative pronoun into reported speech.

1. I wondered: <<Why hasn't Mike turned up yet?>>

2. I wondered: <<How often does the old lady leave her house?>>

3. I wondered: <<Why doesn't he come?>>

4. I wondered: <<What are Gerald and Caroline doing?>>

5. I wondered: <<Whose dog is this?>>

6. He wondered: <<What had they done to the woman in the yard?>>

7. The king wondered: <<What might I give the queen for her birthday?>>

8. They asked: <<What did people do with their leisure before there was television?>>

9. Now that he has been in America for three years, I asked him: <<What was your first impression?>>

10. The theft once again raised the question: <<What happens to stolen paintings?>>

11. Much had been written on the question: <<How should a teacher try to gain the positive interest of unco-operative pupils?>>

12. She stood before him very upright as though she was wondering: <<Why was he so slow to act?>>

13. The police were going to wonder: <<Where the hell does he go to?>>

14. As he was curiously watching a gang of workmen putting in long pipes, he began to wonder: <<What is this all about?>>

15. I wondered: <<Why did he have that idea?>>

16. I do not know how long I waited and I rather wondered: <<What could I possibly have looked like.

17. I was always asking him: <<How do you spend your time?>>

18. Daniel wondered: <<What will the Germans and Dutch think if they see his father sailing his boat down their busy canals?>>

19. If you asked them: <<What do you do for a living?>> They said: <<I work for standard.>>

Die Umwandlung von Befehlen, Aufforderungen

1 Put the following commands into reported speech.

1. He said: <<Write neatly.>>

2. He proposed: <<Try the examination again.>>

3. The officer told them: <<Lower the flag. >>

4. I proposed: <<Give me six hundred dollars in traveller's cheques.>>

5. They were told: <<Lie on the grass beside the line and don't look up at any cost.

6. They told me: <<Go to the information desk.>>

7. I told them: <<Don't forget to lock the door.>>

8. His wife told him: <<Don't drive too fast.>>

9. His mother told them: <<Don't be greedy.>>

10. My father said: <<Let's go up to the restaurant to have a good look at the planes taking off.>>

11. People exerted pressure on the state: <<Take action to eliminate unhappiness and discomfort.>>

12. I told them: <<Don't let him go just yet.>>

13. I proposed: <<Let's have a conversation this evening.>>
14. I said: <<Don't do so.>>
15. I told him: <<Don't bother about having failed. >>
16. He said: <<I shouldn't have said this.>>
17. The judge ordered: <<Send the juvenile delinquent to a home.>>

Die Umwandlung von indirekter Rede in direkte Rede

1 Put the following sentences into direct speech.

1. We thought that there were very fundamental problems in their family.
2. Some experts believed that prices would eventually drop.
3. He cried that he was going to save me.
4. He suggested that they should go up to the restaurant.
5. I told him not to be a fool.
6. He asked what had gone wrong.
7. They were whispering. I wondered what they were saying.
8. He asked him if he had read a book by a certain Harry Williams.
9. I wondered whether she had been out, for she was breathing hard as though she had been running.
10. He said that they made heavy complaints of ill treatment on the part of the government.
11. He saw himself confronted by a dozen policemen asking him where David Adams was.
12. I thought that swift motion across a countryside did not necessarily take away all appreciation of its charm.

13. We believed that in some marriages the roles should be reversed, with the wife as breadwinner and the husband as household manager.

14. Some critics argued that Parliament could contribute to the processes of government and administration more effectively if it strengthened its system of 'select committees'.

15. Egypt demanded that Britain withdraw its forces, and the Sudan be incorporated in Egypt.

☞ Die entsprechenden Lösungen befinden sich im Lösungsheft auf Seite 51ff.

Das Konditional (The Conditional)

1 Put the verbs in brackets into the correct tense (type I).

1. He **(kill)** me if I do that again.
2. Before the end of this century, if current trends continue, China **(have)** over a billion people.
3. A solution of the present crisis **(not take place)** unless men and women work for it.
4. What (you, **do)** if someone talks to you in Chinese?
5. What will you do if your neighhour **(pull)** your hair? I'll scream.
6. I will punish him if he **(not behave)** properly.
7. They will get wet if it **(rain)**.
8. You **(can)** ask Jane, if you like. She will tell you.
9. If an English person **(have)** enough money and security, he will probably buy a house for himself to live in.
10. If the Opposition **(not like)** a bill they will vote against it.
11. You (soon, **be able to)** swim if you practise hard.
12. If things continue on their present course, there **(be)** 600 million people living at the edge of survival.
13. What **(be)** the consequences if his advice is widely followed?
14. It **(be)** very simple for you to reach me if I am needed.
15. He hasn't yet decided whether to accept a promotion that would require moving to his firm's Kyoto branch, but if he **(do)**, he'll be ready.
16. If a candidate **(can)** make it appear that his activities at Washington have brought benefits to his district he will win votes for that reason.
17. A person elected as Vice-President expects that he **(have)** no defined function unless he happens to be thrust into the highest office through the chance of the President's death.

18. If a body **(be)** at rest, it will remain at rest unless it is acted upon by some force.

19. If he is sent to prison - he who loves the freedom of the open air, I **(not answer)** for what might come to him.

20. If I can't live here, neither **(will)** you.

2 Put the verbs in brackets into the correct tense (type II).

1. You would catch the train if you **(leave)** earlier.
2. He would come if you **(ring)**.
3. If men **(be)** more reasonable, there would be no more war.
4. If she **(have)** Simon back, she would probably just explode with happiness.
5. It would be just as well if I **(not mention)** it to anybody.
6. He **(come)** if you waited.
7. If all the seas were one sea, what a big sea that **(be)**!
8. That's a beautiful mahogany bed, or at least it **(be)** if you could get the bugs out of it.
9. What would you do if a bee **(sting)** you?
10. If you **(can)** choose, would you prefer to live then or now?
11. He felt he would faint if he **(stay)** one minute longer in the dimly lighted foyer.
12. If I went back there to live, my father **(be)** after me to work in London.
13. If he wanted to leave us he **(have to leave)** the country.
14. It would be easier if we **(not have to)** tell the passengers.
15. If I **(be)** you, I would say nothing about it.
16. If there **(be)** a real fire alarm now, everything I have seen would repeat itself, wouldn't it?
17. Bob did not know who would attack him, if he **(attack;** passive voice**).**
18. If things **(to be to)** be done twice, all would be wise.

19. If the workers **(not give;** passive voice**)** decent wages, they would leave the factories to settle in the West.

20. If the powers of rulers were carefully defined and limited in legal terms they **(not use;** passive voice**)** oppressively.

21. What places do you think he **(be likely to)** go if he wanted to hide out?

3 Put the verbs in brackets into the correct tense (type III).

1. If she had opened the door immediately, the burglars **(run away)** or **(catch)** her.
2. If she had not missed her lucky brooch, she **(not go back)** to the school building.
3. If the police had not arrested the burglars, Caroline **(not get)** a prize.
4. If Peggy **(not try)** on her new costume, she would not have found out about the missing brooch.
5. If the men **(not carry)** out the TV set and the other things, she would not have thought they were burglars.
6. I would not have done anything to her if she **(not hit)** me.
7. Bob would have fallen from the raft if we **(not hold)** him.
8. About how long **(take,** Mr Palmer**)** to get home, if all had gone well?
9. **(not be,** it**)** cheaper and simpler if the lady had just rung up the subscribers and asked them if there were any complaints?
10. He **(be)** in a position to procure the job for you, if he only had wanted to.
11. If you had done as I told you, you **(have)** more success.
12. The whole thing **(die out)** on its own much sooner if the police hadn't arrived.
13. If they had opened the window, they **(have)** fresh air.
14. They would have done better if they **(buy)** something else.
15. It would have made no difference if it **(be)** the other way about.
16. If he **(can move)** he would have stretched out a hand.

17. If it **(be)** possible he would have cowered deeper into the bed.

18. It **(be)** inconceivably dangerous even if he had known how to set about doing it.

19. If Robinson had read the letter to the end, he **(have)** Burton in at once and accused him.

20. The Government **(take;** passive voice) less by surprise by the famine if the press had done a better job of reporting.

21. What (he, **say)** if it had been possible for him to set his scattered thoughts in order.

22. If Mike had not been surrounded by experienced nurses, he (most inevitably, **kill**; passive voice) in no time.

23. Sheila would unquestionably have denounced him to the secret police if she **(not happened)** to be too stupid to detect the unorthodoxy of his opinions.

4 Make up three sentences using the tenses of type 1 – 3.

1. **(Help)** me if I **(need)** you?

2. There **(not be)** enough oxygen to breathe, if the present development **(go)** on.

3. You **(catch)** the train if you **(take)** a taxi.

4. If she **(not calm down)**, she **(faint)**.

5. If I **(lose)** my way in London, I **(ask)** a policeman.

6. Bob **(pay)** their hotel bill if Simon **(agree)** to stay overnight.

7. If she **(run away)**, the burglars **(get away)** with the things.

8. He **(come)** if you **(ring)**.

9. We can comfort ourselves with the thought that if war or ecological catastrophe **(intervene)**, we (better **equip;** passive voice**)** to survive it.

10. If a cleaner kind of car engine **(invent;** passive voice**)**, air pollution **(become)** less dangerous.

11. What (you, **do)** if I **(lend)** you my bicycle?

12. You **(can)** ask Pamela if you **(like)**.

13. If they **(have)** a board of experts, they probably **(be able)** to tell that the three signatures were forgeries.

14. If they **(discover)** that the will was a forgery, they **(have)** no mercy on him.

15. How much better **(be,** it**)** if he **(**just, **sit down)** in one of the cafés down at the beach.

16. If they **(read)** the small print they **(understand)** the difference.

17. If neither a transfer nor retraining **(be)** possible then workers who accept jobs with less status and pay **(pay**, passive voice**)** a compensatory bonus.

18. If the pipeline **(build;** passive voice**)** above ground it **(hinder)** movement of animals which normally migrate across its projected course.

5 Put the verbs in brackets into the correct tense and decide whether to use type 1, 2, 3.

1. If it **(rain)** this afternoon, it **(be)** too wet to play the match tomorrow.

2. It **(be)** impossible for me to finish my work if you **(not cease)** this chatter.

3. Most of the women with small children **(like)** to work, if the children **(can be cared for)** during mothers' working hours.

4. What subjects **(**you**, choose)** to take if you **(be)** an American High School student?

5. If the burglars **(not go back)** to the house, the police **(not catch)** them.

6. If he **(know)** English was so difficult, he **(**never, **take)** it up.

7. The world's supplies of oil **(exhaust;** passive voice**)** fairly soon unless they **(preserve;** passive voice**)**.

8. If present trends **(continue)**, immigration **(add)** at least 35 million people to the current U.S. population by the year 2000.

9. If I **(be)** in Parliament I **(build)** enough roads.

10. The village ladies had long expected that Robinson would marry Miss Palmer, and perhaps he **(not escape)** if the Stevens **(not come)** to live here a year ago.

11. If our planetary eco-system **(to be to)** recover, then countries like Britain **(have to be)** the first to give up environmental pollutants like car exhaust gases.

12. If a bill **(give;** passive voice**)** a second reading, it **(have)** no prospect of getting through both Houses in the present session.

☞ Die entsprechenden Lösungen befinden sich im Lösungsheft auf Seite 59ff.

Der Infinitiv (The Infinitive)

Der Present Infinitive Active

1 Put in **to** where necessary.

1. Little children were made ..... work in factories for twelve hours or more every day.
2. Dr Davies made Billy ..... open his mouth wide.
3. Let ..... come what may.
4. You had better ..... begin by reading this article.
5. On the way back he heard the telephone ..... ring.
6. He saw her ..... throw the letter into the waste-paper basket as he came into the office.
7. Bob watched Simon ..... help Carol into the boat.
8. From time to time innocent people have been made **.....** suffer unjustly.
9. He did not know what had made him ..... pour out this stream of rubbish.
10. That wonderful opportunity was let ..... slip.
11. We had better ..... get started.
12. I was amazed to hear him ..... tell her a lie.
13. They were heard **.....** come.
14. What did you see him ..... do after that.
15. For the first time since he had first known Ben, Philip could feel him ..... hesitate.
16. Great efforts are being made **.....** ensure that such people are helped.
17. The more you try to make him ..... do something, the more determined he is not ..... do it.
18. I wouldn't have let him ..... go off.

19. You had better ..... let me ..... give you one of these tablets.

20. Would you have him ..... come up please?

21. There are many words and phrases which are peculiar to Scottish use, and this is felt ..... maintain national distinctness quite enough.

22. I could not but smile to hear her ..... talk in that way.

2 Replace the following sentences in bold type by an infinitive construction and rewrite the sentences.

1. **You should say something.** I want .....
2. Would you like **that I help you**?
3. **Peter said that you should go home now.** Peter wanted .....
4. **You must leave in the morning.** He wanted .....
5. It's true that the unemployment rate is still appalling - the rate was recently around 12.5 % and we consider **that it will go over 13%.**
6. People think **that Mr Templeton has been a very cautious man all his life**.
7. I should hate **that you ask him a favour**.
8. Not for an instant did he believe **that Daniel spoke the truth**.
9. It is said **that the natives of these islands are cannibals.** (passive voice)
10. We believed **that she lied.** (passive voice)
11. He supposed **that we stand to attention**. (passive voice)
12. He considered **that he had been lucky beyond reason.**

3 Replace the following sentences by one and rewrite the sentences with an infinitive construction.

1. The suitcase is too heavy. I can't carry it.
2. The coffee is too hot. I can't drink it.

3. He was quick. He followed their advice.
4. I think you were right. You told us.
5. You are very kind. You don't say that.
6. She was naughty. She pulled the kitten's tail.
7. The opportunity was too favourable. We can't miss it.
8. It is sure. He will succeed.
9. He racked his brain. He wanted to say something sensible.

4 Replace the subordinate clauses in bold type by an infinitive construction and rewrite the sentences.

1. She bought a small camera **with which she wanted to take snapshots.**
2. He hasn't got a chair **on which he can sit.**
3. There's a table **on which you can write.**
4. This is a depressing message **that I must send to you** and I regret it.
5. Apparently Mrs Miller was the first **who discovered the broken window.**
6. There was no broom **with which we could sweep**.
7. I don't know **who I could speak to.**
8. He was the very last **who left the office**.
9. Peter was the next **who arrived at the bottom of the hill.**
10. Peter was the only one **who returned to the hotel**.
11. It was the best thing **that we could do.**
12. She didn't really mind having no friend **with whom she could play.**
13. He is not an easy man **with whom you can get along.**
14. You think that it's the easiest way **how you can get rid of us** if you give us what we want.

15. In New York I have nine channels **from which I can choose**, and most times I can find nothing.

16. Carol was the most likely person **who could come to Rome**.

17. In 1964, the millionth guestworker **who entered the country** was given an honorary welcome before the press.

18. For most women without young children **after whom they have to look**, life at home and shopping are unsatisfying.

19. To the American, who has to travel five days and four nights by railroad to get across the continent, a few hundred miles are just no impediment **of which he would** speak.

20. He would have been the first **who would have resented the imputation** that he was a snob.

5 Replace the indirect interrogative sentences in bold type by an infinitive construction and rewrite the sentences.

1. Without TV people would not know **what they should do in their spare time.**

2. Peter and Mike could not make up their minds **where they should go for a holiday**.

3. I have so many questions to ask that I don't know **where I should start.**

4. Charles halted, stood for several seconds wondering vaguely **what he should do**, then turned round and began to retrace his steps.

Der Present Infinitive Passive

1 Put the verbs in brackets into the present infinitive passive.

1. This parcel is **(handle)** carefully.

2. The news had **(keep)** secret.

3. Even Julia seemed **(impress)**.

4. The opinions seem **(divide)**.

5. I want **(trust)**.

6. There was no fire **(see)**, only clouds of smoke.

7. It is too urgent **(put off)**.

8. His age has **(take account of).**

9. It is **(doubt)** if she will ever make it.

10. She was very much what has come **(call)** a personality.

11. Education, too, needs **(give)** more practical objectives.

12. I don't want **(see)** by my future boss in a bar.

13. The south and the east were the first areas **(settle)** because of their temperate climate.

14. It is the custom for boys of the upper class **(send)** to a public school.

15. There are details **(settle)**.

16. The only light **(see)** came from the window of the sheriff's office.

17. For some reason, I continued to urge him, but Robinson was not a man **(persuade)**.

18. He is the second man **(kill)** in that way.

19. The long-term effects of oil pollution are only now beginning **(study)** in depth.

20. Once we'd finally got in front of a TV set, we were not going **(pull)** away again so easily.

21. In every school the head teacher has a great deal of autonomy in deciding what is **(teach)** and how the teaching is **(carry out)**.

22. Another factor **(consider)** of new communications when thinking about the future systems is the rapid pace of technological progress.

23. She is great fun **(marry to)**.

2 Decide whether to use the present infinitive active or the present infinitive passive.

1. He was busy and didn't want **(disturb).**

2. I propose **(have)** a conversation with you this evening.

3. Mr Atkinson didn't seem **(notice)** the difference.

4. The chief carpenter called his apprentice and ordered him **(make)** a bed.
5. The paper is **(find)** in the first drawer to the right.
6. The plants have **(water)**, or they'll not thrive.
7. We'd love your friends **(come).**
8. Do I have **(blame)** for that?
9. English drivers are so considerate, and they never seem **(get)** excited or lose their tempers.
10. He caused the engine **(go)** slower, so that he could stop at any time.
11. He is **(address)** as captain.
12. He spoke quite openly, and I found nothing **(suspect)** in his manner.
13. Many people would be needed if Australia's industry was **(build up)** and if the rich resources of the continent were **(exploit)**.
14. Mrs Brown had known all the time that Robinson's Park was going **(turn)** into a car park.
15. Reality is something that we must learn **(live)** with.
16. You had better **(dismiss)** it from your mind.
17. By inventing the spinning machine, Hargreaves caused many workers **(lose)** their jobs.
18. The fat boy waited **(ask)** his name.
19. Hoping to raise themselves in society, they decided **(collect)** antique furniture.
20. By whom are the two sections of each stanza supposed **(sing)**?

Der Perfect Infinitive Active

1 Put the verbs in brackets into the perfect infinitive active.

1. They were relieved **(cross)** the Atlantic.
2. It seems **(get)** colder.
3. They ought **(know).**

4. He is thought **(leave)** the house at 7 p.m.

5. They are supposed **(lose)** their way.

6. **(Make)** the same mistake twice was unforgivable.

7. She appeared not **(see)** him.

8. The introduction of the health service seems **(do)** much to improve the condition of people's teeth in general.

9. He was understood **(lose)** his fortune.

10. He oughtn't **(go)** near the lion.

11. He heard Mrs Miller's cheerful halloo to him as he went by, but he pretended not **(hear).**

12. It was an inconceivably stupid thing **(do).**

13. It was curious that he seemed **(lose)** the power of expressing himself.

14. I was **(meet)** her at the station.

15. The President has to work to gain support in Congress for the bills which he wants **(pass).**

16. He ought, surely, **(rejoice)** in this just retribution for the harm inflicted upon him.

17. Foreign demand remains high; the last three months for which data are available show export orders **(rise)** 15 % on a year-on-year basis.

Der Perfect Infinitive Passive

1 Put the verbs in brackets into the perfect infinitive passive.

1. For a moment he seemed even **(deprive)** of the power of speech.

2. Nothing seems **(disarrange)** and the drawers haven't been interfered with.

3. **(Educate)** at one of the private universities of high prestige is a great advantage in the pursuit of a good job.

4. Oxford's first college claims **(found)** in 1249, Cambridge's first in 1348.

5. The customer called the waiter and complained that the soup was cold, adding that it ought **(serve)** in a hot dish.

2 Put the verbs in brackets both into the present infinitive active and the perfect infinitive active and translate every sentence.

1. Parents don't seem **(change)** much.
2. I am sorry **(displease)** you, sir.
3. The sun seemed **(grow)** hotter.
4. I am sorry **(keep)** you waiting.
5. We seem **(lose)** something.
6. She ought not **(say)** that.
7. I should like **(see)** it.
8. We ought **(trust)** him.
9. I pretended not **(understand)** her.
10. They are supposed **(commit)** the crime.
11. They seem **(do)** that job pretty well.
12. Scotland Yard still seems **(make)** little progress in the case of the ten valuable paintings, which were stolen from the London home of Lord Carrington last Sunday.

☞ Die entsprechenden Lösungen befinden sich im Lösungsheft auf Seite 63ff.

Das Gerund (The Gerund)

Das Present Gerund Active

1 Put the verbs in brackets into the gerund.

1. I just didn't feel like **(go)** to pack my stuff, so I threw the burden on Bob.
2. She hasn't finished **(do)** her exercise yet.
3. I can't help **(laugh)**.
4. My father doesn't mind **(wash up)** on Sundays.
5. My sister enjoys **(travel)** by train, but some people may prefer **(fly)**.
6. He suggested **(go).**
7. It seemed impossible that he could avoid **(be)** discovered.
8. Don't keep **(ask)** me.
9. We are looking forward to **(see)** you.
10. I could have died **(laugh)**.
11. How can I help **(see)** what is in front of my eyes?
12. We expect our unemployment to keep **(increase)** even if an economic recovery arrives.
13. Not that I minded your **(spend)** the night there, but I thought you were in Munich.
14. He had polished the suitcase with a special English leather dressing, not that it needed **(polish)** because he took such good care of it, but for its protection.
15. The relief of seeing her was so great that he could not resist **(stare)** directly at her for several seconds.

2 Put the following nouns which are gerunds into the corresponding sentence.

1. At the **.....** of the nineteenth century, a canal was opened between the Hudson River and Lake Erie.

feeling

2.	A group of men had come on to the balcony of the ..... across the street.	**meaning**
3.	The driver didn't stop at the ...... He went on at full speed.	**beginning**
4.	I walked into the .....-..... and sat down to breakfast.	**crossing**
5.	In the dim, grey light of early morning he woke up with a strange	**building**
6.	Synonyms are words which have similar .....s, but not the same	**dining-room**
7.	I regret to tell you that the ..... will not take place.	**driving-test**
8.	Do you want Bob to do the ..... this morning?	**blessing**
9.	Try to be a human	**meeting**
10.	It is a ..... for her to get that job.	**shopping**
11.	Although it was summer, the temperature dropped below .... and our .... froze solid.	**being**
12.	If an American moves to a new state he must pass its .....-..... before he can get a licence.	**living**
13.	As private citizens we have to work for our ..... as well.	**freezing point** **drinking water**
14.	These Scottish pipers are playing at the ..... of a High-land games meeting.	**landing**
15.	The ..... of roads, streets, houses and factories and commercial zones, occupies both local and central government more and more.	**training**
16.	There is a popular ..... that Australia lives on the sheep's back.	**misunderstanding**
17.	America's third attempt at a moon ..... in April 1970 failed because of an explosion of fuel cells on board the spacecraft.	**opening**

18. They took a ..... to the beer as soon as they had tasted it. **saying**

19. If the ..... and qualifications are equal, nine times out of ten the job will go to the white man. **planning**

20. There appears to be a ...... **liking**

3 Put the verbs in brackets into the gerund.

1. Father likes the idea of **(go)** to Scotland.
2. He does not take any interest in **(read).**
3. He pretended to have difficulty in **(express)** himself.
4. I went on **(eat)** breakfast.
5. Jugglers are always very good at **(toss)** and **(catch)** balls.
6. Keep on **(try).**
7. Lee was so good at **(jump)** that he nearly won the prize.
8. She had a habit of **(break)** off her sentences in the middle.
9. She insisted on **(get)** the address.
10. She is interested in **(read)** stories about crime.
11. Such a campaign has little chance of **(be)** successful.
12. They did not discuss the possibility of **(get)** married.
13. He hurried to the child's room, but was prevented from **(enter)** by his brother.
14. It gave me an opportunity of **(settle)** the affair.
15. Rockets are the only known motors that are capable of **(propel)** a vehicle in empty space.
16. She succeeded in **(convince)** him.
17. The computer is extremely good at **(work)** rapidly, at **(work)** in a unique way on well-presented data.

18. Whom did Mr Winterbottom suspect of **(be)** the thief?

19. Far from **(be)** necessary this agreement will help in **(solve)** the problem.

20. He smiled apologetically, as though conscious of **(say)** something slightly ridiculous.

21. It is no use talking on the subject of **(drive),** without first laying really tremendous emphasis on the importance of **(read)** the Highway Code.

22. Miners are always warned against **(cave)** in.

23. The commercial supremacy which England possessed in the nineteenth century further preserved the Englishman from the necessity of **(learn)** foreign languages.

4 Replace the following sentences in bold type using the gerund and rewrite the sentences.

1. **After they had defeated the Norwegians at Stamford Bridge**, King Harold and his tired men marched south.

2. We asked a solicitor for advice **before we went to court**.

3. She taught the class **although she was feeling bad**. She taught the class in spite of ...

4. Her father smiled, then looked at her seriously **before he replied.**

5. She had a headache **because she was sitting in the sun.**

6. **Although he had a cold,** the swimmer succeeded in crossing the channel. In spite of...

7. **Although I trust you,** I must make some inquiries. In spite of ...

8. He was sent to prison **because he stole.**

9. The boy was reprimanded **because he was disobedient.**

10. If you were any good, you'd help me **and you would not stand there criticising.**

11. They quarrelled, then left each other **and didn't make friends again.**

12. She had been waiting for the traffic lights to change, **when they didn't turn green** but went out.

13. **Since he finished college** Mr Miller has partly supported himself by teaching creative writing in several colleges and universities.

14. You can walk for miles **and don't meet anybody.**

15. I studied him quietly **but did not appear to do so.**

5 Decide whether to use the gerund or the infinitive or both.

1. In the afternoon she sat down in front of the cabin and began **(knit)** a jacket for Mike.
2. Have you started **(learn)** to drive yet?
3. I hate **(interfere)** in other people's affairs.
4. The tramp said he didn't like **(work).**
5. I think I prefer **(stay)** outside.
6. Simon proposed **(leave)** before the show was over.
7. You must remember **(post)** the letter.
8. Bob remembered **(go)** to a cocktail party at the Stevens' with Simon Atkinson.
9. I don't know what you want me **(say).**
10. Mother didn't mind Betty **(climb)** mountains.
11. I couldn't help **(cry)** when I heard the news.
12. He took his shoes off so he could put his feet up on the sofa, lay back on a pillow, and continued **(read)** Bob's letter.
13. A growing number of people prefer **(watch)** sporting events on TV to **(attend)** them.
14. All the petunias want **(water),** very badly.
15. When the girls saw that Mary did not like the questions, they at once stopped **(ask).**
16. He had not stopped **(rest)**.
17. It's no use **(object)** to his taking risks.

6 Put the verbs in brackets into the gerund and the personal pronouns either into the object case or use the corresponding possessive pronoun.

1. I strongly resent **(you, come)** late.

2. My sister Caroline hates **(I, eat)** with dirty fingers.
3. That shouldn't prevent **(you, go)**.
4. Forgive **(I, leave)** you alone.
5. Laura likes **(her friend, read)** aloud.
6. I rely on **(you, return)** the book soon.
7. She taught the class in spite of **(her mother, be)** ill.
8. You know, your father's very concerned about **(you, come)** home.
9. How do you think I can do only Latin with **(you, interrupt)** every few seconds?
10. Mary can't remember **(he, post)** the letter.
11. I won't have **(you, smoke)** at your age.
12. Will the new job involve **(you, be)** away.
13. I don't think there'll be any trouble now about **(you, have)** Christmas Day off.
14. It can get hold of you without **(you, know)** it.
15. There is no avoiding **(he, leave)** the club.
16. We shall not always expect to find **(they, support)** our view.
17. I won't have **(you, talk)** me over with him.

Das Present Gerund Passive

1 Put the verbs in brackets into the present gerund passive.

1. She kept quiet for fear of **(fire).**
2. He said nothing for fear of **(misunderstand).**
3. I came as near to them as I could without **(see).**
4. She hates **(stare at).**
5. Adults rightly resent **(treat)** as children.

6. It seemed impossible that he could avoid **(discover).**

7. After **(welcome)** by the headmaster, they were shown round the building.

8. After **(capture),** escaping and finally **(recapture),** Charles I was executed in London on 30 January, 1649.

9. If there was any sensation he hated, it was that of **(follow)** by anybody.

10. He is faced with the danger of his secret **(know).**

11. Nobody likes **(laugh at).**

12. Attempts at controlling the 10 % of fifteen year-olds who resent **(oblige)** to stay at school absorb much of the teachers' efforts.

13. When the lady protested at **(tell)** to open her suitcase for inspection, the customs official firmly but politely pointed out that she must do as she was asked.

2 Decide whether to use the present gerund active or the present gerund passive.

1. He avoided **(answer)** directly.

2. Mary and Bob burst out **(laugh).**

3. On a rainy day the girls couldn't go **(swim).** So they went to the museum.

4. He was not a man who would forgive **(deceive).**

5. He bit hungrily into his bread and swallowed a couple of mouthfuls, then continued **(speak).**

6. He may have an opportunity of **(appoint)** a Queen's Counsel.

7. Kennedy's success, first in **(choose)** as Democratic candidate and then in **(elect)** President, was partly due to the fact that very many Catholics voted for him because he was a Catholic.

8. He passed by with studied indifference, his face averted, eyes fixed straight ahead, as though to avoid **(see)** her.

9. Not **(bind)** to the direction of time - as so many other media are - the printed book is still the most valuable medium for teaching and learning.

10. Suppliers of software for personal computers are locked in a battle of wits with their customers over the making and breaking of devices designed to stop programmes from **(copy).**

11. There is virtually no erosion on the moon and footprints can last for 500,000 years before **(erase)** by the invisible rain of micrometeorites.

12. There was a deal table under the window where he and the old man could talk without fear of **(overhear).**

Das Perfect Gerund Active

1 Put the verbs in brackets into the perfect gerund active.

1. First we thank you for **(accept).**
2. At least you have the satisfaction of **(do)** your duty.
3. She denied **(eat)** it.
4. We remember **(leave)** the book on the table.
5. He got an award for **(save)** the boy's life.
6. He remembered **(see)** the man the evening before.
7. Does he regret **(study)** so hard?
8. I told him not to bother about **(fail).**
9. Of course he could not pay at once, **(give up)** all his money.
10. After **(grow)** outward, Los Angeles is now in the process of growing upward.
11. After **(appoint)** a Prime Minister the Queen appoints other ministers and public servants on his advice.
12. The police had questioned three youths on suspicion of **(do)** the horrible deed, but the youths had been later released.
13. M.P.s often vote without **(hear)** a debate, and perhaps without knowing exactly what is the question.
14. I am forty years old, in perfect health, never **(know)** a day's illness.

15. After **(receive)** Mr and Mrs Barton graciously, the Consul proposed a stroll round the garden.

Das Perfect Gerund Passive

1 Put the verbs in brackets into the perfect gerund passive.

1. Both President Ford and Vice-President Rockefeller held office without **(elect),** but appointed through consultation.
2. After **(recognize)**, he could not go and sit at a table with an unattended girl.
3. His sister, conscious of **(rob)** of something, had set up a feeble wail.
4. After **(tell)** the news, the men returned to work.
5. After **(sentence)** to death for his crimes Cunningham was taken to a small single room with a fireplace and a barred window.

2 Put the verbs in brackets into the present gerund active or the perfect gerund active or both.

1. I regret **(trouble)** you, Sir.
2. Please return the enclosed letter after **(read)** it.
3. He remembered **(see)** the man.
4. After not **(find)** this article he left the shop without **(buy)** anything.
5. After **(reach)** the mouth of the River Thames, Roger joined a gang of smugglers.
6. After **(try)** to get a job in a restaurant without success, he wanted to find a place to sleep in a park.
7. When questioned by the master about the disappearance of a bicycle from the school cycle sheds 2 days before, the boy flatly denied **(have)** anything to do with it.
8. Finding the evening extremely dull, Mr Burton cursed himself for **(accept)** the invitation.
9. After **(leave)** the bus, he was suffused by an agitation so acute he scarcely dared approach the solitary house.

☞ Die entsprechenden Lösungen befinden sich im Lösungsheft auf Seite 68ff.

Die Partizipien (The Participles)

Das Present Participle Active

1 Put the verbs in brackets into the present participle.

1. I heard her **(whistle)**.
2. Remain **(sit)**.
3. When I saw him **(run down)** the drive I called him from the kitchen window.
4. It doesn't sound **(encourage)**.
5. She was found **(lie)** in the street.
6. Do you know what they heard me **(say)**?
7. He lay there **(listen)** to what they were arguing so loud over.
8. Geraldine, dressed in black, was very pale and sat **(twist)** her hands together.
9. We stopped outside a big film studio and stood **(watch)** the people going in and out, hoping to see a famous film-star.
10. Oh, you look **(starve)**.
11. We must fully explore all the consequences and possibilities, even when these possibilities seem **(frighten)**.

2 Put the following present participles used as adjectives into the corresponding sentence.

1. To me the most **.....** programmes are films with ghosts in haunted castles.	**interesting**
2. **.....** college dormitories will be used.	**following**
3. China is one of the most **.....** countries in the world.	**existing**
4. If you ever go to London, you will see many **.....** things there.	**exciting**

5. George promised to ring them up the ..... week.
6. Australia today is a rapidly ..... land.
7. His heart bumped in his breast with ..... loudness.
8. A ..... number of people prefer watching sporting events on TV to attending them.
9. The ..... influence of the mass media has caused a steady infiltration of American words and expressions into British English.
10. As centuries had gone by, the village had climbed further and further up the ..... hills.

fascinating

surrounding

growing

developing

frightening

increasing

3 Shorten the following subordinate clauses in bold type using the present participle.

1. I've fallen into a bad habit, eating dinner **while I am watching television**.
2. **Although he is rich**, he is not happy.
3. Most American jazz musicians **who come to Europe** settle in Paris.
4. I was passing the main gate, when I nearly ran into a man **who was hurrying along**.
5. Such little scenes **which interrupt a programme every now and again** are known as Commercials on American TV.
6. **As she fell downstairs** she twisted her ankle.
7. A few days after the end of the war, Abraham Lincoln was shot by a fanatic Southerner **while he was attending a theatre in Washington.**
8. **While they are going about their normal work** the police do not carry guns: they themselves prefer to be unarmed.
9. **When I entered the house** I knew at once that something terrible had happened.
10. **As he was lying there in the darkness**, he knew he was an outcast.
11. **When he turned quickly,** he found the door of the room open and Harrison standing in front of him.

12. **Persons who enter or leave the train** when it is in motion do so at their own risk.
13. The proportion of the people **who live in the fifty biggest metropolitan areas** is growing steadily.
14. **When he came home** he found his wife in tears.
15. If an accent is so broad that it makes understanding difficult, then the speaker is at a disadvantage **when he is talking to people from elsewhere**.
16. **While I was packing a suitcase**, I came across an envelope that Donald gave me in Munich, and which for some unaccountable reason I had forgotten until now.
17. **When he looked up** he caught a glimpse of something red.
18. **While he was waiting bareheaded in the rain**, he lost all count of time.
19. With so great a proportion of the young people **who enter higher education** there is a problem of maintaining academic standards.
20. The House of Lords consists of the Lords Spiritual and the Lords Temporal, as well as peers **who hold a life peerage**.
21. She was to go away with Ronald by the night-boat to be his wife and to live with him in Tokyo, where he had a house **that was waiting for her.**

Das Past Participle

1 Put the verbs in brackets into the past participle.

1. He looked **(depress).**
2. He lay **(injure)** at my feet.
3. Carol's voice sounded **(lose)** already.
4. They felt **(relieve)** after the walk-out.
5. John, however, seemed **(occupy)** with his own thoughts.
6. Bob stood **(petrify)** with fear.
7. He remained **(seat)** for some minutes.
8. He felt **(discourage)** and only the prompt appearance of his father prevented him from bursting into tears.

9. Simon seemed **(please)** that Bob was taking his study of Dutch seriously.

10. Some students, who fail to be elected to fraternities feel **(reject).**

2 Put the following past participles used as adjectives into the corresponding sentence.

1.	I won't pay for the **.....** window, it wasn't my fault.	**fallen**
2.	I'll be very glad to help if I can, Bob said in a properly **.....** voice.	**surprised**
3.	She must have fallen right on the **.....** arm.	**broken**
4.	McDonald stood up with a **.....** air.	**injured**
5.	They heaved the **.....** boy to the platform and let him lie.	**excited**
6.	Peter stared back at the Professor with **.....** perplexity.	**satisfied**
7.	Many jobs in factories demand special skills, and only **.....** workers can carry them out.	**complicated**
8.	As a result of modernization fewer manual workers and many more white-collared workers are needed to operate the new **.....** machinery in factories.	**learned**
9.	The rapid development of internal trade and overseas commerce gave **.....** power and wealth into the hands of an expanding middle class.	**trained**
10.	Many a state university has on its faculty the world's most **.....** scholars in literature and the other humanistic studies.	**increased**

3 Shorten the following subordinate clauses in bold type using the past participle.

1. **When he was questioned,** the young man admitted that he was James Rushman's brother Jason.

2. Does monarchy **as it is practised in England today** interfere with the principles of democracy?

3. **If the letter is posted at once**, the letter will arrive in time.

4. **Unless we were forced to return**, we should be there in time.

5. The dangers of living in a hurricane zone seem acceptable **when we compare them with the other dangers** which have to be faced every day.

6. **When it is focused to a sharp point at very close range**, the laser can vaporize any substance on earth.

7. David stood **as if he was turned to stone**.

8. **As she was determined to earn her own living**, Martha had become a housemaid.

9. **As it is provided with thousands of solar cells**, these active transmitters can receive and re-transmit several TV programmes and hundreds of telephone calls simultaneously.

10. He never speaks of himself except **when he is compelled**.

11. **While he is being accompanied by his friend**, the Consul quitted the house and strode down the gravel path towards the tool shed.

12. Windsor Castle **which was founded by William the Conqueror**, stands on the Thames, 22 miles west of London.

13. Manhattan Island **which was bought for 25 dollars from the Indians in 1626**, is now the centre of New York, one of the largest and richest cities in the world.

4 Put the verbs in brackets into the present participle or the past participle.

1. We can't sit here **(talk).**
2. He sat **(hunch)** forward in an armchair, **(smoke)** and **(think).**
3. It began to sound **(excite)** to him.
4. She sounded **(please).**
5. She looked **(disappoint),** but wanting to appear polite, she smiled at him.
6. In the warm dim light the place looked **(invite).**
7. I had the strong feeling that **(excite)** times were coming.

8. I'll be very glad to help if I can, Bob said in a properly **(excite)** voice.

9. For a while they sat in **(depress)** silence.

10. This is a **(depress)** message to send to you and I regret it.

11. In nature, excessive animal numbers are controlled by an **(increase)** death rate, a **(decrease)** birth rate, or migration.

12. An **(increase)** number of married women have taken jobs in offices, shops, factories.

13. **(Leave)** alone, Consul Carrington had no stomach for his customary after-breakfast cigar.

14. **(Leave)** her with her mother, I hurried downstairs and met Ben coming from the kitchen.

15. I expected to find him **(wait)** for me at the station.

16. It is a way of life they find **(suit)** to their wants.

17. Seeing that the Constitution says that no person shall be deprived of his liberty without due process of law it would seem **(surprise)** that slavery could be allowed to exist.

18. His attention seemed **(focus)** upon Donald.

Das Perfect Participle Active

1 Shorten the subordinate clauses in bold type using the perfect participle.

1. **As I had laboured hard** I was very tired.

2. **As I have lost his telephone number** I couldn't ring him back.

3. **When I had finished my homework** I watched TV.

4. **If you had your car repaired**, be sure to get an estimate.

5. **As he had been cheated once**, he never trusted anybody.

Das Present Participle Passive

1 Put the verbs in brackets into the present participle passive.

1. Something was **(do)**.
2. The strange thing is that I didn't know I was **(look for)**.
3. The orders were given so fast that I could scarcely understand what was **(say)**.
4. By now a second car in the family garage is **(feel)** to be a tiresome necessity rather than a sign of opulence.
5. He was **(wait for)** in the garden.
6. There was of course no way of knowing whether you were **(watch)** at any given moment.

2 Put the verbs in brackets into the present participle active or passive.

1. As I lay **(watch),** I saw the boat draw near to the shore.
2. He could hear Laura **(sing)** to her doll.
3. It was awful to see her **(run)** straight into the lorry.
4. They were **(look at).**
5. We find him **(have)** an early breakfast, and he is already at work.
6. What is **(do)** about the situation?
7. When the car drove off Mr Harris remained **(stand)** upon the portico.
8. All employers are **(ask)** to examine their own practices in appointing staff, at all levels, to ensure that they do not in fact discriminate, without intending to, through habit.

Das Perfect Participle Passive

1 Put the verbs in brackets into the perfect participle passive.

1. Bob glanced over the newspapers from Paris for an item about a scuttled boat's **(find)** near Monaco.

2. Most primary schools are wholly owned and controlled by the local authorities, but about one-third belong to churches, either Anglican or Roman Catholic, **(found)** by religious bodies.

3. The disputes **(settle),** the men returned to work.

4. **(Bite)** twice the postman refused to come into our house.

☞ Die entsprechenden Lösungen befinden sich im Lösungsheft auf Seite 73ff.

Das deutsche *lassen*

1 Rewrite the following sentences using **to have** to express the German *lassen.*

1. I **(cut, my hair;** past tense simple**)** at the barber's.
2. Mrs Stevens **(clean, the windows;** present tense simple**)** every month.
3. I **(wash, my car;** present tense continuous**)** while I am doing my shopping.
4. I **(wash, my car;** past perfect simple**)** before coming here.
5. I **(wash, my car;** future tense simple**)** before going to the check-up.
6. She **(dye, her hair;** present perfect simple**).**
7. We **(redecorate, our house;** future tense simple**).**
8. You **(must take, another picture;** present tense simple**).**
9. In order to be able to vote in the U.S.A., you **(to have to enter, your name;** present tense simple**)** in a list called the electoral register.
10. Any person **(may test, his eyes;** present tense simple**)** free of charge by an optician or eye specialist, but must pay part of the cost of any spectacles that may be provided**.**
11. In June 1688 James II **(born, a son;** past tense simple**)** to him.
12. The houseowner called the tenant and told him **(to make, the roof;** present infinitive**).**
13. Why **(**he, **train, the boy;** present tense simple**)** as a runner?

2 Rewrite the following sentences using **to let** to express the German *lassen.*

1. Please **(hear, me;** present tense simple**)** from you as soon as possible.
2. She **(go out, her cigarette;** past perfect simple**)** and was listening intently.
3. Calmly he **(approach, them;** past tense simple**)** and not until they were within a hundred yards of him did he turn into a lane barred by a gate.
4. By the way, Smith old boy, I suppose you haven't got any razor blades you can **(have, me;** present tense simple**)**?

5. Oh please God, (**not get away, him;** present tense simple**).**

6. I was going to tell you that my brother threw my cap into the river, but you **(not finish, me;** past tense simple**)**.

7. They just **(not do, you;** future tense simple**)** what you'd like to do.

8. Your father ever **(drive, you;** present perfect simple**)** his car?

9. He **(know, her;** conditional**)** his address as soon as he had one.

10. We both had taken on quite a lot of martinis, but he looked capable of driving or naturally I **(not go off, him;** conditional perfect**)**.

11. At first her parents refused **(go, her;** present infinitive**)** but at last Mary managed to persuade them.

12. One knew that it was all rubbish so why **(worry, oneself;** passive infinitive**)** by it?

13. **(not trap in, yourself;** negative imperative, passive infinitive**)** there.

3 Rewrite the following sentences using **to make** to express the German *lassen*.

1. She swept the house and did the dishes and sent out the laundry, and then she **(get up and wash and dress, the children;** past tense simple**).**

2. Mrs Atkinson, Bob said gently, I want you to know that I do everything I can to **(come back, Simon;** present tense simple**)**.

3. Discussion **(think, the students;** present tense simple**).**

4. What do you think **(write, Consul Carrington;** past tense simple**)** this letter?

5. If I told what strange things I made, it **(laugh, you;** conditional**)** at me?

6. What **(think, people;** present tense simple**)** that there may be intelligent beings on Mars?

7. What **(forget, Mary;** present perfect simple**)** that it will soon be Christmas?

8. She talked with an open jeering hatred which **(feel, Ben;** past tense simple**)** uneasy.

9. Civil courts deal with offences against individuals libels, etc.- and a wrongdoer **(compensate,** usually; present tense simple, passive voice**)** the sufferer by a payment to cover the damages.

4 Rewrite the following sentences using **to keep** or **to leave** to express the German *lassen*.

1. They can **(lie about, everything;** present tense simple**)** about.
2. He **(wonder, me;** past tense simple**)**.
3. I **(discuss, them;** past tense simple**)** the matter and went to bed.
4. **(Play, them;** imperative**).**
5. Ben **(wait, her;** past perfect simple**)** on a date?

5 Rewrite the following sentences using **to allow** to express the German *lassen.*

1. Peter thought his father might not **(go, him;** present tense simple**)** to the party.
2. Her parents realized that they must **(lead, her;** present tense simple**)** her own life.
3. Of course they **(talk, him;** conditional**)** to Mary.
4. Would they **(ring up, him;** present tense simple**)** his family?
5. Some states **(impose, local communities;** present tense simple**)** their own speed limits.
6. He turned pale but **(be intimidated, himself;** past tense, negative**).**

6 Decide whether to use **to have, to let, to make, to keep, to leave** or **to allow** to express the German *lassen* and rewrite the following sentences.

1. He wondered what **(think, Mary;** past tense simple**)** his father had been a sissy.
2. I **(not wash, my car;** present perfect simple**)** ever since I have it.
3. I **(wash, my car;** past tense continuous**)** while I went to see the film.
4. **(show, me;** imperative**)** you what I've bought.
5. They had to **(lie, the wounded soldiers;** infinitive**)** in the blazing sun.
6. We must not **(grow, our hair;** present tense simple**).**
7. William **(build, strong castles;** past tense simple**)** all over his kingdom to keep the Saxons down.

8. Why you **(cut, your hair;** past tense simple**)**?

9. We are only going to have about three months **(organize, a programme;** present infinitive**)**.

10. I feel sure that she **(know, me;** future tense simple**)**.

11. **(run free, the dog;** negative imperative**).**

12. **(see, the others;** negative imperative**)** you.

13. For distances of less than 100 kilometres it is not necessary **(endorse, your passport;** present infinitive).

14. He agreed **(help, Perkins;** present infinitive**)**.

15. He was so pleased with our work that he introduced us to a friend of his who also wanted **(paint, his house;** present infinitive).

16. I advise you **(go, him;** negative present infinitive**)**.

17. I am sorry **(wait, you;** perfect infinitive**)**.

18. It happened that whole families of ten people **(live;** past tense simple, passive voice**)** in one room and wages were so low that people could hardly feed themselves.

19. It'll take a little time **(make, the sandwiches;** present infinitive**)**.

20. **(Let's go, it;** imperative**).**

☞ Die entsprechenden Lösungen befinden sich im Lösungsheft auf Seite 78ff.

Der bestimmte und unbestimmte Artikel (The Definite and Indefinite Article)

1 Put in the definite or indefinite article where necessary.

1. She is very good at drawing **.....** animals.
2. **.....** animal whose neck is very long is called **.....** giraffe.
3. If you play **.....** ball with us, we'll play **.....** ball with you.
4. We should prefer to go by **.....** car.
5. She was taken away by **.....** ambulance.
6. Strong young **.....** girls do not easily faint.
7. The boat was rowed by **.....** boy who jumped into the water crying that he was going to save me.
8. In some states of the U.S.A. **.....** boys and **.....** girls are allowed to drive a car at the age of sixteen.
9. Who is **.....** boy who is standing near the window?
10. He congratulated him before all **.....** employees.
11. This is **.....** book I have been speaking of all the time.
12. When I was **.....** child, I used to be read to out of **.....** book of fairy tales I had been given for my birthday.
13. She was **.....** daughter of **.....** leading New England Presbyterian minister and **.....** wife of **.....** professor of theology.
14. Among them there was **.....** mother with her two children.
15. Surely **.....** mother can be trusted to look after her own child.
16. When focused to a sharp point at very close range, the laser can vaporize any substance on **.....** earth.
17. For a long time the Chinese have been, as they are now, among the poorest people on **.....** earth.
18. The computer is just as valuable as **.....** man using it.

19. ..... man must eat to live.

20. If ..... men were more reasonable, there would be no more war.

21. Were I only given ..... chance!

22. Is there ..... chance that machines may learn more than ..... man?

23. People who like to be more fully informed get their bulletin-type news from television and ..... radio, and their depth news from newspapers.

24. His body felt leaden and slow, as if he were trying to raise himself out of deep ..... water.

25. ..... computer doesn't compare with ..... human brain in handling data that haven't yet jelled.

26. I was at a loss for ..... answer.

2 Add the definite or indefinite article to the following names where necessary.

1. I will tell ..... Mr Robinson that you are here.

2. The woman we visited was my ..... aunt Martha.

3. Peter lived in London, and he was visiting ..... aunt in New York for a few months.

4. ..... Tom came home from school the other day, and his mother asked him: Are you getting on well at school, ... Tom?

5. Soon after Christmas ..... Robinsons went to Aspen, Colorado.

6. ..... little Bob couldn't remember the names very well.

7. Of course ..... young Simon and his friends often went into the city.

8. ..... Mrs Burton wrote a postcard to ..... Harrison family.

9. Wasn't there ..... Ben Cunningham in Simon's address book?

10. If ..... Johnson had lived, he would certainly have changed his will.

11. The letter to ..... Atkinsons began as a polite greeting and a thank-you for the bon voyage basket and the comfortable accommodations.

12. The children can, however, be very naughty, especially when they are at ..... Aunt Jenny's.

13. Whom would you call ..... father of railroading?

14. When are you going to let ..... Susan know? Not until you're picked up.

15. My dear ..... Caroline, what are you talking about?

16. On his passage through the outer office he observed, from the corner of his eye, that ..... Cliff had already returned.

17. ..... Burtons were wealthy people, and ..... Samantha led a sheltered life.

18. If ..... House of Lords should reject a bill which has been passed by ..... Commons, the bill can go no further for a few months.

19. The village ladies had long expected that ..... Robinson would marry his housekeeper, ... Miss Adams, and perhaps he would not have escaped if ..... Stevens had not come to live here a year ago.

20. Those who do the will of ..... Father are brethren of ..... Jesus Christ.

3 Add the definite or indefinite article to the following titles, titles of occupation, social, political and religious expressions where necessary.

1. Trafalgar Square is one of the largest and best-known squares in London. It is named after ..... Admiral Nelson's victory at Cape Trafalgar.

2. Sheila Anderson's father was ..... acrobat in a famous circus, which travelled all over England.

3. The Queen was crowned, like her predecessors, by ..... Archbishop of Canterbury in Westminster Abbey.

4. The committee appointed Mr Stevens ..... chairman.

5. ..... Chairman of the House of Commons is ..... Speaker.

6. Who's ..... boss here?

7. Jimmy Carter was ..... Baptist preacher.

8. ..... Cosmonaut Alexei Leonov had shown that a space-suited man could survive in space and ..... Astronaut Edward White demonstrated that he could maneuver freely in it.

9. To be ..... barrister a man must be a member of one of the four Inns of Court and pass the Bar examination.

10. ..... Archbishop Cranmer, author of some of our most magnificent collects, was publicly burned alive at Oxford.

11. ..... Lord Chancellor of England presides over the debates from his position on the Woolsack - a red cloth couch stuffed with wool.

12. He was raised to the rank of ..... Colonel.

13. Until the beginning of the twentieth century, it would be true to say that there were really only two parties: first, ... Whigs and ..... Tories, then, ... Liberals and ..... Conservatives.

14. Parliament is ..... sovereign.

15. The great length of the medical training does not necessarily make it difficult for a poor man to become ..... doctor, because medical students, like other students, may receive grants to cover the cost of their studies.

16. He was a commonplace, mean-looking man who might have been ..... engineer or technician of some kind.

17. These days it is quite usual for the office of ..... mayor or ..... lord mayor to be held by a woman, as many women are elected in their own right to local councils.

18. ..... Lord Mayor of London is the chief officer of this small area only, presiding over the needs of 4,000 inhabitants while ..... Chairman of the Greater London Council deals with 7 million.

19. Each year the taxes are authorised by a Finance Act, which is based on the Budget presented by ..... Chancellor of the Exchequer in April.

20. It is almost impossible to be elected without being ..... Republican or ..... Democrat, but the need to work within one of these parties does not force a man to adopt any narrow opinion.

4 Add the definite or indefinite article to the following geographical expressions where necessary.

1. Bob boarded the bus for ..... Athens.

2. In 1984 the Olympic Games returned to ..... city of LA.

3. ..... Australia is a federation of six states with a Federal Parliament and a Parliament for each of the states.

4. The legislative power in ..... Great Britain resides in the House of Commons.

5. Every year thousands of visitors from ..... Continent come to ..... England by boat from ..... Ostend or ..... Calais.

6. Because ..... England is old, ... Englishman lays great store by tradition.

7. I am ..... Englishman, said I and I wish to help you.

8. The Everglades National Park near ..... Miami in ..... South Florida is a vast swampy area more than 100 kilometres from ..... north to ..... south and from ..... east to ..... west.

9. Some 50 years after Cook landed in ..... Botany Bay, free settlers began to arrive in larger numbers from ..... Britain.

10. Sir Edmund Hillary was the first conqueror of ..... Mount Everest.

11. ..... Matterhorn was first scaled in 1865.

12. We shall need an oxygen apparatus, such as the climbers in ..... Himalayas have.

13. Founded by William the Conqueror, Windsor Castle stands on ..... Thames, 22 miles west of ..... London.

14. We had about a dozen sick people on board when we crossed ..... Channel.

15. It was in the nineteenth century that ..... Australia, ... New Zealand, ... South Africa, and in part ..... Canada, received their English-speaking populations.

16. More than 2,000,000 migrants have arrived since the war, the largest groups coming from ..... United Kingdom and ..... Ireland, from ..... Italy, ... Greece, ... Germany, and ..... Netherlands.

17. From ..... Boston to ..... Los Angeles is as far as from ..... France to ..... Central Asia, and from ..... east to ..... west there are five time zones.

18. All but a few years of my life have been spent in and around ..... New York City, but I cannot claim an intense feeling of identification with the city.

19. The Royal Opera House at Covent Garden, in central ..... London, is leased by the government to the Covent Garden Opera House Trust, which receives a government grant.

20. Far below us now we can see ..... London with the silver ribbon of ..... Thames running through it.

21. The plains run from ..... Gulf of Mexico in ..... south up to the Canadian border and beyond-an endless open space comparable with ..... Siberia.

22. Tourism often leads to unrestrained development, well illustrated in the case of **.....** Côte d'Azur.

23. Huge national parks have been created in **.....** Rocky Mountains to preserve the beauty of the landscape and to protect wild life.

24. People who wanted to get from **.....** East to **.....** West could go by three routes, all long and dangerous: round **.....** Cape Horn, across **.....** Isthmus of Panama, overland by wagon.

25. I have never been taken for **.....** Englishman before, though I was once spoken to as if I were **.....** American.

26. Up to the outbreak of the 1914-18 war, **.....** Europe was largely ruled by hereditary monarchies.

27. **.....** Australia ranks second only to **.....** Argentina as an exporter of beef and veal.

28. **.....** London will continue to be a world centre of finance.

29. The Celts were a group of related tribes, linked by language, religion and culture that gave rise to the first civilization north of **.....** Alps.

30. **.....** Chicago, sprawling in boisterous disorder along the south-western shore of **.....** Lake Michigan, is the central terminal of **.....** United States.

31. Thus growing trade between **.....** East and **.....** West was accompanied by an increase in trading at home.

32. **.....** Chicago is an industrial and commercial city, dominating the five industrial mid-western states **.....** east of **.....** Mississippi.

5 Add the definite or indefinite article to the following names of streets, places, bridges, buildings where necessary.

1. **.....** Regent Street runs from **.....** Piccadilly Circus to **.....** Oxford Street.

2. **.....** Mall and **.....** Strand are two famous London streets.

3. Linda was standing at the corner of **.....** Broadway.

4. **.....** St James's Park is near **.....** Buckingham Palace.

5. Harold marched north and defeated the Norsemen in a great battle near **.....** Stamford Bridge.

6. ..... Tower of London used to be a state prison.

7. William the Conqueror was crowned King of England in ..... Westminster Abbey.

8. ..... church is a place where people can meet others with whom they would like to make friends.

9. In the morning a lot of people go to ..... church.

10. ..... hospital is opposite the museum.

11. Her weak point is not listening in ..... class.

12. She taught ..... class in spite of feeling bad.

13. We asked a solicitor for advice before going to ..... court.

14. As a result he was sent to ..... jail as a horse thief.

15. When I was at ..... university I had a coloured boy friend.

16. However, by six o'clock ..... school is empty and the caretaker and the cleaners can finish their work in peace.

17. I shall see you at ..... office tomorrow.

18. I won't be able to go to ..... theatre tomorrow.

19. ..... Parliament in London makes laws for all the countries in the U. K.

20. Even today it is ..... Parliament, rather than the Queen, which governs England and makes the laws.

21. Side streets to the right of ..... Fifth Avenue are called 41st ..... East Street etc. while streets to the left are called 41st ..... West Street etc.

22. If I were in ..... Parliament I would spend enough money on hospitals.

23. ..... St Paul's Cathedral is the second largest Christian church, second only to ..... St Peter's in Rome.

24. The separation of ..... church and state is a cardinal American principle.

25. The Queen is also Head of ..... Church of England to which, at least nominally, the vast majority of Englishmen belong.

26. ..... court is presided over by a judge, but the decision on guilt or innocence is made by a jury of twelve citizens chosen by lot from the list of persons entitled to vote in elections.

27. The chief building in Washington is ..... Capitol, the meeting-place of the American parliament, known as Congress.

28. ..... Congress decided that a new star should be added every time when a new state joined the Union.

29. The National Health Service provides free medical treatment both in ..... hospital and outside.

30. The dormitories and houses are important assets to ..... college.

31. Nothing but an old woman airing her dog, and a weaving old man coming around the corner from ..... Third Avenue.

32. As she rounded the corner of ..... Atlanta Hotel and came in full view the depot and the tracks, she halted, horrified.

33. The family doctor gives treatment or prescribes medicine, or, if necessary, arranges for the patient to go to ..... hospital or to be seen at home by a specialist.

34. When Harry was arrested and jailed in Dodge City, a mob gathered, broke into ..... jail, removed him, and hanged him from a telegraph pole.

35. At ..... office he is the boss, but at home he plays second fiddle.

36. ..... school has been added to several times.

6 Add the definite or indefinite article to the following names of months, week-days, holidays where necessary.

1. We are going to Italy next ..... summer.

2. Ken wants to know how often Susan and John went to Cornwall last ..... summer.

3. ..... summer of 1987 was very hot.

4. Thousands of holiday-makers visit the Highlands in ..... summer, hoping for good luck with the weather.

5. Scotland is not particularly cold, and the west is in ..... winter one of the mildest parts of Britain.

6. He's not coming back all ..... winter?

7. Mrs Taft lives in Florida during ..... winter.

8. The tramp who came on ..... April 1st was a friendly man.

9. No more school till ..... Monday morning.

10. What's he going to do about ..... Christmas?

11. He'll stay all ..... night.

12. He remembered having seen the man ..... evening before.

13. He has been writing all ..... morning.

14. Tomorrow the wind will change during ..... morning, and there will be rain in ..... afternoon.

15. Hurricanes afflict the south-east particularly during ..... autumn.

16. In ..... autumn of 1621 the settlers celebrated their first year in America with Thanksgiving Day.

17. Tennis in ..... summer, skiing in ..... winter will keep you lithe.

18. The last time Adam was seen by anybody is ..... February fifteenth, when he got off the boat in Calais, coming from Dover.

19. The only one of his friends he felt like telling about his European trip was Susan, and he went to see her on ..... Thursday before he sailed.

20. I don't think there'll be any trouble about you having ..... Christmas Day off.

21. I saw he had possibly slept all ..... night in the chilly room he didn't know.

22. On ..... evening of her coronation day, June 2, 1953, Queen Elizabeth II made her first broadcast to her people.

23. The plane stops twice during ..... night to refuel and to pick up more passengers, and at six o'clock ..... next morning we are circling over a great port, ready to land.

24. The Highland tradition is seen at its colourful best in the clan gatherings which take place throughout ..... summer and ..... autumn in Scotland.

25. The house was well built and usually so oriented to the sun that he could keep it reasonably cool in ..... summer and make it reasonably warm in ..... winter.

26. Her fury at his apparently having been with Simon all ..... winter was water under the bridge.

27. ..... April can't be trusted.

28. In the dim, grey light of early ..... morning he woke up with a strange feeling.

7 Add the definite article or the corresponding possessive pronoun to the following articles of clothing or parts of the body.

1. Look me in ..... eyes.
2. Caroline pushed past me and put ..... arm round the girl.
3. He crossed the road by the zebra-crossing and caught her by ..... arm.
4. Take her by ..... hand.
5. I rose to ..... feet, bowed and left the room.
6. Don't pick stamps up with ..... fingers.
7. Try to pull ..... right leg out.
8. He was struck on ..... head from behind.
9. Little children can't put on ..... shoes. So their parents must help them.
10. She looked him straight in ..... face, then walked quickly on as though she had not seen him.
11. Bob swung with his fist at Philip and caught him on ..... ear.
12. Struck in ..... eye by a Norman arrow, King Harold lay dead on the battlefield.
13. Britain is a parliamentary democracy with the Queen at ..... head.
14. He took ..... shoes off so he could put ..... feet up on the sofa, lay back on a pillow, and continued reading Steven's letter.
15. He ran ..... eye over the text.
16. She refuses to listen when I say that Mr Stevens died of a disease of ..... stomach, made worse by the habit of overdrinking strong spirits.

17. She shrank back, clapping **.....** hand to **.....** mouth, feeling that she was going to be sick.

18. He was sweating so heavily, he took off **.....** jacket so as not to soil it.

19. He pushed open the door, and a hideous cheesy smell of sour beer hit him in **.....** face.

20. They have winter staring them in **.....** face.

☞ Die entsprechenden Lösungen befinden sich im Lösungsheft auf Seite 81ff.

Die Stellung des Artikels (The Position of the Article)

1 Add the definite or indefinite article to the following adjectives and nouns in brackets and put it into the correct position.

1. Mr Brenton asked Bob how **(close, friend)** Simon had been of Daniel Robins.
2. Henry had seldom tasted so **(good, dish).**
3. I have lost my key and have been looking for it for **(half, hour).**
4. This is too **(important, question)** to leave open.
5. The news was **(quite, relief)** to him.
6. How **(terrible, prospect)**!
7. A few years ago, Mrs Smith took lessons in cooking **(twice, week).**
8. The more education a woman has, the more likely she is to be at work, and more than **(half, women)** college graduates are employed.
9. TV keeps families together and prevents **(many, man)** from spending his evenings in the pub.
10. That sounds **(quite, possibility).**
11. It was too **(small, reward)** for such a great deed.
12. We have more than **(twice, acreage)** of woodland than we inherited at the turn of the century.
13. While unemployment has remained slightly below its year-ago level since May, **(both, degree)** and the pace of its decline have been disappointing.
14. Everyone should have as **(good, chance)** as everyone else of achieving wealth by his own efforts.
15. With so **(great, proportion)** of the young people entering higher education there is a problem of maintaining academic standards.
16. With **(half, million)** blacks aged between 19 and 24 enrolled in institutions of higher education, the proportion amounted to nearly one-quarter of that age-group.

17. The majority of the jobless are white but the unemployment rate among Negroes and school-leavers is **(twice, average rate).**

18. Washington is hot and moist, and has just about as **(unpleasant, climate)** as can be found in the whole country.

19. You have **(quite, opinion)** of yourself.

☞ Die entsprechenden Lösungen befinden sich im Lösungsheft auf Seite 85.

Das Geschlecht des Substantivs (The Gender of the Noun)

1 Put in the corresponding personal or possessive pronouns.

1. Since the second world war **Australia** has enjoyed **.....** greatest period of economic growth.
2. Under the rule of the Tudor monarchs, among them Henry VIII and Elizabeth I, **England** regained **.....** national unity.
3. When did you feed the **dog**? I fed **.....** an hour ago.
4. This is our **dog**, **.....** name is Jimmy.
5. That's Brian's **girl friend**. What's **.....** name. Sheila.
6. I want some of your special stamps: They're for my German **pen-friend Klaus**. **.....** collects stamps.
7. If there was a **snake** we'd hunt **.....** and kill **.....**.
8. No **teacher** would profess that **.....** knows all the answers.
9. Our **teacher Miss Taylor** said this morning **.....** can't teach me anything.
10. **America** is convinced that all **.....** institutions and achievements are the biggest and best in the world.
11. **Canada** won **.....** freedom without rebellion, or without major national heroes.
12. The **cat** lay on **.....** side on the floor, panting.
13. Don't tease the **dog**, lest **.....** should bite you.
14. His mother drew her arm round the **child** and pressed **.....** face against her breast.
15. The **passenger** cannot claim **.....** seat unless he takes possession of it by the time the train leaves the station.
16. For me, **America** is not determined by **.....** enormous vastness, nor by the might of material means, nor by the unlimited resources of strength.
17. For a hundred years after Waterloo, **Britain** and **.....** colonies were peacefully protected by the sword of naval power.

☞ Die entsprechenden Lösungen befinden sich im Lösungsheft auf Seite 86.

Der Numerus des Substantivs (The Number of the Noun)

Die Bildung des Plurals

1 Put the following nouns into the correct plural form and insert them into the corresponding columns of the following table.

box - buffalo - church - crisis - difficulty - journey - key - life - roof - sky - studio - success - wish - inquiry - butterfly - tie - guy - toy - progress - tax - bush – speech - basis - thief - proof - hero - ghetto - facility - delay - chimney - witness - ax - flash - witch - hypothesis - loaf - motif - echo - casino

	Endung auf	Singular	Plural	Endung auf	Singular	Plural
1.	**-y →**			**-y →**		
	-ie →					
2.	**-ch +**					
	-sh +					
	-ss +					

	Endung auf	Singular	Plural	Endung auf	Singular	Plural
	-x +					
3.	**-sis →**					
4.	**-f(e) →**			**-f(e) →**		
5.	**-o →**			**-o →**		

Substantive, die nur im Singular oder Plural vorkommen

1 Fill in the corresponding form of **to be** in the present tense simple.

1. **Athletics .....** my favourite subject.
2. I think a pair of **binoculars .....** just as expensive as a camera.
3. Part of the **class .....** late.
4. The **majority .....** poor and untutored.
5. His **mathematics .....** not so good as it was.

6. Every **means .....** tried.

7. **The Netherlands .....** an agricultural country.

8. And then, indeed, he saw that the **news .....** of the first importance.

9. Curious **people .....** standing round the car.

10. **Physics .....** a science.

11. The **stairs .....** steep and slippery.

12. Although the **United States .....** a rich society, poverty exists in it, and the concern of government and people over the problem of poverty has become acute in the past few years.

13. Although judges are well paid their current **earnings .....** less than those which successful barristers can make.

14. This means that either they have some sort of disease, or that somehow the **fish .....** being killed.

15. The **news .....** received in a silence of incomprehension and disbelief.

16. **People .....** unpredictable.

17. The **police .....** going to wonder where the hell he went to.

18. The strikers being bad marksmen, none of the **police .....** hurt; but about a dozen of the mob **.....** wounded.

19. Southern **politics .....** different.

20. I think **politics .....** also passive.

21. His **progress .....** continuous.

22. Automation and technological **progress .....** essential to the general welfare, the economic strength, and the defense of the nation.

23. The **public .....** taught that up-to-dateness is one of the first duties of man.

24. The **public .....** warned of the dangers of drinking.

25. His lips quiver and the **spectacles .....** dimmed with mist.

26. The **United States** ..... less than 200 years old, but the Chinese people can trace their national history back more than 4,000 years.

27. His **trousers** ..... wringing wet, and his face streaked with sweat.

28. It's always one bloody war after another, and one knows the **news .....** all lies anyway.

29. America's **people** ..... still enthusiastic about the future, still willing to take a chance, still like to have a roaring good time.

30. The **police** ..... unable to catch the mastermind behind this most rewarding of all train robberies.

31. Still, no animal **species** ..... likely to prove more intelligent than Homo sapiens.

32. The customers have been made to realize the **staff** ..... always available to deal with situations as they arise.

33. The **United States** ..... bigger in area than the whole of Europe, and includes a spread as great as from Paris to Karachi in Pakistan.

☞ Die entsprechenden Lösungen befinden sich im Lösungsheft auf Seite 87ff.

Common und Possessive Case

Die Bildung des Possessive Case

1 Put the following nouns in bold type into the possessive case.

1. Before the children go back to school, parents sometimes invite their **children.....** friends to a party.
2. Oliver doesn't know **Jenny.....** address.
3. How many times have you washed **father.....** car since the holidays ended?
4. St **James.....** Park is the largest of the London parks. You can walk on the grass, row a boat, ride a horse and go for a swim.
5. The boys and girls and their teachers had great fun on All **Fools.....** Day.
6. Mother went to a **parents.....** evening at school and heard about the homework.
7. At the weekend, a group of the **Scotts.....** friends got together and decided that they would fight to save the park.
8. I can hardly wait to see the **boys.....** faces at school tomorrow, when we tell them what we have done.
9. Joan took a post as superintendent of a **women.....** hospital.
10. The blue envelope containing **Mrs Stevens.....** letter had disappeared.
11. The worst thing I can imagine is to forget **one.....** exercise-book.
12. He was a welcome guest at **gentlemen.....** parties, and he often accompanied his new friends when they went hunting.
13. He had a good knowledge of the **Indians.....** language, and during the following years he led many trading expeditions into the interior.
14. **Smith.....** companions were killed and he himself was captured.
15. I might have made a good light with **bees.....** wax, but I had no bees' wax.
16. I hate interfering in other **people.....** affairs.
17. Finally he could see it: it was a cat - the **stewardess.....** cat.

18. Smiling, Mike shook his head and laid his hand lightly on **Nicholas.....** shoulder.

19. The first beginnings of permanent settlement in North America were nearly a hundred years after **Columbus.....** first voyage.

20. The most daring of the **colonists.....** leaders was Captain Sean Smith.

21. It is not possible for me to express the fear and sickness of my mind at seeing the shore covered with heads, hands, feet and other bones of **men.....** bodies.

22. The first hundred years after Christopher **Columbus.....** journey of discovery in 1492 did not produce any settlement on the north American continent.

23. The Constitution gives the lawmaking power to Congress, but allows the President to propose measures for **Congress.....** consideration.

Die Verwendung von Common und Possessive Case und der Beifügung mit of

1 Decide whether to use the possessive or the common case or an attribute with **of.**

1. He is a drinker and he would sell his soul for a **(bottle, wine).**

2. Mr Robinson drew **(a hundred, pounds)** from the bank yesterday to pay wages and so on.

3. **(Ben Robinson, wife)** had died of drink, and **(Mrs Stevens, husband)** had also been a heavy drinker.

4. The **(chairman, the House of Commons)** is the Speaker.

5. In 1290, it was thought for a time that the Spaniards under the **(Duke, Parma)** might attempt an invasion.

6. Oxford University is the oldest of **(Britain, universities)** and was founded in the 12th century.

7. In the spring of 1775 the **(city, Boston)** on the east coast of America was full of English soldiers.

8. The church whose dome looks like half a football is called **(St Paul).**

9. The **(River, Thine)** is longer than the **(River, Thames)**

10. He wanted to fly to Paris to stay there for three weeks with the Dubois, some friends of his **(father).**

11. There isn't much bread left. Someone must go to the **(baker).**

12. Bob's father had a good job as a train driver on the London Underground and his mother worked part-time in **(Woolworth).**

13. The third of the **(five-year, plans)** has been a sad disappointment.

14. Without checking every **(piece, baggage)** leaving the country the chances of customs officers intercepting the stolen pictures are small.

15. For more than **(a hundred, years)** Britain was **(Australia, chief customer)** for wool and meat.

16. The full union of Ireland with Great Britain took place only in 1810, when the new political unit was called the **(United Kingdom, Great Britain and Ireland)**.

17. Having reached the mouth of the **(River, Thames)**, Jones joined a gang of smugglers.

18. She never rests till she knows every detail of **(everybody, family secrets)**.

19. In terms of power the British monarchy has shrunk drastically from its high point in 1876, when Queen Victoria was proclaimed **(Empress, India)**.

20. The death penalty for murder was first abolished for a **(five-year, period)** in 1965.

21. The Greyhound Bus company provides tickets for unlimited travel all over the United States for a **(three months, period)**.

22. Where shall we be in **(10 years, time)?**

23. The discovery of oil, uranium, and other minerals has increased **(Canada, prosperity)** in recent years.

24. The **(majority, the jobless)** are white but the unemployment rate among negroes and school-leavers is twice the average rate.

25. Americans who have had the good fortune to visit Britain begin to understand the **(pride, the British)** in the achievements of their forbears.

26. A **(Scout, honour)** is to be trusted.

27. I cannot deny that I value in some degree the status which attaches to the **(rank, Consul)**

28. To the American, who has to travel five days and four nights by railroad to get across the continent, **(a few hundred, miles)** are just no impediment to speak of.

29. Until 1951 there was no limit to the number of **(four-year, terms)** for which a person could be elected as President.

30. **(dozens, new office and apartment buildings)** are rising pell-mell above the potholes.

☞ Die entsprechenden Lösungen befinden sich im Lösungsheft auf Seite 89ff.

Die Steigerung des Adjektivs (The Comparison of the Adjective)

Die Bildung der Steigerungsformen

1 Put the adjectives in brackets into the comparative or superlative by adding **-er** or **-est** and fill these forms into the table on the right hand.

	Positiv	Komparativ	Superlativ
1. Venus is the planet **(close)** to the Earth.			
2. New York is the most active city on earth, with the world's **(busy)** station.			
3. He was growing **(fat)** and **(strong)** every day.			
4. Isn't it **(good)** to leave things as they are?			
5. He is **(bad)** than yesterday.			
6. He has (**little**) money since he is unemployed.			
7. **(Large)** than China in territory, Canada has **(few)** people than Ethiopia.			
8. As he reached this decision his heart beat became **(heavy)** and **(fast).**			
9. For thousands of years the **(fit)** have always survived.			
10. She considers him to be the **(good)** candidate.			
11. The **(bad)** enemy of man is man himself.			
12. Alsace is beautiful, the Lorraine no **(little)** so.			

	Positiv	Komparativ	Superlativ
13. Her **(old)** sister has married Mr Gray.			
14. **(Old)** schoolchildren often help to look after old people.			
15. The **(early)** use of a word does not always occur most frequently.			
16. It was the **(hot)** and **(sleepy)** hour of the afternoon.			
17. Families with children have the (**much**) need of more money.			
18. He is **(far)** from believing it than ever before.			
19. The Vice-President succeeds the President if the **(late)** dies or resigns.			
20. The post office is **(near)** than the station.			
21. This hat-box belongs to the lady who sat **(near)** to me.			
22. He is always taking the line of **(little)** resistance.			

2 Put the adjectives in brackets into the comparative or superlative by adding **more** or **most** and fill these forms into the table on the right hand.

	Positiv	Komparativ	Superlativ
1. Peacefully eating, the elephant looked no **(dangerous)** than a cow.			
2. Spring in England is far **(lovely)** than the same season in America.			
3. That's the **(fantastic)** story I've ever heard.			

		Positiv	Komparativ	Superlativ
4.	'The Times' is the **(famous)** of all British newspapers.			
5.	Among local daily papers those published in the evenings are **(important).**			
6.	Welsh people are **(conscious)** of family connection than the English.			
7.	Football and baseball are the two **(distinctive)** American sports.			
8.	This rescue boat was built last year. It has all the **(modern)** electronic instruments.			
9.	In the big cities a tremendous heat is **(disagreeable)** than in the country.			
10.	Letters were frequent at first, but soon became **(distant)** in tone.			
11.	Of all American ideals the notion of equality has perhaps been the **(influential).**			
12.	Very often it is the **(frequent)** meaning of a word that comes to be regarded as the basic meaning.			

Die Verwendung der Steigerungsformen

1 Put the adjectives in brackets into the comparative or superlative by adding **-er** or **-est** or **more** or **most**.

1. Digital technology will make teleconferences **(cheap)** as well as **(easy)** to arrange.
2. He was **(pale)** than before and breathless.
3. It proved to be a **(difficult)** operation than they had thought.
4. Nearly everything in New York is **(big), (large), (noisy), (mad)**, and **(fascinating)** than in most other cities in the world.

5. The importance of comprehensives is that they allow all children to mix out of class with other children **(clever)** or **(stupid)** than themselves.

6. The **(massive)** a body is the **(big)** is its pull.

7. The **(stupid)** a servant, the more he offers them his sympathy.

8. Denmark comes out as the **(civilised)** country, Ireland as the **(little).**

9. You are **(early)** today.

10. Rapid economic growth, bringing greater prosperity to most of western Europe, made it less attractive to leave Europe with its **(varied)** scenery and culture.

11. The curse of noise around airports was being attacked by the development of **(quiet)** jet engines.

12. The **(simple)** and the least disturbing way of moving heavy loads, provided that there is no great hurry, is by water.

13. We have some of the **(good)** education in Europe, and we have **(few)** industrial accidents.

14. New York represents the **(full)** expression - for good or ill - of our urban culture.

15. Many a state university has on its faculty the world's **(learned)** scholars in literature and the other humanistic studies.

16. The immediate availability of data for management allows **(efficient)** planning and therefore higher machine loading.

☞ Die entsprechenden Lösungen befinden sich im Lösungsheft auf Seite 91ff.

Das Adjektiv mit dem Stützwort one (The Adjective with the Prop-Word **one**)

1 Put the prop-word **one, ones** after the following adjectives in bold type where necessary.

1. There was not a single bad ..... among the eggs.
2. What do you think of these two cars? - I like the blue ..... better than the red ......
3. I had a secretary who was with me for 9 years and then she decided to get married and I had to get a new ......
4. The bridges in London are the highest ..... I ever saw.
5. The Millers have three children. The eldest ....., Kevin, is at a boarding school, so he only comes home during the holidays.
6. Millions of American whites admired Martin Luther King. Few ..... had ever seen him face to face.
7. The most important of these amendments are the first ....., fifth ..... and tenth ......
8. Alexander Graham Bell was one among many ....., who were experimenting with the possibility of transmitting speech by wire.
9. His hypnotic eyes gazed into his own ......
10. A survey of teenagers made by the magazine LIFE found that six ..... out of seven expressed belief in God.
11. If you kept the small rules, you could break the big .....
12. In the post-war years a great number of new industries have grown up and expanded, while the established ..... have been modernized.
13. Although the United Kingdom is a unitary state, not a federal ....., a very large part of the public services are administered by local authorities.
14. California has filled up with people: her valleys are richly farmed, her cities are among the greatest ..... in the world, her industries are fabulous.
15. The two armies were about equal in number, but Duke William's was the stronger ....., because his men had been trained to fight on horseback.

16. Of a population of about 50,000 aborigines, today only few **.....** still live a primitive life as nomadic hunters.

17. Some areas of Mars are covered by curious streaks, which are believed by many **.....** to be artificial canals constructed by Martian engineers.

18. All the 37 states added to the Union since its foundation have constitutions based on the same principles as those of the original thirteen **......**

19. Unemployment over a long period is one cause for poverty, old age another, large family combined with low income is a third **......**

20. Was it reasonable that individuals should put the community good above their own **.....**?

21. It is possible to introduce bills in the Lords, though usually they are not controversial **......**

22. America is still continuing its explosive growth, begun in Colonial times, and its history remains a dynamic **......**

23. Not wanting to wait a year for our house, we built a prefabricated **......**

24. America has the reputation of being a rich society and it is indeed the richest **.....** the world has seen, in terms of total possessions.

25. The least skilled and least educated are the last to be hired and the first **.....** to be fired when automation changes labour requirements.

26. The peaceful purposes to which the laser may be put are so many **.....** and so varied as to suggest magic.

☞ Die entsprechenden Lösungen befinden sich im Lösungsheft auf Seite 93.

Der Vergleich (The Comparison)

1 Fill in **than, like** or **as**.

1. He found Venice much bigger **.....** he had supposed.
2. He moved **.....** Simon would have done.
3. I see you do not trust me **.....** Miss Sheila trusts me.
4. I think fishing is just as exciting **.....** a boat trip.
5. I'm afraid I'm not so clever **.....** Charles is.
6. She behaved **.....** an angle.
7. They act **.....** amateurs.
8. Today there are no less **.....** 10 million scouts in 70 different countries.
9. From our space lab, the sun, the moon and the stars look brighter **.....** they did from the earth because there is no atmosphere between them and us.
10. He felt **.....** an automaton, compelled by forces which he himself had set in motion, and were now out of his control.
11. His tiny sister, clinging to her mother with both hands, exactly **.....** a baby monkey, sat looking over her shoulder at him with large, mournful eyes.
12. In some western states there are already more than half as many cars **.....** people.
13. It was impossible to move so much **.....** a centimetre in any direction.
14. The contrast between old and new is often very striking, modern buildings and factories existing side by side with jungle tribes who still live **.....** their fathers lived for centuries before them.
15. The steam-engine did not put the horse out of action **.....** motors have done.
16. There's such a shortage of trained secretarial staff in London today that you have to be satisfied with rather less **.....** maximum qualifications.
17. America, with all its college graduates, buys only about half as many dailies per person **.....** the United Kingdom.

18. He ran his fingers through his hair, ... Simon sometimes did when he was irritated.

19. His knees bent and he went down ..... a bull hit between the eyes with a hammer.

20. His smooth face was pale ..... bone and his mouth hung down, livid ..... a wound.

21. Less ..... one-tenth of one per cent of polluting materials can kill fish life by consuming oxygen in the waters.

22. The Consul's tone bit ..... acid.

23. Bob wanted his Swedish to be as good ..... Bob's, and he thought he could make it that good in another month, if he kept on working hard at it.

24. What effect the existence of nuclear weapons will have upon the coexistence of nations is a question less understood and less explored ..... any other affecting our future.

☞ Die entsprechenden Lösungen befinden sich im Lösungsheft auf Seite 94.

Die Bildung des Adverbs (The Forms of the Adverb)

1 Change the following adjectives into adverbs and put them into the corresponding column of the following table.

angry - attentive - careful - cool - cruel - dry - due - dull - extreme - full - gay - gentle - heroic - idle - lucky - pale - practical - radical - shrill - shy - sole - sure - terrible - true - unique - vague - vile – whole

	Umwandlungs-merkmal	Adjektiv	Adverb	Umwandlungs-merkmal	Adjektiv	Adverb
1.	**-y →**					
	Ausnahmen					
2.	Endung **-e** nach Konsonant			Endung **-e** nach Vokal		
3.	**-le** nach Konsonant			**-le** nach Vokal		
	Ausnahme					

4.

Umwandlungs-merkmal	Adjektiv	Adverb	Umwandlungs-merkmal	Adjektiv	Adverb
-l →			-ll →		

5.

-ic →		

☞ Die entsprechenden Lösungen befinden sich im Lösungsheft auf Seite 95.

Die Steigerung des Adverbs (The Comparison of the Adverb)

Die Bildung der Steigerungsformen

1 Put the adverbs in brackets into the comparative or superlative by adding **-er** or **-est**.

1. It was a pity that they had not made up their minds **(early).**
2. I do **(good)** in French than in German.
3. Most of the houses are far from town centres and **(good)** reached by car.
4. He knew **(little)** than I did.
5. You should have known **(good)** than believe all those lies.
6. If party candidates are chosen in public elections it will be **(little)** easy for bosses to exercise power.
7. He did not look the **(little)** surprised or suspicious.
8. Officials said that these delicate activities were **(good)** conducted in secrecy.
9. If the crowd pushes forward the police ask the people to move **(far)** back.
10. I think it is not necessary to inquire **(far)**.
11. Nowadays the rituals surrounding marriage have become **(little)** elaborate and less rigid than in the past.
12. He settled **(deep)** into the arm-chair and put his feet up on the fender.
13. He lives **(high)** up the road.
14. Who knows **(much)** says **(little)**.

2 Put the adverbs in brackets into the comparative or superlative by adding **more** or **most.**

1. If the driver had watched the traffic **(carefully)**, the accident might not have happened.
2. The others took the matter **(coolly).**

3. I hope we can reach you **(easily)** the next time we have questions to ask you.

4. Big cities are **(heavily)** polluted than small towns.

5. Miller! repeated the voice **(loudly)**.

6. He told us to write **(neatly)** and to speak **(distinctly)**.

7. Wishing to examine these things **(closely)**, I lifted the lid.

8. Because of the Puritan influence education has for a long time been **(easily)** accessible to the people and more democratic than in England.

9. Although there are great extremes of cold in winter and of heat in summer the plains are **(favourably)** placed than those of Siberia.

10. Stand easy! barked the instructress, a little **(genially)**.

11. Japanese goods sometimes sell **(cheaply)** in suburban London than in suburban Tokyo.

12. His forehead was furrowed, **(darkly)** thoughtful than before.

13. The farmer of the 21st century will be **(deeply)**, **(intricately)**, and **(learnedly)** involved with the land than ever before.

14. The earliest use of a word does not always occur **(frequently)**.

15. People who like to be **(fully)** informed get their bulletin-type news from television and radio, and their depth news from newspapers.

Die Verwendung der Steigerungsformen

1 Put the adverbs in brackets into the comparative or superlative by adding **-er** or **-est** or **more** or **most**.

1. I will put it **(precisely)**.

2. If I should return **(late),** you might put the key in the place known to both of us.

3. She began walking **(close)** and **(close)** toward me.

4. Tell them to work **(fast)**.

5. The pilot flew **(low)** and tried the landing.

6. They were pleased that he was writing **(often)**.

7. As much as we pilots hate to admit it, the computer can operate the machinery much **(efficiently)** and **(accurately)**.

8. During the terrible poverty of the Hungry Forties, many industrial and agricultural workers who could no **(long)** make a living in Britain, arrived in New Zealand.

9. The Chancellor said that if the nation were to work **(hard)** and increase output, wage increases would be fully justified.

10. Actions speak **(loud)** than words.

11. George's eyebrows lifted a trifle **(high).**

12. He had no **(soon)** seated himself at his desk when Charles knocked and entered.

13. Carol quizzed him **(acutely)** than any police officer.

☞ Die entsprechenden Lösungen befinden sich im Lösungsheft auf Seite 96ff.

Die Stellung des Adverbs (The Position of the Adverb)

1 Decide whether to put the adverbs in brackets before or after the verb.

1. Philip spoke (**absently**).
2. He wants to spend the winter in Miami. **(apparently)**
3. I shall telephone to Rome, the officer answered, **(calmly)** and picked up the telephone on his desk.
4. The hunter followed the trace (**cautiously**).
5. It can be very lonely out there. (**certainly**)
6. We are not concerned with it. (**directly)**
7. The dawn was breaking over London. (**just)**
8. He drew himself up and took off his tie. (**calmly)**
9. This parcel is to be handled. (**carefully)**
10. The plan was worked out, (**thoroughly and carefully**) but within a year it was judged to have been a failure.
11. As soon as the first settlers followed the explorers and adventurers, women were wanted and needed in America. (**desperately)**
12. I wish that he may be successful. (**heartily)**
13. A matter of extreme importance has been brought to my notice. (**just)**
14. His information went to show that the situation might become worse. (**easily)**
15. The unemployment rate was still higher among blacks than among whites, but the gap had narrowed. (**enormously)**
16. And this was what was aimed at. (**exactly)**
17. Since he had taken his decision two nights before, he knew that there was no looking back and his mind was fixed upon (**firmly**) what must come to pass (**inevitably)**.
18. Do not think at all **(just)**, he told himself.

19. You watch now (**just**) and do what you should.

20. The Government cannot spend any money without the permission of the House of Commons (**legally**).

2 Decide whether to put the adverbs in brackets before or after the adjective or adverb.

1. A patient must normally go to the doctor with whom he is actually registered. (**only**)

2. Claire had her hat on and had just come from the village (**clearly**).

3. He hoped Philip wouldn't land just when the police were here. (**here**)

4. I could see it clearly and I felt uneasy (**enough**).

5. She was brought here. **(last night)**

6. The house was certainly big. (**enough**)

7. The package had arrived on January sixth. (**only**)

8. George was smoking a Victory Cigarette which he held horizontal. (**carefully**)

9. You shouldn't go by bus, it's a bad service. (**awfully**)

10. His wife felt extremely annoyed but George seemed unreasonable and stubbornly refused to listen to her complaints. **(absolutely**)

11. I don't want to be reminded of all those hours alone here. (**last night)**

12. I like this hotel with its hallways barely wide to walk through. (**enough**)

13. Somebody went, just before us. (**there)**

14. We were nearly broke when we arrived - 50 cents left. (**only**)

15. The hair of the little monkeys in the paintings was well done. (**really, astoundingly)**

16. After trying on several pairs of shorts that did not fit him or at least not adequately to serve as a bathing suit, (**enough**) he left the shop.

17. Clearly Mr Robinson himself could have opened the door. (**only**)

18. He would go often. (**there)**

19. The bay was beautiful with white sails moving across its ruffled surface under the sun. **(certainly, extraordinarily)**

20. The proportion of those holding hereditary titles who take an active part in the affairs of the House of Lords is small. (**comparatively**)

3 Put the adverbs in brackets at the beginning or the end of the sentence.

1. No one had found anything. (**apparently**)
2. He folded the letter and put it back into his pocket. (**carefully**)
3. They reached the Grand Union Canal, which runs from London to Birmingham. (**eventually**)
4. A little girl did come along and she was carrying a basket of food. (**finally**)
5. The British people readily accept the fact that obeying the law is necessary for the smooth running of national and neighbourhood affairs. (**generally**)
6. Segregation and discrimination are strange paradoxes in a nation founded on the principle that all men are created equal. (**indeed**)
7. A warm wave of relief flowed through him. **(instantly**)
8. He let them approach, and not until they were within a hundred yards of him did he turn into a lane barred by a gate. (**calmly**)
9. People have shown themselves quite ready to build houses in areas which are particularly subject to danger from hurricanes. (**curiously**)

4 Put the adverbs in brackets into the correct position.

1. He was sitting on the sofa, listening. (**attentively)**
2. Some experts believe that the prices will drop. (**eventually**)
3. Corporations merge into big trusts. (**frequently**)
4. It is nice to hear those kind words. (**certainly)**
5. The doctor on the rescue boat treated the injured people. (**badly**)
6. He turned his head away. (**abruptly)**

7. The wide-spread motorization of the population, especially since World War II, has created new occupations and reduced others. (**drastically**)

8. Henry washed, brushed his teeth and changed his shirt. (**hurriedly**)

9. He felt his legs give way under him but saved himself from falling. (**just**)

10. It was by chance that they had met. (**actually**)

11. We do not hope, but, we hope. (**greatly, still)**

12. Alone, the Captain straightened himself in the empty compartment. (**completely**)

13. She seemed to have become spiritless. (**completely**)

14. The rocks are full of the bones of extinct animals which lived long before man was ever heard of. (**here)**

15. Our air is dirty. But there is no such thing as 'pure air', and never has been. (**there**)

16. Cricket has been adopted in the Commonwealth. (**seriously and extensively, only)**

☞ Die entsprechenden Lösungen befinden sich im Lösungsheft auf Seite 98ff.

Adverb oder Adjektiv (Adverb or Adjective)

1 Change the words in brackets into adverbs or adjectives.

1. All he cared for was to lie **(quiet)** on his bed.
2. Behind him was Harry, fighting to get **(close).**
3. He came to my house in the **(early)** hours of the morning.
4. He remained **(attentive)** to all his wishes.
5. He shouted **(angry)** at his wife and demanded an explanation.
6. He stood **(close)** to the wall.
7. Her face seems **(bad)** hurt.
8. I haven't the **(little;** superlative**)** idea where Philip is at the present moment.
9. It makes **(little)** difference.
10. Elizabeth seldom had an evening **(complete)** free.
11. If they gave their pony **(little;** comparative**)** sugar, it would be better for its teeth.
12. Many severe hurricanes have caused **(much)** material damage but no loss of life.
13. May the **(good;** superlative**)** man win.
14. One by one the larger countries of the Empire became **(independent)**.
15. Martha grew **(silent)** and **(scornful).**
16. She brought the glass paperweight over to the bed to have a look at it in a **(good;** comparative**)** light.
17. The **(bad;** superlative**)** thing I can imagine is to be late for school.
18. They all sat **(attentive)** and listened **(attentive)** to the speaker.
19. Things have changed very much since the **(last)** time.
20. Arthur stopped **(abrupt)** and turned.

21. In a flash of understanding the situation became **(clear)** to him.

22. It does not take **(much)** imagination to think of the courage and other admirable qualities needed by the early settlers.

23. It seems likely that the formerly under-developed areas will now continue to grow **(fast)**.

24. Many football teams cannot be sure of attracting **(enough)** spectators to fill the grounds.

25. Someone gripped his head from behind, forcing him to look **(straight)** in front of him.

26. The coastal region suffers from mist and drizzle, though only a **(little)** way inland the weather is commonly very much clearer.

27. The plates **(constant)** interact at their boundaries.

28. Time is getting **(short)** and we ought to start back soon.

29. Today a supersonic airliner can fly round the earth in **(little;** comparative**)** time than it took me to travel from the Continent to Britain.

30. You are the **(bad;** superlative**)** boy to worry I ever knew.

31. His face remained **(complete)** inscrutable.

32. Instead of being discouraged or falling into despair, David remained **(calm)** and **(cheerful).**

33. But the English have never had **(much)** reputation for their appreciation of good food or good cooking.

34. Early American society kept women in a domestic role, and with no courts, no aristocracy, there was **(little;** comparative**)** scope for female influence even than in the Europe of those times.

35. He had grown **(old)** and **(stiff)** and **(spiteful)** before he was twenty.

36. I can only tell you that they built **(good)** and **(true)**, and they calculated **(correct).**

37. Since 1958 it became **(possible)** for the Queen to confer a peerage-membership upon a man or woman.

38. The train, having furiously rattled itself downhill to a **(little)** valley, was now met by a noticeably steep ascent.

39. The **(bad; superlative)** enemy of man is man himself.

40. There are days when I am so overcome by suffering and exhaustion I can **(bare)** concentrate upon my work.

2 Change the words in brackets into adverbs or adjectives.

1. I've been doing quite a lot of night work **(late)**.
2. They were all below, eating their **(late)** dinner, he supposed.
3. In the teaching profession there is no **(clear)** distinction between elementary and advanced-level school-teachers.
4. Speak **(clear)**.
5. Enjoy a voyage that will take you through the beautiful countryside, **(pretty)** villages, and old towns of England.
6. This is **(pretty)** difficult.
7. The Negro slaves tried to forget their **(hard)** life by singing religious songs during and after work. Such songs have become known as Spirituals.
8. George, suddenly motionless, stared at Arthur in a **(hard)** kind of way.
9. The patient will **(hard)** live to see another day.
10. Charles is giving me a **(hard)** time all the while.
11. In 1941-45 thousands of Negroes became officers in the army and navy; a few attained **(high)** rank.
12. This news, if it can be relied upon, is **(high)** significant.
13. The **(high)** ratio of teachers to students and the large amount of personal contact between them constitute the chief merit of the English universities in general.
14. There is almost nobody in political life who has a recognised claim to **(high)** office because of his political standing.
15. Most of the poor people could not read or write and thus the **(only)** way they could make a living was by poorly-paid manual work.
16. You can **(only)** wait.

17. Although immigration has been **(fair)** small for fifty years, the population has recently grown much faster than ever before.

18. Our new boss is a **(fair)** man.

19. He feels **(just)** ashamed.

20. It is something of which we can be **(just)** proud.

21. The Equilibrium Society is indeed being mistaken for the **(just)** society.

22. From the earliest days of their formation in the 17th century, Quakers have been **(deep)** concerned for the suffering of mankind.

23. His body felt leaden and slow, as if he were trying to raise himself out of **(deep)** water.

24. Can you tell me the (**near**; superlative) way to the station?

25. She was **(near)** drowned.

☞ Die entsprechenden Lösungen befinden sich im Lösungsheft auf Seite 100.

Das Personalpronomen (The Personal Pronoun)

Das deutsche *es*

1 Fill in **it** + the corresponding form of **to be** in the past tense simple in order to express the German *es.*

1. ..... 22 hours after the explosion.
2. The boatkeeper might remember that ..... two Americans who had not come back with the boat.
3. ..... the merchants of Liverpool that encouraged Stephenson to build his railway in 1830.
4. His instinct told him that ..... bad news that was coming.
5. From the group one man detached himself and looked towards her. ..... the doctor.
6. ..... his friend Arthur, who worked in the Research Department.
7. ..... Consul Carrington who entered.
8. George looked up at a man standing near the desk. ..... the man who had missed the plane.
9. How can you be sure that ..... the prisoner that you saw?
10. ..... (present tense simple) rich Peters who are taxed to pay poor Pauls.

2 Fill in **there** + the corresponding form of the verbs in brackets in the past tense simple or the tense indicated in brackets.

1. After a few days ..... **(come)** a fearful storm.
2. ..... **(be)** nobody near me.
3. Mrs Collins might have watched TV if ..... **(be,** past perfect simple**)** no blackout.
4. ..... **(be)** no sausages at the butcher's today.
5. She was in a hurry, for today ..... **(be)** work for everyone to do in the little village.
6. ..... **(be)** no proof that anyone else was in the room.

7. ..... **(be)** something strange about them.

8. ..... **(be)** little more to say.

9. ..... **(be)** no such thing. Nowhere in the world.

10. ..... **(appear)** to be a misunderstanding.

11. ..... **(remain)** only one more step for them to take.

12. ..... **(be)** at least a dozen dead fish in the river.

13. ..... **(be)** bitter quarrels but the quarrels had been settled, usually by compromise.

14. For many people ..... **(seem;** present tense simple**)** to be the problem of what to do in the hours away from work.

15. From behind him ..... **(emerge)** a broad-chested guard with a long black truncheon in his hand.

16. Opposite Charles ..... **(sit)** a man with a chinless, toothy face.

17. ..... **(step)** out a tall man with shining black air of shoulder length.

18. Suddenly ..... **(spring)** into his mind, the image of a certain Mr Winterbottom.

19. The last four years had been for the most part a waste, ... **(be)** no denying that.

20. Some people complain that ..... **(be,** present tense simple) not enough hard learning in the schools.

3 Fill in **so** in order to express the German *es.*

1. Are you sure that an oxygen apparatus will save him? I hope ......

2. She hated him and said ..... in the crudest words.

3. Where does he go now? Home. I suppose ......

4. Haven't we met before. No, I don't think ......

5. He is a really poor guy ...... am I, Bob thought.

6. I'm not sure if I have locked the door, but I hope ......

7. Every few minutes the old man kept repeating: We didn't ought to have trusted them. I said **......**

8. We've found St Paul's. Do we climb to the top? I suppose **......**

9. Have you anything to declare? I don't think **......**

10. The new book is a great success. **.....** I've heard.

11. I wanted to spend my holidays in the Himalayas but my father prayed me not to do **.....**

4 Fill in **it**, or **there,** or **so** + the corresponding form of the verbs in brackets in the past tense simple in order to express the German *es.*

1. When I had finished I was surprised to find someone waiting for me. **..... (be)** Miss Davies.

2. During October **..... (come)** heavy rains, so that I could not go out of my house.

3. It was clear that **..... (be)** not Philip Barton in the study at nine-thirty, for he had already left.

4. Are you two all right? I think **......**

5. **..... (be)** your neighbours that have spread the rumour.

6. A hundred years ago, **..... (be)** no radio, **..... (be)** no aeroplanes, no cars and buses.

7. He arrived in London late that afternoon, and **..... (be)** no bus to Milchester until tomorrow morning at eleven.

8. **..... (be)** my sister Caroline who was the cause of my few minutes delay.

9. If he has an alibi, why doesn't he come forward and say **.....**?

10. **..... (be)** deep lines of fatigue and haste in his face.

11. **..... (be)** the areas nearest to the coasts which suffered most severely.

12. **..... (remain)** usually about sixty days for discussion of the bills which the Government wanted to have passed.

13. You're going to ask her, aren't you? Well, I suppose **......**

14. **..... (seem)** to be some confusion here.

15. **..... (be)** always a reason behind my action.

16. **..... (be)** talk of a national student service, with an obligatory term or two of Peace Corps work in the villages.

☞ Die entsprechenden Lösungen befinden sich im Lösungsheft auf Seite 101ff.

Das Reflexivpronomen (The Reflexive Pronoun)

1 Fill in the corresponding reflexive pronoun.

1. First I'd better tell you about **.....** and my country.
2. Oh dear, you've cut **.....** badly.
3. What information about **.....** did he give to the reporter?
4. They knew they would need rifles to defend **.....** with.
5. Last week a TV reporter visited our school and filmed us. Tomorrow night we'll see **......**
6. Parts of the Houses of Parliament, including the Commons Chamber **.....**, were badly damaged in an air-raid in 1941.
7. One knew that it was all rubbish so why let **.....** be worried by it.
8. If you doubt me, ask her **......**
9. Simon was bored with living by **......**
10. You'll never find the house by **......**
11. Don't deceive **......**
12. For her own sake, whatever the pain to **.....**, she must do it.
13. Are you sure the guy you were talking to wasn't under the influence of dope **.....**?
14. I feel a terrific urge to be by **......**
15. All by **.....** ? the man asked.
16. Everyone who works has the right to just and favourable remuneration, ensuring for **.....** and his family an existence worthy of human dignity.
17. Settling **.....** on the wooden bench he prepared to endure the usual delay.
18. The conception of each person's freedom and responsibility for **.....** is at the centre of the idea of the American way of life.
19. No one today can disassociate **.....** from the dangers that technology multiplies.
20. By **.....**, this would not be alarming.

2 Fill in the corresponding reflexive or personal pronoun.

1. A sound behind ..... made him turn.
2. Half an hour later Mr Cunningham, my mother and ..... were in the train on the way to London.
3. He looked around ......
4. He saw the accident and Mrs Taylor's bleeding face before ..... all the time.
5. He swore to ..... he would stick to a job once he got it.
6. He thought that he could do the housekeeping for his daughter and ......
7. It was one of the few times in his life that he felt pleased with ......
8. McDonald was thinking the same thing as ......
9. She made porridge for him, George and ......
10. She preferred to be by ......
11. When he was twenty-one, Arthur Robinson married a beautiful woman some years older than ......
12. Charles wondered whether his friend Arthur was engaged on the same job as ......
13. He felt surer of ..... now in every way.
14. He was beside ..... with rage.
15. It was left to George, Mrs Robinson and ..... to do the talking, for Cunningham as usual had little to say.
16. May I express the hope, sir, that you will honour Mrs Rose and ..... by a visit to our apartment in the King's Road?
17. McDonald was a being in all ways larger than ......
18. Obviously with a total of 2,000 universities and colleges there must be great differences in quality and reputation among ......
19. The United Kingdom includes four nations, and there are discernible differences between ......

20. Through the darkness we speed southwards and, as day breaks, we see far below **.....** the long coast-line of Australia.

21. We have often gone on strike on our own claims, and we have decided that it was time we did something to help those who are worse off than **.....**.

22. He saw **.....** as if he were standing apart from **.....** and watching the scene.

23. She married beneath **.....**.

24. He laid the stick beside **.....**, and huddled **.....** down in the blackness.

☞ Die entsprechenden Lösungen befinden sich im Lösungsheft auf Seite 103.

Das Reziprokpronomen (The Reciprocal Pronoun)

1 Fill in **each other** or **one another.**

1. It was more than a week since they had seen **......**
2. Sean and Jack are twins. They are like **.....** in every way.
3. Nearly all English people now live in towns or suburbs and most towns are very like **......**
4. The boys and girls looked at **.....** with startled faces.
5. The pupils from the two rival houses were doing their best to shout **.....** down.
6. They had been talking to **.....** for a couple of minutes at the most.
7. We could hear them call to **......**
8. What caused the police and the mob to start firing at **.....**?
9. They could do nothing except stand gazing into **.....** eyes.
10. You could see the whole field from there, and you could see the two teams bashing **......**
11. The prisoners seemed terrified of speaking to anybody, and above all of speaking to **......**
12. There have been times in which the members of the Court have greatly disagreed with **......**
13. Candidates for the Democratic nomination rival **.....** in their attempts to win the Democratic voters.
14. Reconnaissance vehicles of the U.S. and U.S.S.R. now crisscross **.....** territory with perfect legality.
15. In the past, nations could pledge themselves to **.....** aid in case of attack.
16. Arthur and Philip smiled at **.....** with shy liking.
17. All political discussions balance the opposing views against **......**

☞ Die entsprechenden Lösungen befinden sich im Lösungsheft auf Seite 104.

Das Possessivpronomen (The Possessive Pronoun)

Das attributive Possessivpronomen

1 Fill in the corresponding possessive adjective or the definite article.

1. He bought two evening newspapers, tucked them under **.....** arm, and walked on.
2. The shot hit the king in **.....** breast.
3. In **.....** eyes of the law one should not make a distinction between one person and another.
4. Shaking off one, and hitting the other one in **.....** face with his fist, he escaped.
5. The man in the boat shook **.....** head, and Peter saw a big smile on **.....** face of the swimmer.
6. Bob felt a painful wrench in **.....** breast, and he covered **.....** face with **.....** hands.
7. Bob sank back in his chair, pulled **.....** cap down over **.....** eyes and folded **.....** hands over **.....** waist.
8. Bob's fists were clenched tight in **.....** trousers pockets.
9. You must clean **.....** shoes.
10. A direct hit in **.....** eye by a strong laser beam can cause instant blindness.
11. He got up, patted her on **.....** shoulder, and gave her an affectionate peck on **.....** cheek.
12. He sank **.....** arms to his sides and slowly refilled **.....** lungs with air.
13. I lost my temper, picked up an ash tray off the mantelpiece, and hit her on the back of **.....** head.
14. She gathered **.....** skirts and ran down the street.
15. The child felt **.....** heart sink.
16. The doctor's sister told me of a place in Liverpool where her brother used to send people not quite right in **.....** head.
17. Whether an advertisement misleads or a package deceives, lies in **.....** eye of the purchaser.

18. He began to feel a tingling fear at the end of ..... spine, tingling over ..... buttocks.

19. He could just stop ..... teeth from chattering, but ..... knees were beyond his control.

20. It was a noise that set one's teeth on edge and bristled ..... hair at the back of one's neck.

21. What he saw turned ..... bones to rubber.

Das substantivische Possessivpronomen

1 Fill in the possessive pronoun or the possessive adjective.

1. Does a scientist have to think about possible consequences of ..... work?

2. He is no true friend of ......

3. Hello stewardess, those umbrellas there are ......

4. Many people do not like Helen, but she can be very charming to ..... friends.

5. Mr O'Neil saw his hat. He told the stewardess it was ......

6. One third of the apples are ......

7. Out of the corner of ..... eye, I saw him running.

8. Philip begged Mary to keep ..... marriage secret.

9. She had no money of ..... own and was dependent on her brother-in-law's generosity.

10. That is no concern of .....

11. The children I invited were ..... classmates.

12. These flowers are ......

13. He thought suddenly of one summer day when he had been on a cross-country trip with Aunt Elizabeth and a woman friend of ....., and they had got stuck in a bumper-to-bumper traffic jam somewhere.

14. Make good use of ..... time.

15. Her eyes met ......

16. ..... time was made good use of.

17. Perhaps it was merely that this pathetic look of ..... ceased to wring his heart-strings.

18. The investiture of ..... Royal Highness the Prince of Wales at Caernarvon Castle means little to us.

2 Change the following possessive adjectives in bold type into the possessive pronouns and rewrite the sentences.

1. Look at **his** car.
2. Bob left Liverpool by taxi around six o'clock, after a cup of tea at Arthur's, where he said good-bye to Arthur, George, and **his** other village acquaintances.
3. I had hoped that **my** visit would remain unnoticed.
4. Were they **your** friends?
5. I was talking recently to **your** friend who is certainly an expert.
6. The book on the table is **my** book.
7. Which glass is **your** glass?
8. He is my countryman and I am **his** countryman.
9. What about **your** interest in my patients?
10. Some Commonwealth countries are maddened to find that Britain's voice seems to carry more weight than all **their** voices put together.

☞ Die entsprechenden Lösungen befinden sich im Lösungsheft auf Seite 105.

Das Demonstrativpronomen (The Demonstrative Pronoun)

1 Fill in **this, these** or **that, those**.

1. Give me **.....** book on London. This little one? Yes.
2. Give me **.....** telephone books over there.
3. I must get some sleep, even if it means taking four of **.....** tablets which you gave me.
4. I'm not against water-skiing, or sawing, or any of **.....** noise-making pastimes.
5. Look Mary, there are our umbrellas. Hello, stewardess, **.....** umbrellas there are ours.
6. Look, how **.....** man over there is running. He wants to catch a plane I guess.
7. People say a girl fell off the roof of **.....** boat-house there. Was her name Helen?
8. Some centuries ago, there were only very few roads, and even **.....** roads were narrow and bad.
9. The captain felt very anxious when he saw the helicopter coming so near and sent **.....** radio message: Impossible to land on board.
10. We are flying across the pacific. Land is in sight. **.....** city over there on the coast is Vancouver.
11. What has become of **.....** articles of value which you kept in the little box upon your dressing table.
12. Every year a student must take an examination in each of his courses. If he fails a course, he must only repeat **.....** course.
13. Fiji consists of 250 small islands. It is said that the natives of **.....** islands used to be cannibals.
14. I don't want to be reminded of all **.....** hours alone here last night.
15. I had just got to the bottom drawer of the desk when **.....** girl Sheila Adams came in.
16. In an article Professor Andrews explained why cigarette smoking is dangerous. The TIMES published **.....** article last week.
17. In front of the factory was a large pile of very old, dead fish, and on top was a notice: McCarthy's factory killed **.....** fish, we hope you will enjoy the dish.

18. It is possible for a student to move between one university and another, though **.....** is not in fact done as a regular practice.

19. Two Englishmen succeeded in building steam-engines which could pump water out of deep coal-mines. James Watt found ways of improving **.....** engine.

20. A lot of students are continually faced with the problems of economies, even though **.....** problems may be temporarily solved by scholarship grants.

21. A visitor to Liverpool arriving by boat is first impressed by the sight of the waterfront and all the bustle of an enterprising community that has been typical of **.....** city for a long time.

22. He has a reputation for caution in his attitudes and **.....** reputation is on the whole deserved.

23. I told you **.....** job I was after in Rome didn't pan out.

24. In all instances the men and women of the Peace Corps will go only to **.....** countries where their services and skills are genuinely needed and desired.

25. Let us explore what problems unite us instead of belabouring **.....** problems which divide us.

2 Fill in **this, these** or **that, those**.

1. By 1850, the South of America had long been an area of large cotton plantations and most of the world's cotton came from plantations in the Southern States in **.....** years.

2. He asked me if I would go out **.....** night and I said I wouldn't.

3. I am flying to Paris **.....** evening.

4. If it rains **.....** afternoon, it will be too wet to play the match tomorrow.

5. I'll put our ideas before the Mayor at the end of **.....** week.

6. I'm going to see my mother **.....** afternoon.

7. Mr Witherspoon, being himself an author, knows well enough how hard it is for a young poet to find a publisher **.....** days.

8. We shall see you in Paris one of **.....** days.

9. Coming back from an unsuccessful shooting-party he was very cross. He had not shot a single bird **.....** afternoon.

10. Cromwell's Puritans did bad things in Tewkesbury Abbey; you can see that to **.....** day.
11. Protestants not belonging to the Church of England suffered much persecution in the 17th century. In **.....** days they were called dissenters.
12. The guests protested to the courier because dinner was late again **.....** evening.
13. Until about 1700 new peerages were given very sparingly, and at **.....** time there were only 70 temporal peers.
14. You're so damned cautious **.....** days! Bob said.
15. He has been on several trips **.....** year.
16. He spoke well **.....** morning.
17. In 1975 there were 120,000 divorces, or one for every four marriages in **.....** year.
18. In the hey-day of imperialism in 1897, Joseph Chamberlain, the British foreign Secretary at **.....** time, explained in a speech what he thought to be the true conception of the British Empire.
19. **.....** days it is quite usual for the office of mayor or lord mayor to be held by a woman.
20. We look upon the distant past and the wonders of **.....** times with awe and respect.

3 Fill in **this, that** or **these, those** and add **one** where necessary.

1. Don't ask for another book until you've finished **......**
2. I went up and down the shore, but I could see no mark except **......**.
3. It was getting dark, so we pushed the van off the road and decided to stay there for the night. **.....** was the coldest night I have ever spent.
4. Now we know **.....** is the right place.
5. Push this button here. Nothing is happening. Try **......**
6. That boy is taller than **......**
7. The shop-assistant said: **.....** is quite a good model. I use it myself.
8. There are two committees responsible for government expenditure. One of **.....** is the Public Accounts Committee.

9. This gentleman is much nicer than ......

10. Though there are many different accents of English people are mostly used to speak the same English: ..... is Standard English.

11. Where is that wooden case? Which one? ..... under the Captain's bed.

12. Which key is .....? I don't know.

13. Which of the questions can you answer? I think I can answer ......

14. Which of these books do you prefer? I prefer ..... to ......

15. Arthur did not feel nearly as sure about tramps as he had been a few days before because ..... had a black beard and black eyebrows, and his hat was pulled down over his eyes.

16. The Pilgrim Fathers wanted to build a new society which was free of the bad elements of the old, while preserving ..... which seemed to them good.

17. Up to the Boer War in 1902 the British Empire had suffered only one setback. ..... was the loss of the thirteen American colonies in 1776.

18. In having government responsibility for the mails the United States is following a universal practice among modern states...... is the only public service that has not been left to private enterprise.

19. In the formal election there is rivalry between the Democratic and Republican candidates. One of ..... is sure to have an overall majority.

☞ Die entsprechenden Lösungen befinden sich im Lösungsheft auf Seite 106.

Das Determinativpronomen (The Determinative Pronoun)

Das substantivische Determinativpronomen

1 Fill in **that of, those of** or **the one, the ones.**

1. The area of Greater London is 620 square miles, almost twice ..... New York City.
2. Across the road there was another hotel, an identical twin to ..... where he was staying.
3. He handed Simon his letter and stuffed ..... from Mr Atkinson into his pocket.
4. Robert liked the shops in London better than ..... in his hometown.
5. Would you like a cappuccino or an espresso? Which is ..... with milk? Cappuccino.
6. All the thirty-seven states added to the Union since its foundation have constitutions based on the same principles as ..... the original thirteen.
7. Australia is more than twice as big as India, yet it has a population of only 10 millions - not much larger than ..... London.
8. Each American is subject to two governments, ... his state and ..... the Union.
9. Ghandi's most distinctive doctrine was ..... non-violence.
10. Irrigation systems like ..... in Arizona were let go.
11. The Queen confers peerages and other honours and makes appointment to all important State offices including ..... judges, governors and diplomats.
12. Britain's economic comeback in many ways parallels ..... the U.S.
13. If there was any sensation he hated, it was ..... being followed by anybody.
14. The signs of his disease are very like ..... poisoning.
15. The very beginnings of America arose from rejection of established rules and authority - ..... England and the rest of northern Europe.

2 Fill in **he who, those who** or **that which, those which** or **the one who, the ones who.**

1. He is ..... showed me how to do it.

2. ..... is not for us is against us.

3. It was ..... asked the questions.

4. It was ..... won the game.

5. Many settlers died and ..... survived lived in miserable conditions.

6. Of all my friends, they are ..... told me about you.

7. The Pilgrim Fathers, and many of ..... followed them, left Europe to be free.

8. There are usually more than two candidates for each seat, but ..... receives most votes is elected.

9. Which of the brothers drove the car? ..... lived at this hotel, the main said.

10. Although judges are well paid their current earnings are less than ..... successful barristers can make.

11. Evening classes are flourishing immensely, and not only ..... prepare people for examinations leading to professional qualifications.

12. Everywhere in England the education committee of the local elected council is responsible for all the schools, except for ..... are independent.

13. ..... doesn't take advice can't be helped.

14. Motor boats, many of them fast and noisy, often arouse bitter resentment among ..... sail or paddle canoes more peacefully.

15. Students may take up to eleven years to repay the loans, though ..... themselves become teachers in public schools only have to repay a portion of the loan.

16. The House of Commons spends many more hours in session each year than any other parliamentary assembly, but for most of the time less than fifty M.P.s are present listening to ..... is speaking.

17. The working week for most Americans is forty hours, though this does not apply to ..... have senior positions in management.

18. ..... says what he likes shall hear what he does not like.

19. If he is sent to prison - ..... loves the freedom of the open air - I will not answer for what might come to him.

20. The word 'plankton' means ..... is made to 'wander'.

Das attributive Determinativpronomen

1 Fill in **those who, the who** or **the which.**

1. She was one of ..... people ..... can go to sleep at any hour and in any position.
2. ..... birds ..... ran across the road were geese.
3. ..... countries ..... belong to the Commonwealth today were once colonies of the British Empire.
4. ..... man ..... was hurt died soon after.
5. ..... noise ..... was coming from the saloon could be heard down the street.
6. ..... pupils ..... live near the school walk or cycle home for lunch.
7. Who could have a better knowledge of what killed Mr Stevens than .... doctor ..... was attending him?
8. As the number of unemployed rose so ..... number ..... suffered for this reason grew.
9. He was one of ..... people ..... never looked at anyone they were talking to.
10. Many of ..... stories ..... are told in Westerns are very much alike.
11. Many people wanted to escape from the oppressive religious and social atmosphere of ..... England ..... they left behind.
12. On big occasions the chamber is overcrowded, but most of the time the benches provide more than enough room for all ..... members ..... are present.
13. Human ingenuity has not yet found any means of mitigating .....damage..... hurricanes may cause to buildings and property in general.
14. I cannot deny that I value in some degree ..... status ..... attaches to the rank of a Consul.
15. The essence of automation is the replacement of ..... worker ..... operates the machine by the machine that operates machinery.

☞ Die entsprechenden Lösungen befinden sich im Lösungsheft auf Seite 107.

Das Relativpronomen (The Relative Pronoun)

1 Fill in **who** or **whom.**

1. Mary worked day and night among the wounded, **.....** she found crowded together in indescribably dirty barracks.
2. I don't know **.....** you mean.
3. It was she **.....** I had seen on Sunday.
4. It was the Millers **.....** called us.
5. Peggy was thinking only of Linda **.....** a doctor had to look after.
6. The chairman's wife **.....** you met recently, was also bored.
7. There were few passengers **.....** escaped without serious injuries.
8. There were two letters, one to him from Simon's father, one to Simon from someone in New York **.....** Bob didn't know.
9. After a period of uncomfortable change stability was reached under Queen Elizabeth, daughter of the Queen **.....** Henry had married in 1533 and beheaded three years later.
10. Americans **.....** have had the good fortune to visit Britain begin to understand the pride of the British in the achievements of their forbears.
11. David is a delicate boy **.....** one shouldn't laugh at all the time.
12. During the terrible poverty of the Hungry Forties, many industrial and agricultural workers **.....** could no longer make a living in Britain, arrived in New Zealand.
13. Charles was just taking his place in one of the middle rows when two people **.....** he knew by sight, but had never spoken to, came unexpectedly into the room.
14. Women **.....** tried to break away from their accepted, conventional backgrounds had neither right nor sympathy on their side.
15. Many of the great inventions which were the foundation of modern industrial processes were made by Englishmen or Scotsmen, and there were men at the same time **.....** possessed the vision and ability to put the new inventions to use.
16. The President is elected by all the people, but the Constitution originally provided that he was to be indirectly elected by an electoral college **.....** the people were to choose, each state voting separately.

17. The proportion of those holding hereditary titles ..... take an active part in the affairs of the House of Lords is comparatively small, and it is noticeable that those holding life peerages are particularly active.

2 Fill in **which** or **that, who** or **whom.**

1. About one-third are women - mostly housewives ..... do not have paid jobs.
2. After some days George went to take his father back to his home in one of the boats ..... the men had left.
3. Simon closed a book of poems ..... had been lying face down on his studio couch before he followed Bob out of the room.
4. Had he any enemies ..... you know of?
5. He is the only man ..... can speak English here.
6. I ordered one of the men ..... we had taken with the boat to speak to them.
7. One of the girls over there was a girl ..... he often passed in the corridors.
8. Alvin was one of the people ..... worked for the Associated Press.
9. Bob felt completely comfortable, as he had never felt before at any party ..... he could remember.
10. You're the gentleman ..... bought the young lady's keepsake album.
11. By about 1960 the division of children between the two types of secondary school was widely unpopular, particularly among people ..... were politically on the left.
12. He had the appearance of being a person ..... you could talk to.
13. I've got a wife ..... I can't get rid of.
14. Navigation was one of the practical sciences ..... gained from the new inventions.
15. The most important task is to concentrate on improving standards throughout our educational system, reducing the size of classes and removing the social distinctions ..... exist today.
16. The officer asked another question ..... Bob pretended not quite to grasp.
17. This is a problem ..... is maintained to be among the most pressing.

18. When English people use the word 'hunting' they usually mean fox-hunting, a sport ..... is popular among a small but important minority.

19. I'm trying to get a medium-sized, medium-priced place ..... I can heat completely without spending a fortune for it.

20. It has been brought about to some extent by those of my colleagues ....., quite rightly, wish to encourage wider public appreciation of the importance of the new biological science.

21. One of the many purposes ..... a laser may be put to is the measurement of very long distances.

22. The old professor, fine scholar ..... he was, soon solved the problem.

23. There are areas over the country ..... are pretty solidly one political party or the other.

3 Fill in **whose** or **of which.**

1. After passing the second reading stage the bill must then go to a committee for detailed examination, in the course ..... there may be many proposals for amendment.
2. All members recognize the Queen as Head of the Commonwealth whether or not such states are republics or countries ..... she is Queen.
3. Each chamber has galleries, parts ..... are kept for the use of the public.
4. He looked around the little lobby and into the hotel bar ..... door was off the main hall.
5. Is it the member of a fire department ..... business it is to extinguish fires?
6. Of the three, it was Arthur ..... appearance had most impressed Charles.
7. On the surface, the children of divorce don't seem any different from the kids ..... families are still intact.
8. The church ..... dome looks like half a football is called St Paul's.
9. The Conservative Party is a party ..... basic aim is the protection of the individual.
10. The man ..... car broke down in the forest had a pistol with him.
11. And yet during all those years she had never found out the name of the priest ..... yellowing photograph hung on the wall above the broken harmonium.
12. California has one place ..... fame goes back to the early days of the great rush to prosperity and growth: Hollywood.

13. In a world ..... inhabitants are more and more involved with one another across the frontiers of politics and language, it is obvious that translation is a daily necessity.

14. Several colleges and universities have recently begun programmes designed particularly for women ..... education or creative work was interrupted by family responsibilities.

15. Supplementary benefits are provided for people ..... incomes are too low for them to be able to live at a minimum standard.

16. The British Commonwealth of Nations, as given legal shape by the Statute of Westminster, 1931, is a free association of sovereign, independent states and their dependencies, if any, each member ..... is equal in status and has joined of its own choice.

17. The flats are built round a quadrangle and in four blocks, one block ..... is the community centre which houses the large dining-room, hall, waiting area, surgery, small shop, and telephone kiosk.

18. Miró died on the island of Mallorca, but came from Catalonia, the Spanish province ..... language and humour had fuelled his imagination all his life.

19. On the opposite side of the alley there was a dingy little pub ..... windows appeared to be frosted over but in reality were merely coated with dust.

4 Fill in **whoever, whichever** or **whatever.**

1. ..... he may promise, I don't give in.

2. ..... way you turned, the telescreen faced you.

3. ..... we do we're laughed at.

4. Hands up, said Kevin strongly, ... wants Philip not to be chief ?

5. ..... happened to him nothing mattered if George remained his loyal, his loving friend.

6. Good stories, ... the theory or lack of theory behind them, have one bond in common: They produce an impact upon the reader.

7. ..... selected the packaging material was apparently not too well advised.

8. The civil servants have constituted a rather special kind of profession whose main role is to be ready to serve the ministers in power, ... their party.

9. The United States is a system of separate states, and ..... state a person lives in is responsible for the whole of the ordinary business of government which affects him.

10. ..... is beautiful in this world is worth looking at.

11. Every man has got a right to live, to come and go as he pleases and to have a good time ..... way he likes, so long as he don't interfere with nobody else.

12. The person, ... it was, gave a small cough, evidently as a prelude to speaking.

13. Shirley always had the lights on, dim ones, which gave a nocturnal atmosphere ..... the time of day.

5 Fill in **that, when, whenever, where** or **wherever.**

1. Both he and Simon excluded her from their travel plans ..... they discussed them.
2. He was walking back to his car ..... a sports car came down the street, with William Taylor at the wheel.
3. Investors can withdraw their money ..... they wish to.
4. It was in the nineteenth century ..... Australia, New Zealand, South Africa, and in part Canada, received their English-speaking populations.
5. Many large organisations provide canteens ..... their staffs can get lunch quickly and cheaply.
6. The twelve members of the jury are taken to a room ..... they are locked in and left alone until they agree on a verdict.
7. There were very few days ..... they could go for walks in the mountains.
8. Was this the first time ..... this had happened?
9. A Commission on Civil Rights tries to detect discrimination ..... it can be identified.
10. At length he came to a clearing in the forest ..... rock prevented vegetation from growing.
11. Congress decided that a new star should be added every time ..... a new state joined the Union.
12. Gone is the time ..... parents could exact unquestioning obedience.
13. The pueblo came under American occupation in 1846, was incorporated in 1850 - the same year ..... California received statehood.

14. Though I could not understand the words, yet they were good to hear, for they were the first sound of a man's voice which I had heard for all these years **.....** I had been on the island.

15. Three million people go regularly to bingo sessions **.....** they enjoy the company as well as the prospect of some small success.

16. It was not until the 17th century **.....** Parliament was able to assert itself with regard to the King and gain greater influence.

17. The Civil War of 1861 to 1865 was fought over the claim by the southern states to the right to secede from the Union and form a separate nation **.....** slavery would continue.

18. We have come a long way from the days **.....** primitive man roamed the earth in small groups of fifty to sixty.

19. When James Meredith became the first Negro to enter the University of Mississippi in 1962 he met with so many threats of violence that he had to be protected by large bodies of armed soldiers **.....** he went.

☞ Die entsprechenden Lösungen befinden sich im Lösungsheft auf Seite 108ff.

Das Interrogativpronomen (The Interrogative Pronoun)

1 Replace the words in bold type by **who, whom** or **whose** and rewrite the sentences.

1. **He** told me that.
2. I am calling **my mother.**
3. I believe **Bob.**
4. I blame **Sheila.**
5. I want **your hat.**
6. I'm going to share my room with **Peter.**
7. It is an **architect's** job to make plans for houses.
8. **My neighbour** is going to look after my children.
9. **My sister** helps me with my homework.
10. She married **a friend of mine.**
11. She was talking to **the headmaster.**
12. The black bag belongs **to my brother**.
13. **The inspector** might have asked the following question.
14. The inspector suspects **the prisoner**.
15. These are **my socks.**
16. They began to help **the poor boy**.
17. This was **my fault.**
18. We were making fun of **Larry.**
19. He was shielding **a criminal.**
20. I would call **Stephenson** the father of railroading.
21. Mr Burton suspected **Peter** of being the thief.

22. **Mr Winters** is to be blamed for Jack's failure to get the job.

23. **Peter** would have thought you had so much courage.

2 Fill in **which** or **what**.

1. **.....** are you two going to do?
2. **.....** did they argue about?
3. **.....** do you think is wrong with him?
4. **.....** key is this one? Let me count up.
5. **.....** must he adjust himself to?
6. **.....** people can possibly live in this desert?
7. **.....** of the brothers drove the car? The one who lived at this hotel, the man said.
8. **.....** of the following statements are true?
9. **.....** qualifications do you think a worker needs to get a well-paid job in a modern factory?
10. **.....** qualities do you think programmes must have to get high ratings?
11. **.....** of the two men leads the conversation?
12. **.....** wicked nonsense is this?
13. **.....** of these two bicycles would you buy? - I think I'd buy the red one.
14. **.....** one of you two wants it?
15. **.....** did the judge find Harold Evans guilty of?
16. **.....** general rules would you consider important for successful team-work?
17. **.....** is being done about the situation?
18. **.....** is the best means of transport for oil from Alaska to the USA?
19. **.....** people are likely to read The Times?
20. **.....** of the two countries pioneered railroading - Britain or the United States?

21. ..... scope is there for youth activities in secondary schools, and how could these activities be extended?

22. ..... subjects would you choose to take if you were an American High School student?

23. ..... of these reasons appear to you the most important?

3 Fill in **how** or **what.**

1. ..... is your Uncle Edward?
2. ..... long would it take him to reach the house? Not more than five minutes.
3. ..... was the weather like?
4. ..... is your answer?
5. ..... much did Mr Tillot pay you to keep your mouth shut?
6. ..... sort of people might have made these remarks?
7. ..... about a drink?
8. ..... does it work?
9. ..... many men were there?
10. ..... was he like?
11. ..... is your judgement?
12. ..... old is he?
13. ..... kind of interesting things happened on your trip?
14. ..... well do you know the story?
15. ..... is the ship called? The White Shark.
16. ..... colour is your car?
17. ..... size are you?
18. ..... could the advance of urbanization be slowed down or stopped?
19. ..... is it you are accusing me of?

20. ..... far have advances in science in the last few decades given hope for the solution of many of our technical, economic, medical and social problems?

21. ..... much will you charge me?

22. ..... was I to know that?

4 Fill in **when, where** or **why.**

1. ..... do I have to be ready?
2. ..... did Philip Rogers wish to keep his marriage secret?
3. ..... are we going?
4. ..... did you leave in such a hurry?
5. ..... did the Pilgrim Fathers cast anchor on the rocky coast of the New World?
6. ..... were the first locomotives for the American railroads built?
7. ..... in fact did he try to persuade her not to see Miles?
8. ..... ever doesn't he come forward himself?

☞ Die entsprechenden Lösungen befinden sich im Lösungsheft auf Seite 110ff.

Das Indefinitpronomen (The Indefinite Pronouns)

Some und any

1 Fill in **some** or **any.**

1. All white American-born citizens today are descended from people who at **.....** time made the great decision to move from Europe.
2. Are there **.....** last instructions?
3. Did you ask **.....** of the people?
4. He said if **.....**thing ever happened to him, he wanted me to have his rings.
5. I wonder if **.....** strangers have been seen round here.
6. Is there **.....** hope of help coming?
7. It is reported that Roger Brenton, for whom the police have been looking for **.....** days has been found at Brighton.
8. If his flight weren't a military secret he could ring up **.....** military department.
9. **.....** Member moves a motion; the House debates it and finally decides whether to agree or to disagree with it.
10. The climate of the United States is extremely varied, and in **.....** ways hostile.
11. I could not see **.....** fields or huts on the island, nor any marks to show that there were men on it.
12. The inspector was excited, hoping to get **.....** important information.
13. The Mayor has not found **.....** of our ideas good enough.
14. They said that the army did not need **.....** female nurses.
15. This little town has 4,000 inhabitants and hardly **.....** hotels.
16. Hardly **.....** households employ domestic servants and few women work as servants.
17. He could so easily have pretended to be **.....** friend of Simon's.
18. Laser light can bore holes through steel in the wink of an eye, detect art frauds, subdue **.....** cancers.

19. Poverty means not enough suitable food, inadequate clothing, inadequate living conditions, or ..... of these.

20. She had walked ..... distance, for her shoes were worn to pieces; but where she came from, or where she was going to, nobody knows.

21. Suppose you are really a slave to the drug habit. Is there ..... cure?

22. The English legal system is built up out of precedents, not on ..... general principles.

23. While a Frenchman may think it most unlikely that he will leave France, an American accepts the idea that it is quite likely that he will move to ..... other state during his lifetime.

24. He made it very funny and Carol laughed like .....one who hadn't had .....thing funny to laugh at in years.

25. Can .....one conceive of .....thing more confusing than that?

26. He never showed ..... liking for that place, did he?

27. Human ingenuity has not yet found ..... means of mitigating the damage which hurricanes may cause to buildings and property in general.

28. Of course he could not bear to ask his dear Martha to live in ..... but the perfect house, and the perfect house wanted finding.

29. ..... source of power began to pulse in George's body.

2 Fill in **some** or **any.**

1. All men are created equal. Not ..... men. Not white men. All men.

2. ..... person who is entitled to vote in parliamentary elections may now vote in local elections too.

3. Are you saying that it might be a wiser decision not to make use of ..... of these machines?

4. Do you want me to give the wounded man ..... water?

5. Don't you think, under the circumstances, you should take ..... steps?

6. I would buy the car if .....one gave me the money.

7. If only I could do **.....**thing useful!

8. If we had **.....** chewing-gum, we could stop the hole.

9. I'll be at home tonight at **.....** time you like to call.

10. It is usually possible to get a seat in the strangers' gallery of the House of Lords at **.....** time.

11. Should we not make **.....** inquiries here?

12. There's **.....**thing I don't like about her.

13. Was it likely she would be dismissed for disturbing **.....** papers?

14. Was there **.....** technical problem?

15. Would you be kind enough to answer **.....** questions?

16. **.....** bill relating only to Scotland is sent to a committee composed entirely of Members who represent constituencies in Scotland.

17. Both the prosecution and the defence may object to **.....** person who is called out for the jury, and if that happens one of the other waiting jurors is put in his place.

18. If you wish, I can arrange for **.....** money to be paid to you, if you wish.

19. It shall be unlawful for **.....** person to keep **.....** wild animal in captivity.

20. Why did the beat groups originate in Liverpool and not in **.....** other town?

21. Recent research found that there were many old people, and **.....** not so old, living in poverty because they did not receive the benefits to which they were entitled.

22. **.....** people are not reached by the anti-poverty programme, because local authorities and agencies do not want to play their part or do not have the resources to do so.

23. Which would you prefer, an extravagant house that lacks **.....** practical qualities, or a practical house that doesn't satisfy aesthetically?

24. If a body is at rest, it will remain at rest, and if it is in motion, it will remain in motion at a constant velocity in a straight line, unless it is acted upon by **.....** force.

25. The practice of allowing six minutes before Members must enter their lobbies gives enough time for them to come from **.....** part of the Palace of Westminster.

Every und each

1 Fill in **every** or **each.**

1. Simon Atkinson had two banks, one in Paris and one in New York, with about five thousand dollars in **.....** account.

2. Do you have to get up early **.....** day.

3. Every change or amendment must be approved by a two-third's vote in **.....** House of Congress, and by at least three-fourths of the fifty states.

4. **.....** county, district and parish has its council, elected by the inhabitants.

5. Glasgow and Newcastle upon Tyne, **.....** on a convenient river, became great centres of engineering and shipbuilding.

6. He is sure about **.....** single thing.

7. I have my car washed **.....** Saturday.

8. They have holidays of about four weeks over Christmas, two weeks **.....** at Easter and Whitsun, and about eleven weeks - from early August to mid-October - in the summer.

9. We have a constitution for the United States, we have constitutions for **.....** of the fifty states, and **.....** city has its written constitution.

10. A modern Government is arranged in about fifteen departments, **.....** with its ministerial head, normally entitled, for example, 'Secretary of State for Social Services'.

11. At the end of **.....** debate the Speaker puts the question whether or not to accept the motion that has been debated.

12. **.....** means was tried.

13. **.....** trifle must be paid for.

14. In streets where the houses are standing well back from the road, the postman does not come to the door of **.....** house, because **.....** house has a mailbox of standard type by the roadway.

15. Resignation often ends a politician's career as a leading politician, but not in **.....** case.

16. The Queen must appoint the leader of the party with a majority in the House of Commons, and the Members of Parliament of **.....** major party elect their leader.

17. Up to eight million new cars are made ..... year; four households out of five own at least one car, and more than a quarter own two ......

18. Every important city can now be entered and traversed by motorways with two, three or four lines of traffic on ..... side of the central division, and without any level junctions.

19. Los Angeles is already famous for its motorways; more than 1,000 kilometres were already in use by 1976, ... for four, six or more lines of traffic.

20. Until 1958 ..... newly-created temporal peer was succeeded by his eldest son, and then by succeeding generations; so the membership of the House of Lords increased beyond a thousand.

21. We can easily point to inequalities, social and economic, but there is still a deep-seated belief that, no matter what his wealth or his job, ... man is fundamentally equal with ..... other.

All und whole

1 Fill in **all** or **the whole** or **a whole.**

1. As soon as the crime was discovered ..... forest was combed by search parties.
2. He said he would be away for ..... day.
3. In these schools boys can learn ..... about life-saving and rescues.
4. Richard Barton's father was an acrobat in a famous circus, which travelled ..... over France.
5. Now, what's ..... this noise in the middle of the day?
6. Of course, the children did not want to look at buildings and statues ..... day long.
7. One evening Roger was walking along the shore ..... by himself.
8. Sheila is having her birthday party today. She has been very busy ..... week preparing the great event.
9. We have lost ..... day.
10. When Jack and Jenny were back home, their friends Walter and Linda wanted to know ..... about their trip to London.
11. Where do you get ..... the money from? A lot of our money comes from London. A lot is given by big firms. But quite a lot is collected by school children every year.

12. You don't want to look at me ..... the time.

13. He was giving me a hard time ..... the while.

14. In the Management Engineering Department six fully qualified engineers spend ..... time advising the employers on the best way of improving productivity.

15. Mr Jones must give his investigators ..... the backing that they need.

16. Of course she said ..... lot more, but I don't want to bore you, and anyway I soon stopped listening because I'd heard it all so often I knew it by heart now.

17. Social problems, as the words imply, are problems which concern not only society as ..... but also each of us individually.

18. ..... place needs doing up.

19. Everyone knows that in a capitalist economy where everyone follows his own profit-making motive, ... society will automatically benefit.

20. I believe that swift motion across a countryside does not necessarily take away ..... appreciation of its charm.

21. If a single disaster were to occur in a nuclear power plant or in a reactor-driven ship near a large city, thousands of people might die and ..... region be rendered uninhabitable.

22. What must ..... of mankind realize and how must we respond to this challenge?

23. What we refuse to recognize is that modern man has been altering his total environment so rapidly and suddenly that ..... 'great chain of life' on this planet is endangered.

Much und many

1 Fill in **much** or **many.**

1. Did you get ..... birthday presents? Yes I did.
2. He hasn't got ..... money.
3. How ..... chocolate have you got? Six bars.
4. It's surprising how ..... space there is on a boat.
5. I've never seen so ..... buses in my life.

6. Later he could not remember well why he had stopped swimming and taken in so ..... water.

7. ..... of them would rather die than continue living under tyranny.

8. ..... people go by Underground because there is too ..... traffic on the roads.

9. ..... of what you say is not true. Don't say any more. We know most of it anyway.

10. Sheila wants to know how ..... records Laura has got.

11. There isn't ..... bread left. Someone must go to the baker's.

12. Bob hasn't ..... hair, has he?

13. We could take as ..... sweets as we liked.

14. We have as ..... right to be here as the Johnsons or any other family in this street.

15. A show at a prime evening hour can attract as ..... as 70 million viewers.

16. I was here at four o'clock. And that wasn't ..... use. You were asleep.

17. It may be said of both that they had too ..... irons in the fire.

18. ..... remains to be done before I can finish my studies.

19. The jobs have been made so simple that there is not ..... room to move up from one skill to another.

20. When I'm working there is not ..... chance to get a breather.

21. Although ..... pay lip service to the liberal ideal, the effort to achieve a liberal society is a continuous struggle.

22. He has too ..... good sense to be affronted at insults.

23. In Europe, there are ..... oppressed for conscience-sake, and in the United States there are those oppressed which are of a black colour.

24. In the years leading up to the Civil War, women were among the most active and outspoken advocates of the abolition of slavery, and ..... of them linked the emancipation of the slave to their own cause.

25. The English have never had ..... reputation for their appreciation of good food or good cooking.

Little und few

1 Fill in **little** or **few.**

1. A ..... days ago, Richard and John were out for a bicycle ride.
2. Did you catch many fish? No, only a ......
3. He had ..... money and no job.
4. His English is far better than my German, and there are only a ..... mistakes.
5. His speedometer gives him very ..... information at all.
6. It'll take a ..... time to get the sandwiches made.
7. Millions of American whites admired Martin Luther King. ..... of them had ever seen him face to face.
8. Of a population of about 50,000 aborigines, today only ..... still live a primitive life as nomadic hunters.
9. The Millers had very ..... sunshine during their holiday in Scotland.
10. The night was clear, the road was dry, and there was ..... traffic.
11. After a ..... more unsuccessful attempts at getting information, I left, and drove back to London.
12. After walking a ..... yards, turned off the road and through a gate leading into a muddy lane between high grass banks.
13. Behind us the cliff rolled away into the bush-covered hillside with a ..... sheep grazing contentedly.
14. He proposed a treaty of friendship to the Indians, but they remained mistrustful, and his efforts to win their confidence made ..... progress.
15. If a free society cannot help the many who are poor, it cannot save the ..... who are rich.
16. Mr Jackson had ..... hope of doing business here.
17. The advances in science particularly in the last ..... decades have sometimes been spectacular and have given hope for the solution of many of our technical, economic, medical and social problems.

18. You play to win, and the game has ..... meaning unless you do your utmost to win.

19. These people of the real upper class would have you believe that wealth has ..... bearing on their social pre-eminence.

No, none und nobody

1 Fill in **no, none** or **nobody.**

1. At the first ballot there were six candidates, ... of whom gained an overall majority.

2. He liked the fact that Venice had ..... cars.

3. He searched every pocket for a garage ticket, but he found ......

4. I can't run out and leave a tramp in the house with ..... else about.

5. Knowing that there is ..... water and ..... air on the moon, we shan't find men or animals, trees or flowers.

6. ..... had ever seen Mr Miller looking so angry before.

7. ..... knew where he had gone.

8. Of all the games that Americans play and watch, ... is thought more typical of the country than baseball.

9. The phone rang and rang, but there was ..... answer.

10. ..... knows what I've been through in the last twenty-four hours.

11. ..... would take you for an expert.

12. Some professional planners, have lately been preaching the need to improve public transport for the benefit of people who have ..... access to a car.

13. Sometimes there are several Democratic candidates for the Democratic nomination, and in some states there is a second ballot to the primary election if ..... of them gets the majority at the first.

14. Still, ... animal species is likely to prove more intelligent than Homo sapiens.

15. There is, of course, complete religious freedom, and anyone may belong to any religious faith that he chooses or to ..... at all.

16. Britain has ..... brilliant cooking and ..... Alps, and the sea is rather cold; but there are good reasons for enjoying the tolerance and friendliness of the people.

17. Modern industry favours large organisations, and it is ..... accident that the world's biggest commercial firms are American.

18. ..... of the people looked like Andrew, and the shimmering heat waves kept him from making out the people very far away.

19. Only fifty years ago the majority of the working-class population were crowded together in slum dwellings with ..... of the comforts we take for granted today.

20. People ought to choose the kind of government they want themselves, and ..... else ought to have no say in the matter.

21. The state should ensure, as far as it can, than ..... should be without the means of the minimum necessities of life as the result of unemployment, old age, sickness, or over-large families.

Either und neither

1 Fill in **either** or **neither.**

1. «I never drink anything for luncheon,» she said. «..... do I,» I answered promptly.
2. ..... Bob or Sean was responsible.
3. ..... the son or the daughter is married.
4. If I can't live here, well then, ... will you.
5. I'm free now, except that I'm not supposed to leave the hotel today. ..... am I.
6. Judges are ..... practising or former barristers.
7. ..... of them bothered to explain it to her.
8. ..... of us, I think, was really afraid.
9. Perhaps he doesn't want to meet us. I'm not surprised. I don't want to meet him ......
10. Some 3,500,000 Negro slaves had to do all the hard work that white people ..... could not do because of the hot climate or just refused to do.
11. You aren't allowed to walk on the grass ......

12. A debate ends **.....** when every member who wants to speak has done so, or at a time fixed in advance **.....** by informal agreement between the parties or by a vote of the House.

13. Abraham Lincoln made it clear where he stood: My paramount object in this struggle is to save the Union, and is not **.....** to save or to destroy slavery.

14. **.....** side may object to up to seven jurors without giving reasons.

15. Daniel was the son of an American hotel-chain owner, and a playwright - self-styled, Bob gathered, because he had written only two plays, and **.....** had seen Broadway.

16. I have not seen him or heard from him, **.....** on the day of the murder or since.

17. The President, being elected separately, does not owe his office in any sense to either house, and **.....** house can remove the government.

18. They receive a very general education for about three years, then the number of subjects is reduced, usually in favour of **.....** the arts or the sciences.

19. You're all right **.....** way.

20. The village was by now just visible behind her, the cliffs towered up on **.....** side of the bay, and both the mansions were hidden by folds of the hill.

21. Ministers do in fact very often accept proposals for amendment, **.....** in their original form or in some form which is agreed to as a compromise.

☞ Die entsprechenden Lösungen befinden sich im Lösungsheft auf Seite 112ff.

Die Präposition (The Preposition)

1 Fill in the correct preposition.

1. They arrived **.....** Paddington Station.
2. Your flight will be announced **.....** 10:15.
3. They arrived **.....** lunch.
4. Where shall we be **.....** 10 years' time?
5. The door opened, and two men came **.....**
6. They came **.....** the other side of the door.
7. I came **.....** while you were watching the film.
8. Mr Atkinson came **.....** the room.
9. Charles covered his face **.....** his hands.
10. We always have chicken **.....** Sunday.
11. Throwing paper **.....** the ground is forbidden.
12. Your father bought this car **.....** you.
13. I climbed **.....** to the top of the hill.
14. He fell **.....** the stairs.
15. I was reading a book **.....** lunch.
16. We were too close **.....** him.

2 Fill in the correct preposition after the following verbs.

1. I don't agree **.....** you.
2. Bob and Mary can never agree **.....** anything.
3. The driver stopped to ask **.....** the way.
4. His son believed **.....** him.

5. Impossible to call ..... help.
6. They were congratulated ..... their success.
7. You should look ..... your little brother.
8. What are you looking .....?
9. That will be easy, put ..... Harry.
10. Put ..... your hands!
11. I shall just have to put ..... with that.
12. I put ..... my socks.
13. We had to put ..... going on holidays.
14. Send ..... the doctor.
15. Speak .....!
16. I succeeded ..... passing my examination.
17. He did not wait ..... a reply.
18. You will have to account ..... that error.
19. His age has to be taken account ......
20. The children all burst ..... laughter.
21. Mac and Henry burst ..... laughing.
22. What did he die .....?
23. Smiling she gave ......
24. We gave ..... teasing him.
25. What did the bishops and barons live .....?
26. The solution was arrived ..... by chance.
27. Thank you for bearing ..... us.
28. They were not discriminated ..... in employment.

29. If you had only heard him mock ..... you!

30. That's not to be wondered ......

3 Fill in the correct preposition after the following nouns.

1. Note the difference ..... meaning.
2. We had great difficulty ..... translating the text.
3. There is no doubt ..... that.
4. It did not make much impression ..... her.
5. He does not take any interest ..... reading.
6. What is your opinion ..... these questions?
7. He had no opportunity ..... speaking to him.
8. They did not discuss the possibility ..... getting married.
9. The chance ..... meeting him was but poor.
10. My chances ..... promotion aren't so hot.
11. Madam, my congratulations ..... your rehabilitation.
12. She kept quiet for fear .....being fired.
13. The early Americans had great faith ..... the Constitution.
14. The improvement ..... her appearance was startling.
15. I was at a loss ..... an answer.
16. Age is no proof ..... folly.

4 Fill in the correct preposition after the following adjectives.

1. Bob's mother is angry ..... him.
2. He'll get angry ..... nothing.

3. We are not directly concerned ..... it.
4. He was crazy ..... thirst.
5. I was crazy ..... a good Agatha Christie, or something.
6. When I had finished this work, I was very delighted ..... it.
7. Scottish towns look very different ..... English towns.
8. Are you good ..... drawing horses?
9. You are expected to be interested ..... the job you have been offered.
10. The worst thing I can imagine is to be late ..... school.
11. We are prepared ..... the worst.
12. I'm proud ..... you.
13. I feel sorry ..... her.
14. I was surprised ..... the news.
15. Feeling slightly ashamed ..... himself, he sat up against the bedhead.
16. Simon was bored ..... living by himself.
17. Harry's parents are anxious ..... him to receive a good education.
18. All human beings are born free and equal ..... dignity and rights.

☞ Die entsprechenden Lösungen befinden sich im Lösungsheft auf Seite 116ff.

Die Wortstellung (The Word Order)

1 Put the two objects in brackets into the correct order.

1. Your mother sent **(you, some nosedrops).**
2. A policeman gave **(a form, him).**
3. Jack handed (**her, the flag**) without saying a word.
4. Alice handed **(the sugar, her sister)**.
5. Robert brought **(a shell, him).**
6. The officer handed **(him, the passport)** with a little bow and a smile.
7. The money gave **(the leisure, him)** to see Greece.
8. The woman gave **(him, a long, smiling answer)** in Italian and pointed downward toward the sea.
9. A clerk told **(the number of his reserved room, him)** and handed **(a bellboy, the key)**.
10. The Queen gave **(him, the higher honour)** of Knight of the Garter.
11. When the assistant handed **(the sheet, him)** he read it through twice, sat for some minutes in heavy fretful thought, then slowly raised his eyes to the assistant.
12. A relation left **(me, some money)** a year ago, but unluckily I lost it in some foolish plan to make more.
13. Simon showed **(some ship models; me)** that were sitting on a table in his room.
14. People ask **(all kinds of things, me).**
15. May God grant **(these blessings, us).**

2 Put the two objects in brackets into the correct order and insert **to** wherever necessary.

1. When you've chosen a book, bring **(me, it)** and I'll stamp it, said the librarian.

2. Sam gave **(some milk, the cat)**.

3. Mrs Adams wrote **(the Maxwell family, a postcard).**

4. He bent down, cut a large marrow and offered **(it, me)**.

5. Richard muttered **(himself, the name)** and then shouted it to Philip.

6. Mary had promised **(me, her photo)**. Hasn't she promised **(it, your brother)** ? No, she has promised **(me, it)**.

7. Don't do **(me, it).**

8. She didn't understand until I explained **(her, it)**.

9. All committees give **(seats, the parties)** in proportion to their strength in the House or Senate, as the case may be.

10. Tom handed **(him, it).**

11. The Government gives **(money, the universities)** to cover the costs of buildings and to cover almost the whole of their current expenditure.

12. Give **(me, it).**

13. Leave **(me, it).**

14. Simon hadn't had the guts to stand up and deny **(it, her).**

15. He used to say **(me, it)** when I was a little girl.

16. I took the sketch from my pocket and showed **(it, him).**

3 Put the verbs before the subjects and rewrite the following sentences.

1. My mother is there, he called out.

2. Gentlemen, barons, earls, knights of the Garter, all richly dressed and bareheaded, went first.

3. The Queen came next, in the 65th year of her age, very majestic.

4. The day came then when Sitting Bull, the chief of the Kickapoos, lay in his wigwam dying.

5. The keynote speech comes then.

6. Commercial interests were involved there.
7. People were sitting all over the stone-flagged floor there.

☞ Die entsprechenden Lösungen befinden sich im Lösungsheft auf Seite 118.

Kurzfragen (Question Tags)

1 Fill in the correct question tag.

1. He doesn't like me, **.....**?
2. He never showed any liking for that place, **.....**?
3. He wasn't waiting there for us, **.....**?
4. He won't do it, **.....**?
5. He's getting desperate, **.....**?
6. I can't really take all the prize myself, **.....**? No. We both won it, **.....**? Yes?
7. I don't know, **.....**?
8. I tried to do my best, **.....**
9. I won't see you again, **.....**?
10. I'm not selfish, brother, **.....**?
11. Is he an American? I think so, but he doesn't act like an American, **.....**?
12. Sam, I'm going to be all right, **.....**?
13. Somebody could hide it, **.....**?
14. They both look very funny, **.....**?
15. They didn't help, **.....**?
16. They don't actually believe Harry killed him, **.....**?
17. Your uncle wanted to give us something, **.....**?
18. Jack looks weaker than John, **.....**?
19. You know where we go now, **.....**?
20. They have always been making trouble, **.....**?
21. Jack has big ears, **.....**?

22. Bob doesn't look strong, **.....**?

23. Bob hasn't much hair, **.....**?

24. Bob is very fat, **.....**?

25. Bob isn't very good-looking, **.....**?

26. We had better push the barrow together, **.....**?

27. We haven't failed yet, **.....**?

28. We'll be happier now, **.....**?

29. We'll just please ourselves, **.....**?

30. We're not far from London, **.....**?

31. Whatever we do we're laughed at, **.....**?

32. You can watch that on television, **.....**?

33. You don't like Bill, **.....**?

34. You knew, **.....**?

35. You know the trouble, **.....**?

36. You were asleep, **.....**?

37. You weren't very careful, **.....**?

38. You weren't whispering, **.....**?

39. You'll go when we get there, **.....**?

40. You're going to ask her, **.....**?

41. Sit down, **.....**?

42. Let's have a look inside, **.....**?

43. Let's put the sack in the barrow and wheel it, **.....**?

☞ Die entsprechenden Lösungen befinden sich im Lösungsheft auf Seite 119.

Eigene Notizen

Eigene Notizen

Eigene Notizen

Eigene Notizen

Eigene Notizen

Eigene Notizen

Lösungen

Die Konjugation (The Conjugation)

Die Konjugation der Verben

1 Setzen Sie die fehlenden Verbformen ein und verwenden Sie das angegebene Personalprono

Infinitive	Pres. T. Simple	Past T. Simple	Pres. Perf. Simple	Past Perf. Simple
1. to stay	she stays	she stayed	she has stayed	she had stayed
2. to plan	he plans	he planned	he has planned	he had planned
3. to happen	it happens	it happened	it has happened	it had happened
4. to listen	you listen	you listened	you have listened	you had listened
5. to fight	you fight	you fought	you have fought	you had fought
6. to wash	he washes	he washed	he has washed	he had washed
7. to mix	she mixes	she mixed	she has mixed	she had mixed
8. to hate	she hates	she hated	she has hated	she had hated
9. to permit	you permit	you permitted	you have permitted	you had permitted
10. to regret	you regret	you regretted	you have regretted	you had regretted
11. to visit	she visits	she visited	she has visited	she had visited
12. to like	they like	they liked	they have liked	they had liked
13. to teach	he teaches	he taught	he has taught	he had taught
14. to play	she plays	she played	she has played	she had played
15. to miss	she misses	she missed	she has missed	she had missed
16. to stand	he stands	he stood	he has stood	he had stood
17. to tell	she tells	she told	she has told	she had told
18. to prefer	she prefers	she preferred	she has preferred	she had preferred
19. to answer	you answer	you answered	you have answered	you had answered
20. to cover	they cover	they covered	they have covered	they had covered
21. to refer	I refer	I referred	I have referred	I had referred
22. to remember	I remember	I remembered	I have remembered	I had remembered
23. to suffer	he suffers	he suffered	he has suffered	he had suffered
24. to read	she reads [ri:ds]	she read [red]	she has read [red]	she had read [red]
25. to change	I change	I changed	I have changed	I had changed
26. to promise	I promise	I promised	I have promised	I had promised
27. to watch	he watches	he watched	he has watched	he had watched
28. to get	we get	we got	we have got	we had got
29. to lie	he lies	he lay	he has lain	he had lain
30. to lay	he lays	he laid	he has laid	he had laid
31. to spring	you spring	you sprang	you have sprung	you had sprung
32. to continue	he continues	he continued	he has continued	he had continued
33. to ring	I ring	I rang	I have rung	I had rung
34. to arrive	he arrives	he arrived	he has arrived	he had arrived
35. to reply	she replies	she replied	she has replied	she had replied

men.

Future Tense	Future Perfect	Conditional	Conditional Perf.	Cont. Form
she will stay	she will have stayed ◀1	she would stay	she would have stayed ◀1	staying
he will plan	he will have planned ◀2	he would plan	he would have planned ◀2	planning ◀2
it will happen	it will have happened ◀3	it would happen	it would have happened ◀3	happening ◀3
you will listen	you will have listened ◀3	you would listen	you would have listened ◀3	listening ◀3
you will fight	you will have fought	you would fight	you would have fought	fighting
he will wash	he will have washed	he would wash	he would have washed	washing
she will mix	she will have mixed	she would mix	she would have mixed	mixing
she will hate	she will have hated ◀5	she would hate	she would have hated ◀5	hating ◀5
you will permit	you will have permitted ◀2	you would permit	you would have permitted ◀2	permitting ◀2
you will regret	you will have regretted ◀2	you would regret	you would have regretted	regretting ◀2
she will visit	she will have visited ◀3	she would visit	she would have visited ◀3	visiting ◀3
they will like	they will have liked ◀5	they would like	they would have liked ◀5	liking ◀5
he will teach	he will have taught	he would teach	he would have taught	teaching
she will play	she will have played ◀1	she would play	she would have played ◀1	playing
she will miss	she will have missed	she would miss	she would have missed	missing
he will stand	he will have stood	he would stand	he would have stood	standing
she will tell	she will have told	she would tell	she would have told	telling
she will prefer	she will have preferred ◀2	she would prefer	she would have preferred	preferring ◀2
you will answer	you will have answered ◀3	you would answer	you would have answered ◀3	answering ◀3
they will cover	they will have covered ◀3	they would cover	they would have covered ◀3	covering ◀3
I will refer	I will have referred ◀2	I would refer	I would have referred ◀2	referring ◀2
I will remember	I will have remembered ◀3	I would remember	I would have remembered	remembering
he will suffer	he will have suffered ◀3	he would suffer	he would have suffered ◀3	suffering ◀3
she will read	she will have read [red]	she would read	she would have read [red]	reading
I will change	I will have changed ◀5	I would change	I would have changed ◀5	changing ◀5
I will promise	I will have promised ◀5	I would promise	I would have promised ◀5	promising ◀5
he will watch	he will have watched	he would watch	he would have watched	watching
we will get	we will have got	we would get	we would have got	getting ◀2
he will lie	he will have lain	he would lie	he would have lain	lying ◀7
he will lay	he will have laid	he would lay	he would have laid	laying
you will spring	you will have sprung	you would spring	you would have sprung	springing
he will continue	he will have continued	he would continue	he would have continued ◀5	continuing ◀5
I will ring	I will have rung	I would ring	I would have rung	ringing
he will arrive	he will have arrived ◀5	he would arrive	he would have arrived ◀5	arriving ◀5
she will reply	she will have replied ◀6	she would reply	she would have replied ◀6	replying

Infinitive	Pres. T. Simple	Past T. Simple	Pres. Perf. Simple	Past Perf. Simple
36. to make	we make	we made	we have made	we had made
37. to behave	they behave	they behaved [5]	they have behaved [5]	they had behaved [5]
38. to leave	you leave	you left	you have left	you had left
39. to believe	I believe	I believed [5]	I have believed [5]	I had believed [5]
40. to feel	I feel	I felt	I have felt	I had felt
41. to burst	he bursts [8]	he burst [8]	he has burst	he had burst
42. to smile	I smile	I smiled [5]	I have smiled [5]	I had smiled [5]
43. to touch	she touches [4]	she touched	she has touched	she had touched
44. to carry	she carries [6]	she carried [6]	she has carried [6]	she had carried [6]
45. to live	I live	I lived [5]	I have lived [5]	I had lived [5]
46. to grow	we grow	we grew	we have grown	we had grown
47. to advise	she advises	she advised [5]	she has advised [5]	she had advised [5]
48. to build	you build	you built [8]	you have built [8]	you had built [8]
49. to send	they send	they sent [8]	they have sent [8]	they had sent [8]
50. to do	he does [4]	he did	he has done	he had done
51. to catch	she catches [4]	she caught	she has caught	she had caught
52. to set	he sets [8]	he set [8]	he has set	he had set
53. to draw	we draw	we drew	we have drawn	we had drawn
54. to pass	he passes [4]	he passed	he has passed	he had passed
55. to be	we are	we were	we have been	we had been
56. to be	I am	I was	I have been	I had been
57. to be	you are	you were	you have been	you had been
58. to be	he is	he was	he has been	he had been
59. to sing	he sings	he sang	he has sung	he had sung
60. to destroy	he destroys [1]	he destroyed [1]	he has destroyed [1]	he had destroyed [1]
61. to control	he controls	he controlled [2]	he has controlled [2]	he had controlled [2]
62. to quarrel	I quarrel	I quarrelled [2]	I have quarrelled [2]	I had quarrelled [2]
63. to travel	they travel	they travelled [2]	they have travelled [2]	they had travelled [2]
64. to use	they use	they used [5]	they have used [5]	they had used [5]
65. to move	we move	we moved [5]	we have moved [5]	we had moved [5]
66. to recognise	I recognise	I recognised [5]	I have recognised [5]	I had recognised [5]
67. to mean	they mean	they meant	they have meant	they had meant
68. to bring	he brings	he brought	he has brought	he had brought
69. to love	you love	you loved [5]	you have loved [5]	you had loved [5]
70. to know	they know	they knew	they have known	they had known
71. to imagine	I imagine	I imagined [5]	I have imagined [5]	I had imagined [5]
72. to guess	she guesses [4]	she guessed	she has guessed	she had guessed
73. to describe	you describe	you described [5]	you have described [5]	you had described [5]
74. to keep	she keeps	she kept	she has kept	she had kept
75. to notice	you notice	you noticed [5]	you have noticed [5]	you had noticed [5]
76. to sit	they sit	they sat	they have sat	they had sat
77. to think	we think	we thought	we have thought	we had thought

Future Tense	Future Perfect	Conditional	Conditional Perf.	Cont. Form
we will make	we will have made	we would make	we would have made	making ◄5
they will behave	they will have behaved ◄5	they would behave	they would have behaved	behaving ◄5
you will leave	you will have left	you would leave	you would have left	leaving ◄5
I will believe	I will have believed ◄5	I would believe	I would have believed ◄5	believing ◄5
I will feel	I will have felt	I would feel	I would have felt	feeling
he will burst	he will have burst	he would burst	he would have burst	bursting
I will smile	I will have smiled ◄5	I would smile	I would have smiled ◄5	smiling ◄5
she will touch	she will have touched	she would touch	she would have touched	touching
she will carry	she will have carried ◄6	she would carry	she would have carried ◄6	carrying
I will live	I will have lived ◄5	I would live	I would have lived ◄5	living ◄5
we will grow	we will have grown	we would grow	we would have grown	growing
she will advise	she will have advised ◄5	she would advise	she would have advised ◄5	advising ◄5
you will build	you will have built ◄8	you would build	you would have built ◄8	building
they will send	they will have sent ◄8	they would send	they would have sent ◄8	sending
he will do	he will have done	he would do	he would have done	doing
she will catch	she will have caught	she would catch	she would have caught	catching
he will set	he will have set	he would set	he would have set	setting ◄2
we will draw	we will have drawn	we would draw	we would have drawn	drawing
he will pass	he will have passed	he would pass	he would have passed	passing
we will be	we will have been	we would be	we would have been	being
I will be	I will have been	I would be	I would have been	being
you will be	you will have been	you would be	you would have been	being
he will be	he will have been	he would be	he would have been	being
he will sing	he will have sung	he would sing	he would have sung	singing
he will destroy	he will have destroyed	he would destroy	he would have destroyed ◄1	destroying
he will control	he will have controlled	he would control	he would have controlled ◄2	controlling ◄2
I will quarrel	I will have quarrelled ◄2	I would quarrel	I would have quarrelled ◄2	quarrelling ◄2
they will travel	they will have travelled ◄2	they would travel	they would have travelled	travelling ◄2
they will use	they will have used ◄5	they would use	they would have used ◄5	using ◄5
we will move	we will have moved ◄5	we would move	we would have moved ◄5	moving ◄5
I will recognise	I will have recognised ◄5	I would recognise	I would have recognised ◄5	recognising ◄5
they will mean	they will have meant	they would mean	they would have meant	meaning
he will bring	he will have brought	he would bring	he would have brought	bringing
you will love	you will have loved ◄5	you would love	you would have loved ◄5	loving ◄5
they will know	they will have known	they would know	they would have known	knowing
I will imagine	I will have imagined ◄5	I would imagine	I would have imagined ◄5	imagining ◄5
she will guess	she will have guessed	she would guess	she would have guessed	guessing
you will describe	you will have described	you would describe	you would have described ◄5	describing ◄5
she will keep	she will have kept	she would keep	she would have kept	keeping
you will notice	you will have noticed ◄5	you would notice	you would have noticed ◄5	noticing ◄5
they will sit	they will have sat	they would sit	they would have sat	sitting ◄2
we will think	we will have thought	we would think	we would have thought	thinking

DAS VERB

Infinitive	Pres. T. Simple	Past T. Simple	Pres. Perf. Simple	Past Perf. Simple
78. to try	she tries ◀6	she tried ◀6	she has tried ◀6	she had tried ◀6
79. to enjoy	she enjoys ◀1	she enjoyed ◀1	she has enjoyed ◀1	she had enjoyed ◀1
80. to push	he pushes ◀4	he pushed	he has pushed	he had pushed
81. to meet	I meet	I met	I have met	I had met
82. to reach	he reaches ◀4	he reached	he has reached	he had reached
83. to buy	he buys ◀1	he bought	he has bought	he had bought
84. to run	you run	you ran	you have run	you had run
85. to see	she sees	she saw	she has seen	she had seen
86. to lend	we lend	we lent ◀8	we have lent ◀8	we had lent ◀8
87. to begin	we begin	we began	we have begun	we had begun
88. to wake	we wake	we woke/waked ◀5	we have	we had woken/waked ◀5
89. to bear (geboren werden)	I am born	I was born	I have been born	I had been born
90. to bear ((er)tragen)	she bears	she bore	she has borne	she had borne
91. to find	he finds	he found	he has found	he had found
92. to die	he dies	he died ◀7	he has died ◀7	he had died ◀7
93. to shake	you shake	you shook	you have shaken	you had shaken
94. to give	we give	we gave	we have given	we had given
95. to hurry	he hurries ◀6	he hurried ◀6	he has hurried ◀6	he had hurried ◀6
96. to decide	we decide	we decided ◀5	we have decided ◀5	we had decided ◀5
97. to suppose	she supposes	she supposed ◀5	she has supposed ◀5	she had supposed ◀5
98. to cry	she cries ◀6	she cried ◀6	she has cried ◀6	she had cried ◀6
99. to throw	you throw	you threw	you have thrown	you had thrown
100. to learn	I learn	I learnt/learned	I have learnt/learned	I had learnt/learned
101. to swim	we swim	we swam	we have swum	we had swum
102. to hold	he holds	he held	he has held	he had held
103. to have	he has	he had	he has had	he had had
104. to have	I have	I had	I have had	I had had
105. to hurt	he hurts ◀8	he hurt ◀8	he has hurt	he had hurt
106. to lose	she loses	she lost	she has lost	she had lost
107. to wear	she wears	she wore	she has worn	she had worn
108. to finish	she finishes ◀4	she finished	she has finished	she had finished
109. to satisfy	he satisfies ◀6	he satisfied ◀6	he has satisfied ◀6	he had satisfied ◀6
110. to drive	I drive	I drove	I have driven	I had driven
111. to cost	it costs ◀8	it cost ◀8	it has cost	it had cost
112. to develop	she develops	she developed ◀3	she has developed ◀3	she had developed ◀3
113. to stop	she stops	she stopped ◀2	she has stopped ◀2	she had stopped ◀2
114. to wish	she wishes ◀4	she wished	she has wished	she had wished
115. to hear	you hear	you heard	you have heard	you had heard
116. to eat	you eat	you ate	you have eaten	you had eaten
117. to show	I show	I showed	I have shown	I had shown
118. to agree	I agree	I agreed ◀5	I have agreed ◀5	I had agreed ◀5
119. to hope	I hope	I hoped ◀5	I have hoped ◀5	I had hoped ◀5

Future Tense	Future Perfect	Conditional	Conditional Perf.	Cont. Form
she will try	she will have tried ◄6	she would try	she would have tried ◄6	trying
she will enjoy	she will have enjoyed ◄1	she would enjoy	she would have enjoyed ◄1	enjoying
he will push	he will have pushed	he would push	he would have pushed	pushing
I will meet	I will have met	I would meet	I would have met	meeting
he will reach	he will have reached	he would reach	he would have reached	reaching
he will buy	he will have bought	he would buy	he would have bought	buying
you will run	you will have run	you would run	you would have run	running ◄2
she will see	she will have seen	she would see	she would have seen	seeing
we will lend	we will have lent ◄8	we would lend	we would have lent ◄8	lending
we will begin	we will have begun	we would begin	we would have begun	beginning ◄2
we will wake	we will have woken/waked ◄5	we would wake	we would have woken/waked ◄5	waking ◄5
I will be born	I will have been born	I would be born	I would have been born	bearing
she will bear	she will have borne	she would bear	she would have borne	bearing
he will find	he will have found	he would find	he would have found	finding
he will die	he will have died ◄7	he would die	he would have died ◄7	dying ◄7
you will shake	you will have shaken	you would shake	you would have shaken	shaking ◄5
we will give	we will have given	we would give	we would have given	giving ◄5
he will hurry	he will have hurried ◄6	he would hurry	he would have hurried ◄6	hurrying
we will decide	we will have decided ◄5	we would decide	we would have decided ◄5	deciding ◄5
she will suppose	she will have supposed	she would suppose	she would have supposed ◄5	supposing ◄5
she will cry	she will have cried ◄6	she would cry	she would have cried ◄6	crying
you will throw	you will have thrown	you would throw	you would have thrown	throwing
I will learn	I will have learnt/learned	I would learn	I would have learnt/learned	learning
we will swim	we will have swum	we would swim	we would have swum	swimming ◄2
he will hold	he will have held	he would hold	he would have held	holding
he will have	he will have had	he would have	he would have had	having ◄5
I will have	I will have had	I would have	I would have had	having ◄5
he will hurt	he will have hurt	he would hurt	he would have hurt	hurting
she will lose	she will have lost	she would lose	she would have lost	losing ◄5
she will wear	she will have worn	she would wear	she would have worn	wearing
she will finish	she will have finished	she would finish	she would have finished	finishing
he will satisfy	he will have satisfied ◄6	he would satisfy	he would have satisfied ◄6	satisfying
I will drive	I will have driven	I would drive	I would have driven	driving ◄5
it will cost	it will have cost	it would cost	it would have cost	costing
she will develop	she will have developed ◄3	she would develop	she would have developed	developing ◄3
she will stop	she will have stopped ◄2	she would stop	she would have stopped ◄2	stopping ◄2
she will wish	she will have wished	she would wish	she would have wished	wishing
you will hear	you will have heard	you would hear	you would have heard	hearing
you will eat	you will have eaten	you would eat	you would have eaten	eating
I will show	I will have shown	I would show	I would have shown	showing
I will agree	I will have agreed ◄5	I would agree	I would have agreed ◄5	agreeing ◄5
I will hope	I will have hoped ◄5	I would hope	I would have hoped ◄5	hoping ◄5

Infinitive	Pres. T. Simple	Past T. Simple	Pres. Perf. Simple	Past Perf. Simple
120. to speak	I speak	I spoke	I have spoken	I had spoken
121. to break	you break	you broke	you have broken	you had broken
122. to realize	we realize	we realized [5]	we have realized [5]	we had realized [5]
123. to fall	he falls	he fell	he has fallen	he had fallen
124. to drink	they drink	they drank	they have drunk	they had drunk
125. to come	she comes	she came	she has come	she had come
126. to cut	he cuts [8]	he cut [8]	he has cut	he had cut
127. to beat	he beats [8]	he beat [8]	he has beaten	he had beaten
128. to steal	he steals	he stole	he has stolen	he had stolen
129. to go	he goes [4]	he went	he has gone	he had gone
130. to dream	we dream	we dreamt/dreamed	we have dreamt/dreamed	we had dreamt/dreamed
131. to take	they take	they took	they have taken	they had taken
132. to worry	he worries [6]	he worried [6]	he has worried [6]	he had worried [6]
133. to say	he says [1]	he said	he has said	he had said
134. to let	she lets [8]	she let [8]	she has let	she had let
135. to put	he puts [8]	he put [8]	he has put	he had put
136. to spend	I spend	I spent [8]	I have spent [8]	I had spent [8]
137. to choose	he chooses	he chose	he has chosen	he had chosen
138. to sleep	I sleep	I slept	I have slept	I had slept
139. to write	they write	they wrote	they have written	they had written
140. to shut	he shuts [8]	he shut [8]	he has shut	he had shut
141. to hit	she hits [8]	she hit [8]	she has hit	she had hit
142. to forbid	we forbid	we forbade	we have forbidden	we had forbidden
143. to forget	they forget	they forgot	they have forgotten	they had forgotten
144. to fly	she flies [6]	she flew	she has flown	she had flown

Erklärungen und Lernhinweise

1. Dem **-y** geht ein Vokal voraus, daher bleibt das **-y** beim Anhängen von **-s** und **-ed** erhalten.
2. Dem Endkonsonant geht ein kurzer, betonter Vokal voraus, daher verdoppelt sich dieser Endkonsonant
Verben verdoppeln dieses beim Anhängen von **-ed** und **-ing**.
3. Dem Endkonsonant geht ein unbetonter Vokal voraus, daher verdoppelt sich dieser Endkonsonant beim
4. Auf **-ch, -sh, -ss, -x** und **-o** endende Verben hängen in der 3. Person Singular des present tense
5. Auf **-e** endende Verben, verlieren dieses beim Anhängen von **-ed** und **-ing.** Auf **-ee** endende Verben ver
6. Dem **-y** geht ein Konsonant voraus, daher wir das **-y** beim Anhängen von **-s** und **-ed** zu **-ie**.
7. Auf **-ie** endende Verben, ändern dieses in **-y** beim Anhängen von **-ing**, beim Anhängen von **-ed** entfällt
8. Verben, die in allen 3 Stammformen dieselbe Form haben unterscheiden sich im present tense vom
einige Verben auf **-d** dieses in der 2. und 3. Stammform in **-t** ändern.

Nicht markierte Verbformen sind unregelmäßig. Es ist zu beachten, dass **bear** in der Bedeutung von
nur im Passiv gebraucht und erhält in der 3. Stammform kein **-e**.

Es ist zu beachten, dass die Verbformen der 3. Person Singular im present tense simple und das
Future tense und conditional werden mit dem Infinitiv gebildet (also z.B. **will keep** und nicht

Future Tense	Future Perfect	Conditional	Conditional Perf.	Cont. Form
I will speak	I will have spoken	I would speak	I would have spoken	speaking
you will break	you will have broken	you would break	you would have broken	breaking
we will realize	we will have realized [5]	we would realize	we would have realized [5]	realizing [5]
he will fall	he will have fallen	he would fall	he would have fallen	falling
they will drink	they will have drunk	they would drink	they would have drunk	drinking
she will come	she will have come	she would come	she would have come	coming [5]
he will cut	he will have cut	he would cut	he would have cut	cutting [2]
he will beat	he will have beaten	he would beat	he would have beaten	beating
he will steal	he will have stolen	he would steal	he would have stolen	stealing
he will go	he will have gone	he would go	he would have gone	going
we will dream	we will have dreamt/dreamed	we would dream	we would have dreamt/dreamed	dreaming
they will take	they will have taken	they would take	they would have taken	taking [5]
he will worry	he will have worried [6]	he would worry	he would have worried [6]	worrying
he will say	he will have said	he would say	he would have said	saying
she will let	she will have let	she would let	she would have let	letting [2]
he will put	he will have put	he would put	he would have put	putting [2]
I will spend	I will have spent [8]	I would spend	I would have spent [8]	spending
he will choose	he will have chosen	he would choose	he would have chosen	choosing [5]
I will sleep	I will have slept	I would sleep	I would have slept	sleeping
they will write	they will have written	they would write	they would have written	writing [5]
he will shut	he will have shut	he would shut	he would have shut	shutting [2]
she will hit	she will have hit	she would hit	she would have hit	hitting [2]
we will forbid	we will have forbidden	we would forbid	we would have forbidden	forbidding [2]
they will forget	they will have forgotten	they would forget	they would have forgotten	forgetting [2]
she will fly	she will have flown	she would fly	she would have flown	flying

beim Anhängen von **-ed** und **-ing**. Der betonte Vokal ist zur Veranschaulichung unterstrichen. Auf **-l** endende

Anhängen von **-ed** und **-ing** nicht. Der betonte Vokal ist zur Veranschaulichung unterstrichen.

simple **-es** an.

lieren ein **-e** beim Anhängen von **-ed.**

das Endungs-e.

past tense simple nur in der 3. Person Singular (z.B. **he bursts** und **he burst**). Es ist zu beachten, dass

ertragen oder *gebären* in der 3. Stammform ein **-e** erhält, **bear** in der Bedeutung von *geboren werden* wird

Hilfsverb im present perfect simple generell ein **-s** erhalten.
will kept).

Kurzformen (Contractions)

1 Setzen Sie die folgenden Verben in die entsprechende Kurzform.

Bejahte Kurzform	**have**	**had**	**be**	**will/ shall**	**would/ should**
I	've	'd	'm	'll	'd
you	've	'd	're	'll	'd
he, she, it	's ◄1	'd	's	'll	'd
we	've	'd	're	'll	'd
you	've	'd	're	'll	'd
they	've	'd	're	'll	'd

Erklärungen und Lernhinweise

1 Die 3. Person Singular von **have** lautet **has**, demnach lautet auch Kurzform **'s**.

Bitte beachten Sie, dass Kurzformen, die die gleiche Form haben (z.B.: **'d** für **had** und **would** oder **should**) häufig verwechselt werden.

2 Setzen die die folgenden Verben in die entsprechenden Kurzformen.

Verneinte Kurzform	**have**	**had**	**be**	**was**	**will/ shall**	**would/ should**	**do**	**did**
I	haven't	hadn't	'm not ◄2	wasn't	won't/shan't	wouldn't/shouldn't	don't	didn't
you	haven't	hadn't	aren't	weren't	won't/shan't	wouldn't/shouldn't	don't	didn't
he, she, it	hasn't ◄1	hadn't	isn't	wasn't	won't/shan't	wouldn't/shouldn't	doesn't ◄3	didn't
we	haven't	hadn't	aren't	weren't	won't/shan't	wouldn't/shouldn't	don't	didn't
you	haven't	hadn't	aren't	weren't	won't/shan't	wouldn't/shouldn't	don't	didn't
they	haven't	hadn't	aren't	weren't	won't/shan't	wouldn't/shouldn't	don't	didn't

Erklärungen und Lernhinweise

1 Die 3. Person Singular von **have** lautet **has**, demnach lautet auch die verneinte Kurzform **hasn't**.

2 **Am** und **not** können nicht zusammengezogen werden.

3 Die 3. Person Singular von **do** lautet **does**, demnach lautet auch die verneinte Kurzform **doesn't**.

Das Hilfsverb to do (The Auxiliary Verb to do)

To do im verneinten Satz

1 Verneinen Sie die folgenden Sätze mit dem Verb im present tense simple.

1. do not/don't show ◀1 2. do not like ◀1 3. do not seem ◀1 4. does not like/doesn't like ◀2 5. does not belong ◀2 6. does not make ◀2 7. does not help ◀2 8. does not do ◀3 9. do not have ◀3 10. Don't say ◀4 11. do not get ◀1 12. do not find ◀1 13. does not go ◀2 14. does not wish ◀2 15. does not rule ◀2 16. does not take ◀2 17. does not have ◀3 18. Don't do ◀4 19. do not play ◀1 20. Don't keep ◀4 21. does not compare ◀2

Erklärungen und Lernhinweise

▶1 Das Verb ist ein Vollverb, daher wird die Verneinung mit **to do** gebildet. Bei allen Personen, außer bei der 3. Person Singular, steht **do not** bzw. die Kurzform **don't**, die nicht jedesmal aufgeführt ist.

▶2 Das Verb ist ein Vollverb, daher wird die Verneinung mit **to do** gebildet. Bei der 3. Person Singular steht **does not** bzw. die Kurzform **doesn't**, die nicht jedesmal aufgeführt ist. Es ist zu beachten, dass auf **does not** der Infinitiv des Verbs folgt (also z.B. **she does not like** und nicht **she does not likes**).

▶3 Auch bei **to do** und bei **to have**, wenn es nicht als Hilfsverb verwendet wird, d.h. es folgt kein weiteres Vollverb, wird die Verneinung mit **to do** gebildet.

▶4 Dies ist ein Befehl, auch bei verneinten Befehlen wird **to do** verwendet. Befehle beziehen sich auf die 2. Person, daher steht **do not** bzw. **don't**.

2 Verneinen Sie die folgenden Sätze mit dem Verb im past tense simple.

1. did not/didn't send ◀1 2. did not listen ◀1 3. did not write ◀1 4. did not wait, did not feel ◀1 5. did not sleep ◀1 6. did not leave ◀1 7. did not obey ◀1 8. did not find ◀1 9. did not have ◀2 10. did not do ◀2 11. did not notice ◀1 12. did not hear ◀1 13. did not last ◀1 14. did not catch ◀1 15. did not stop ◀1 16. did not quiet ◀1 17. did not explain ◀1 18. did not do ◀2 19. did not have ◀2

Erklärungen und Lernhinweise

▶1 Das Verb ist ein Vollverb, daher wird die Verneinung mit **to do** gebildet. Die Verneinung wird für alle Personen mit **did not** bzw. mit der Kurzform **didn't**, die nicht jedesmal aufgeführt ist, gebildet. Es ist zu beachten, dass auf **did not** der Infinitiv des Verbs folgt (also z.B. **did not listen** und nicht **did not listened**).

▶2 Auch bei **to do** und bei **to have**, wenn es nicht als Hilfsverb verwendet wird, d.h. es folgt kein weiteres Vollverb, wird die Verneinung mit **to do** gebildet.

3 Verneinen Sie die folgenden Sätze, die ein Hilfsverb enthalten.

1. have not/haven't decided ◀1 2. had not/hadn't told ◀1 3. had not left ◀1 4. has not/hasn't for-

gotten ◀1 5. has not had ◀2 6. am not/'m not ◀4 7. 'm not/am not allowed ◀1 8. was not/wasn't ◀4 9. is not/isn't ◀4 10. have not replied ◀1 11. had not waited ◀1 12. are not allowed ◀1 13. were not/weren't ◀4 14. have not been ◀1 15. has not been found ◀3 16. 're not doing/aren't doing ◀1 17. has not been solved ◀3 18. are not served ◀1 19. is not ◀4 20. were not ◀4 21. am not/'m not ◀4 22. is not ◀4 23. were not ◀4

Erklärungen und Lernhinweise

▶1 Es ist ein Hilfsverb vorhanden, daher wird die Verneinung nicht mit **to do**, sondern mit diesem Hilfsverb + **not** bzw. der Kurzform **n't**, die nicht jedesmal aufgeführt ist, gebildet.

▶2 **To have** ist Hilfsverb und Vollverb, es wird das Hilfsverb (das erste **have**) verneint.

▶3 Es sind zwei Hilfsverben vorhanden, es wird das erste Hilfsverb verneint.

▶4 **To be** ist Vollverb, es wird auch in dieser Funktion nicht mit **to do** verneint.

4 Verneinen Sie die folgenden Sätze, die ein Modalverb enthalten.

1. cannot/can't read ◀1 2. could not remember ◀1 3. may not be ◀1 4. might not be ◀1 5. could not let ◀1 6. must not get ◀1 7. shall not/shan't know ◀1 8. cannot come ◀1 9. cannot do, must not give up ◀1 10. ought not to smoke ◀1 11. will not/won't be ◀1 12. should not flood ◀1 13. will not mind/won't mind ◀1 14. would not like ◀1 15. may not have been ◀2 16. might not have happened ◀2 17. should not have given ◀2 18. would not believe ◀1 19. need not take ◀1 20. should not be interrupted ◀2 21. ought not to have said ◀2 22. shall not/shan't always expect ◀1 23. need not have troubled ◀2

Erklärungen und Lernhinweise

▶1 Es ist ein Modalverb vorhanden, daher wird die Verneinung nicht mit **to do**, sondern mit diesem Modalverb + **not** bzw. der Kurzform **n't**, die nicht jedesmal aufgeführt ist, gebildet. Es sind die besonderen Kurzformen von **shall, shan't** und **will, won't** zu beachten. Die verneinte Form von **can** schreibt man zusammen, **cannot**.

▶2 Es ist ein Modalverb und ein Hilfsverb vorhanden, es wird das Modalverb verneint.

5 Verneinen Sie die folgenden Sätze mit dem Verb im present tense simple und verwenden Sie **to do** wo nötig.

1. do not have ◀1 2. cannot tell ◀2 3. must not find ◀2 4. should not talk ◀2 5. does not do ◀3 6. could not hear ◀2 7. might not be ◀2 8. shall not/shan't go ◀2 9. have not had ◀5 10. have not got ◀4 11. will not be able ◀5 12. ought not to lie ◀2 13. do not bite ◀1 14. do not get ◀1 15. does not need ◀6 16. need not leave ◀7 17. need not worry ◀7 18. do not need ◀6 19. do not need ◀6 20. have not been interfered ◀5 21. was not ◀8 22. were not ◀8 23. would not sit ◀2 24. do not need ◀6 25. need not be looked after ◀7

Erklärungen und Lernhinweise

▶1 Das Verb ist ein Vollverb, daher wird die Verneinung mit **to do** gebildet. Bei allen Personen, außer bei der 3. Person Singular steht **do not** bzw. die Kurzform **don't**, die nicht jedesmal aufgeführt ist.
Auch **to do** und **to have**, wenn es nicht als Hilfsverb verwendet wird, sind Vollverben.

▶2 Es ist ein Modalverb vorhanden, daher wird die Verneinung nicht mit **to do**, sondern mit diesem Modalverb + **not** bzw. der Kurzform **n't**, die nicht jedesmal aufgeführt ist, gebildet. Es sind die besonderen Kurzformen von **shall**, **shan't** und **will**, **won't** zu beachten. Die verneinte Form von **can** schreibt man zusammen, **cannot**.

▶3 Das Verb ist ein Vollverb, daher wird die Verneinung mit **to do** gebildet. Bei der 3. Person Singular steht **does not** bzw. die Kurzform **doesn't**, die nicht jedesmal aufgeführt ist. Es ist zu beachten, dass auf **does not** der Infinitiv des Verbs folgt (also z.B. **she does not like** und nicht **she does not likes**).

▶4 Es ist ein Hilfsverb vorhanden, daher wird die Verneinung nicht mit **to do**, sondern mit diesem Hilfsverb + **not** bzw. der Kurzform **n't**, die nicht jedesmal aufgeführt ist, gebildet.

▶5 Es ist ein Modalverb und ein Hilfsverb bzw. es sind zwei Hilfsverben vorhanden, so wird das Modalverb bzw. das erste Hilfsverb verneint.
To have kann Hilfsverb und Vollverb sein, es wird dann das Hilfsverb (das erste **have**) verneint.

▶6 **Need** ist Vollverb, d.h. es folgt kein Infinitiv, daher wird die Verneinung mit **to do** bzw. der Kurzform **don't**, die nicht jedesmal aufgeführt ist, gebildet. In der 3. Person Singular steht **does not** bzw. **doesn't**.

▶7 **Need** ist Modalverb, d.h. es folgt ein Infinitiv, daher wird die Verneinung nicht mit **to do** gebildet, sondern mit **need + not** bzw. der Kurzform **needn't**, die nicht jedesmal aufgeführt ist.

▶8 **To be** ist Vollverb, es wird auch in dieser Funktion nicht mit **to do** verneint.

To do im Fragesatz

1 Bilden Sie Fragen mit dem Verb im present tense simple.

1. Does Harry **know** ◀1 2. Do buses **run** ◀2 3. Do German people **eat** ◀2 4. Does Mrs Summers **teach** ◀1 5. Does she **want** ◀1 6. Does this little bag **have to** be weighed ◀3 7. Do you **have** ◀3 8. Do you **know** ◀2 9. Do you **like** ◀2 10. Do you really **expect** ◀2 11. Do you **think** ◀2 12. Do you **want** ◀2 13. Does your brother **like** ◀1 14. Does your friend **know** ◀1 15. Do you **think** ◀2 16. Does he **regret** ◀1 17. Do drivers **have to** have ◀3 18. Do drivers **have to** give ◀3 19. Does a scientist **have to** think ◀3 20. Does your tyre **want** ◀1 21. Does the translation **do** ◀1

Erklärungen und Lernhinweise

▶1 Das Verb ist ein Vollverb, daher wird die Frage mit **to do** gebildet. Bei der 3. Person Singular steht **does**. Das Subjekt tritt zwischen **does** und Vollverb. Es ist zu beachten, dass auf **does** der Infinitiv des Verbs folgt (also **does Harry know** und nicht **does Harry knows**). Zur Veranschaulichung ist das Vollverb fett gedruckt.

▶2 Das Verb ist ein Vollverb, daher wird die Frage mit **to do** gebildet. In allen Personen, außer der 3. Person Singular steht **do.** Das Subjekt tritt zwischen **do** und Vollverb. Zur Veranschaulichung ist das Vollverb fett gedruckt.

▶3 Auch bei **to have**, wenn es nicht als Hilfsverb verwendet wird, d.h. es folgt kein weiteres Verb, und bei **to do** wird die Frage mit **to do** gebildet. Dies gilt auch für **have to**.

2 Bilden Sie Fragen, mit dem Verb im past tense simple.

1. Did you **catch** ◀1 2. Did you **get** ◀1 3. Did you **buy** ◀1 4. Did you **feed** ◀1 5. Did you **sleep** ◀1 6. Did you **see** ◀1 7. Did Peggy **find** ◀1 8. Did you **go** ◀1 9. Did he really **say** ◀1 10. Did you **get** ◀1 11. Did it **hurt** ◀1 12. Did you **read** ◀1 13. Did you **try** ◀1 14. Did you **send** ◀1 15. Did you **have** ◀2 16. Did your aunt **die** and **leave** ◀1 17. Did he really **have** ◀2 18. Did they **receive** ◀1 19. Did you **know** ◀1 20. Did he **do** ◀2

Erklärungen und Lernhinweise

▶1 Das Verb ist ein Vollverb, daher wird die Frage mit **to do** gebildet. Die Frage wird für alle Personen mit **did** gebildet. Das Subjekt tritt zwischen **did** und Vollverb. Es ist zu beachten, dass auf **did** der Infinitiv des Verbs folgt (also z.B. **did you catch** und nicht **did you caught**). Zur Veranschaulichung ist das Vollverb fett gedruckt.

▶2 Auch bei **to have**, wenn es nicht als Hilfsverb verwendet wird, d. h. es folgt kein weiteres Verb, und bei **to do** wird die Frage mit **to do** gebildet.

3 Formen Sie die folgenden Sätze, die ein Hilfsverb enthalten, in Fragen um.

1. **Was** he ◀1 2. **Had** Linda gone ◀2 3. **Are** you ◀1 4. **Has** your uncle got ◀2 5. **Is** it ◀1 6. **Were** you able ◀2 7. **Are** you getting on ◀2 8. **Has** it stopped ◀2 9. **Is** she hurt ◀2 10. **Have** you spent ◀2 11. **Were** they ◀1 12. **Had** he **been** drinking ◀3 13. **Was** he wanted ◀2 14. **Was** it likely ◀2 15. **Have** you got ◀2 16. **Had** the fellow stopped ◀2 17. **Have** you heard ◀2 18. **Has** the new rocket sufficiently **been** tested ◀3 19. **Are**n't I ◀4 20. **Am** I supposed ◀2

Erklärungen und Lernhinweise

▶1 **To be** ist Vollverb, auch wenn es in dieser Funktion steht, wird die Frage nicht mit **to do** gebildet.

▶2 Es ist ein Hilfsverb vorhanden, daher wird die Frage nicht mit **to do**, sondern mit diesem Hilfsverb gebildet. Das Subjekt tritt hinter dieses Hilfsverb. Zur Veranschaulichung ist das Hilfsverb fett gedruckt.

▶3 Es sind zwei Hilfsverben vorhanden, so wird die Frage mit dem 1. Hilfsverb gebildet.

▶4 **I am not** wird in der Frage zu **aren't I**.

4 Formen Sie die folgenden Sätze, die ein Modalverb enthalten, in Fragen um.

1. **Can** we go ◀1 2. **Could** you shut ◀1 3. **May** I borrow ◀1 4. **Might** I use ◀1 5. **Must** you get up ◀1 6. **Should** we go in ◀1 7. **Will** you take ◀1 8. **Would** you do ◀1 9. **May** I come ◀1 10. **Must** you smoke ◀1 11. **Would** that be ◀1 12. **Shall** we have ◀1 13. **Can** you lend ◀1 14. **Could** I have ◀1 15. **Shall** we do ◀1 16. **Should** the flow of newcomers be diminished ◀2 17. **Will** you do ◀1 18. **Will** you stop ◀1 19. **Shall** I make ◀1

Erklärungen und Lernhinweise

▶1 Es ist ein Modalverb vorhanden, daher wird die Frage nicht mit **to do**, sondern mit diesem Modalverb gebildet. Das Subjekt tritt hinter dieses Modalverb. Zur Veranschaulichung ist das Modalverb fett gedruckt.

Erklärungen und Lernhinweise

▶2 Es ist ein Modalverb und ein Hilfsverb vorhanden, so wird die Frage mit dem Modalverb gebildet.

5 Bilden Sie Fragen und verwenden Sie **to do** wo nötig.

1. **Have** you asked ◀1 2. Did Columbus **discover** ◀2 3. **Has** he been ◀1 4. **Could** Henry see ◀1 5. **Shall** I post ◀1 6. **Was** Mike's business ◀1 7. **Aren't** the pigeons you see in front of St Paul's Cathedral afraid ◀7 8. Do they **serve** ◀4 9. **Had** we switched ◀1 10. Does your mother **write** ◀5 11. Does your sister **talk** ◀5 12. **Have** the gang of eight or nine boys, aged around 18, been caught ◀3 13. **Hasn't** the present owner got ◀8 14. **Have** things been going well ◀3 15. **May** he have had ◀3 16. Doesn't it **mean** ◀8 17. **Hadn't** she been invited ◀8 18. **Hasn't** the matter yet been put ◀8 19. Doesn't he **tell** ◀8 20. Didn't you **pay** ◀8 21. Do/did the private TV stations, mainly supported by the viewers' fees, **broadcast** ◀6

Erklärungen und Lernhinweise

▶1 Es ist ein Hilfsverb bzw. ein Modalverb vorhanden, daher wird die Frage nicht mit **to do**, sondern mit diesem Hilfsverb bzw. Modalverb gebildet. Das Subjekt tritt hinter das Hilfsverb bzw. das Modalverb. Das Hilfsverb bzw. das Modalverb ist zur Veranschaulichung fett gedruckt.

▶2 Das Verb ist ein Vollverb, daher wird die Frage mit **to do** gebildet. Das Verb des bejahten Satzes steht im past tense, also wird die Frage mit **did**, das bei allen Personen verwendet wird, gebildet. Das Subjekt tritt hinter **did**. Es ist zu beachten, dass auf **did** der Infinitiv des Verbs folgt (also z.B. **did Columbus discover** und nicht **did Columbus discovered**). Das Vollverb ist zur Veranschaulichung fett gedruckt.

▶3 Es sind zwei Hilfsverben bzw. ein Modalverb und ein Hilfsverb vorhanden, somit wird die Frage mit dem ersten Hilfsverb bzw. mit dem Modalverb gebildet. Das Subjekt tritt hinter das 1. Hilfsverb.

▶4 Das Verb ist ein Vollverb, daher wird die Frage mit **to do** gebildet. Das Verb des bejahten Satzes steht im present tense, also wird die Frage, bei allen Personen, außer bei der 3. Person Singular, mit **do**, gebildet. Das Subjekt tritt hinter **do**. Das Vollverb ist zur Veranschaulichung fett gedruckt.

▶5 Das Verb ist ein Vollverb, daher wird die Frage mit **to do** gebildet. Das Verb des bejahten Satzes steht im present tense, das Subjekt steht in der 3. Person Singular, also wird die Frage mit **does**, gebildet. Das Subjekt tritt hinter **does**. Es ist zu beachten, dass auf **does** der Infinitiv des Verbs folgt (also z.B. **does your mother write** und nicht **does your mother writes**). Das Vollverb ist zur Veranschaulichung fett gedruckt.

▶6 Das Verb ist ein Vollverb, das in allen 3 Stammformen gleich ist, daher kann die Frage, sofern dies aus dem Zusammhang nicht klar wird, sowohl mit **do** als auch mit **did** gebildet werden.

▶7 **To be** ist Vollverb, auch wenn es in dieser Funktion steht, wird die Frage nicht mit **to do** gebildet.

▶8 Das Verb des Aussagesatzes ist verneint, die Frage wird dann mit diesem verneinten Verb gebildet.

6 Bilden Sie Fragen mit dem Verb in Klammern im present tense simple.

1. Whom do you believe ◀1 2. What does your mother usually drink ◀2 3. When do you usually get up ◀1 4. When does the plane leave ◀2 5. Where does your mother usually buy ◀2 6. Why do

giraffes have ◀3 7. What does an architect do ◀3 8. Who does this black bag belong to ◀2 9. Which bus do I have to ◀3 10. What else do you do ◀3 11. What do you want ◀1 12. When do you usually have ◀3 13. Where does he want ◀2 14. Which rules does he not/doesn't he obey ◀2 15. What does your breakfast usually consist of ◀2 16. What does the National Health Service do ◀3 17. Which of the mass media do you consider ◀1 18. Who do you think ◀1 19. Who do you take ◀1 20. Which condition does he add ◀2 21. What reasons does a trainer give ◀2

Erklärungen und Lernhinweise

▶1 Das Verb ist ein Vollverb und das Fragewort ist nicht Subjekt, denn das Subjekt folgt nach dem Fragewort, daher wird die Frage mit **to do** gebildet. Bei allen Personen, außer bei der 3. Person Singular, steht **do**. Das Subjekt tritt hinter **do**.

▶2 Das Verb ist ein Vollverb und das Fragewort ist nicht Subjekt, denn das Subjekt folgt nach dem Fragewort, daher wird die Frage mit **to do** gebildet. Bei der 3. Person Singular, steht **does**. Das Subjekt tritt hinter **does**. Es ist zu beachten, dass auf **does** der Infinitiv des Verbs folgt (also **what does your mother usually drink** und nicht **what does your mother usually drinks**).

▶3 Auch bei **to have**, wenn es nicht als Hilfsverb verwendet wird, d.h. es folgt kein weiteres Verb, und bei **to do** wird die Frage mit **to do** gebildet. Dies gilt auch für **to have to**.
Bei der 3. Person Singular, steht **does**.

7 Bilden Sie Fragen mit dem Verb im past tense simple.

1. Who did she marry ◀1 2. What did the burglar do ◀2 3. What did he mean ◀1 4. What did she look like ◀1 5. What did he wish ◀1 6. What did you say ◀1 7. When did you come ◀1 8. Who did you send ◀1 9. What did she die of ◀1 10. What did he have to do ◀2 11. Why did the children keep standing ◀1 12. Why did the Americans make ◀1 13. What did the knights live on ◀1 14. Why did Linda Adams ask ◀1 15. Whom did Mr Brown suspect of ◀1 16. What did you see ◀1 17. What did Mr Adams tell ◀1 18. What did the captain make ◀1 19. Where did the girl ask ◀1 20. How did you do ◀2 21. What did the judge find ◀1

Erklärungen und Lernhinweise

▶1 Das Verb ist ein Vollverb und das Fragewort ist nicht Subjekt, denn das Subjekt folgt nach dem Fragewort, daher wird die Frage mit **to do** gebildet. Die Frage wird für alle Personen mit **did** gebildet. Es ist zu beachten, dass auf **did** der Infinitiv des Verbs folgt (also z.B. **did she marry** und nicht **did she married**). Das Subjekt tritt zwischen **did** und Vollverb.

▶2 Auch bei **to have**, wenn es nicht als Hilfsverb, d. h. es folgt kein weiteres Verb, verwendet wird und bei **to do** wird die Frage mit **to do** gebildet. Dies gilt auch für **to have to**.

8 Bilden Sie Fragen und verwenden Sie die angegebenen Fragepronomen.

1. Who gave her ◀1 2. Which of the boys broke ◀1 3. Who goes ◀1 4. Who invaded ◀1 5. Who invited Mike and Walter ◀1 6. Who knows ◀1 7. Who left ◀1 8. Who married her ◀1 9. Who read ◀3 10. Who reads ◀1 11. Who discovered ◀1 12. Who rode ◀1 13. Who sent you ◀1 14. Who taught him ◀1 15. What happened ◀1 16. What irritated her ◀1 17. What made her notice ◀1 18. What moves people ◀2 19. Who gives her ◀1 20. What gives him ◀1 21. What made people think ◀1

Erklärungen und Lernhinweise

▶1 Das Fragewort ist selbst Subjekt, d.h. auf das Fragewort folgt das Verb und nicht das Subjekt des bejahten Satzes, denn dieses wird ja erfragt. Daher wird die Frage, obwohl ein Vollverb vorhanden ist, nicht mit **to do** gebildet, sondern mit diesem Vollverb.

▶2 Das Fragewort gilt als 3. Person Singular, daher steht das folgende Verb ebenfalls in der 3. Person Singular, d.h. im present tense simple erhält es ein **-s**. Dies ist auch dann der Fall, wenn das Verb des Aussagesatzes nicht auf -s endet, da es sich auf ein Subjekt, das nicht in der 3. Person Singular steht, bezieht.

▶3 **Read** hat in allen 3 Stammformen dieselbe Form. Es unterscheidet sich im present tense simple vom past tense nur in der 3. Person Singular durch die Endung **-s**, d.h. **read** ohne **-s** steht es also im past tense.

9 Formen Sie die folgenden Sätze, die ein Hilfsverb enthalten, in Fragen um, und verwenden Sie die angegebenen Fragepronomen.

1. Where **is** ◀2 2. When **are** you leaving ◀1 3. When **was** she born ◀1 4. What **were** you doing ◀1 5. Why **has** he come back ◀1 6. What **have** you been doing ◀1 7. How often **have** you been ◀1 8. How **had** Mr Green spent ◀1 9. What **has** impressed you most ◀1 10. What **was** he promising ◀1 11. Where **will** you go ◀1 12. Where **would** you like to spend ◀1 13. Whose socks **are** these ◀2 14. When **was** I supposed/when **were** you supposed to go ◀1 15. What **is** he accusing you of ◀1 16. What **will** you be having for lunch ◀1 17. Whose job **is** it ◀2 18. How **was** the weather (like) ◀2 19. What **had** he been arrested for ◀1

Erklärungen und Lernhinweise

▶1 Das Verb ist ein Hilfsverb, daher wird die Frage, unabhängig davon ob das Fragewort Subjekt ist oder nicht, nicht mit **to do,** sondern mit diesem Hilfsverb gebildet. Das Hilfsverb ist zur Veranschaulichung fett gedruckt.
Das Pronomen **I** des bejahten Satzes wird im Fragesatz sinnvollerweise meist zu **you**.

▶2 **To be** ist Vollverb, auch wenn es in dieser Funktion steht, wird die Frage nicht mit **to do** gebildet.

10 Formen Sie die folgenden Sätze, die ein Modalverb enthalten, in Fragen um, und verwenden Sie die angegebenen Fragepronomen.

1. Where **can** I get the book ◀1 2. How **could** I do that ◀1 3. What **may** he want ◀1 4. How **should** I know that ◀1 5. Who **must** be sent for ◀1 6. When **shall** we be back ◀1 7. How **could** the advance of urbanization be slowed down or stopped ◀1 8. Why **might** husbands prefer ◀1

Erklärungen und Lernhinweise

▶1 Das Verb ist ein Modalverb, daher wird die Frage, unabhängig davon ob das Fragewort Subjekt ist oder nicht, nicht mit **to do,** sondern mit diesem Modalverb gebildet. Das Modalverb ist zur Veranschaulichung fett gedruckt.

11 Bilden Sie Fragen und verwenden Sie die angegebenen Fragepronomen. Verwenden Sie **to do** wo nötig.

1. Who helps you ➊ 2. Who needs to ask ➊ 3. What makes her realize ➊ 4. What could he have ➋ 5. Who is the young man ➌ 6. Who has the rings ➍ 7. What does your mother need ➎ 8. What do they need these apples for ➎ 9. When do you do ➎ 10. What do people have to have ➎ 11. What suits you ➊ 12. Who has the right ➊ 13. How could she have acted ➋ 14. What has been made ➍ 15. What makes her believe ➊ 16. Who has got ➊ 17. Who has to be blamed for that ➍ 18. How was it always going to be ➋ 19. How can we do better ➋

Erklärungen und Lernhinweise

➊ Das Fragewort ist selbst Subjekt, d.h. auf das Fragewort folgt das Verb und nicht das Subjekt des bejahten Satzes, denn dieses wird ja erfragt. Daher wird die Frage, obwohl ein Vollverb vorhanden ist, nicht mit **to do** gebildet, sondern mit diesem Vollverb.
Dies gilt auch für **need** und **have**, wenn sie Vollverben sind.

➋ Das Verb ist ein Hilfs- bzw. Modalverb, daher wird die Frage, unabhängig davon ob das Fragewort Subjekt ist oder nicht, nicht mit **to do** gebildet.

➌ **To be** ist Vollverb, auch wenn es in dieser Funktion steht, wird die Frage nicht mit **to do** gebildet.

➍ Das Fragewort ist selbst Subjekt, d.h. auf das Fragewort folgt das Verb des bejahten Satzes, daher wird die Frage nicht mit **to do** gebildet. Das Fragewort gilt als 3. Person Singular, daher steht das folgende Verb ebenfalls in der 3. Person Singular, d.h. im present tense simple erhält es ein **-s.** Dies ist auch dann der Fall, wenn das Verb des Aussagesatzes nicht auf -s endet, da es sich auf ein Subjekt, das nicht in der 3. Person Singular steht, bezieht. Dies gilt auch für **have**, wenn es Vollverb und nicht Hilfsverb ist und für **have to**.

➎ Das Verb ist ein Vollverb und das Fragewort ist nicht Subjekt, denn das Subjekt folgt nach dem Fragewort, daher wird die Frage mit **to do** gebildet. Im present tense simple steht bei allen Personen, außer bei der 3. Person Singular, **do**, bei der 3. Person Singular steht **does**. Das Subjekt tritt hinter **do** bzw. **does**.
Dies gilt auch bei **need** und **have**, wenn sie Vollverben sind sowie **have to** und bei **to do**.

Die Modalverben (Modal Auxiliary Verbs)

Can, could und ihre Ersatzverben

1 Setzen Sie **can, could** oder ihr Ersatzverb **to be able to** ein.

1. can ◀1 2. could ◀2/were not able to ◀3 3. could ◀2/was not able to ◀3 4. Can ◀1 5. be able to ◀3 6. be able to ◀3 7. can ◀1/are able to ◀3 8. can ◀1 9. could ◀2/was not able to ◀3 10. be able to ◀3 11. can ◀1 12. could ◀2/was not able to ◀3 13. can/could ◀4 14. can/could ◀4 15. could ◀2 16. could ◀5 17. could ◀6/was not able to ◀3 18. cannot ◀6/am not able to ◀3 19. could ◀4 20. be able to ◀3 21. be able to ◀3 22. could ◀2 23. had so far been able ◀3 24. be able to ◀3 25. being able to ◀3

Erklärungen und Lernhinweise

▶1 Es wird die (geistige, körperliche) Fähigkeit ausgedrückt, daher steht **can**. Das Verb des Hauptsatzes steht im present tense simple, daher wird **can** und nicht **could** verwendet. Es ist zu beachten, dass verneintes **can** zusammengeschrieben wird (**cannot**).

▶2 Es wird die (geistige, körperliche) Fähigkeit ausgedrückt, daher steht **could**. Das Verb des Hauptsatzes steht im past tense simple, daher wird **could** und nicht **can** verwendet. Im Deutschen wird **could** in dieser Bedeutung mit *konnte* übersetzt.

▶3 Es wird die (geistige, körperliche) Fähigkeit ausgedrückt, daher steht **to be able to**. **To be able to, can** und **could** sind häufig austauschbar, **to be able to** steht jedoch mehr bei ganz bestimmten, einzelnen Handlungen (fähig sein, in der Lage sein). Es muss jedoch stehen, wenn die Verwendung der zusammengesetzten Zeiten erforderlich ist oder wenn bereits ein anderes Verb oder sonstiger Ausdruck vorausgeht.

▶4 Es steht **can**, wenn ausgedrückt werden soll, was geschehen kann (z.B.: *ich kann es arrangieren, dass*), **could** steht, wenn ausgedrückt werden soll, was geschehen könnte (z.B.: *ich könnte es arrangieren, dass*). Im Deutschen wird **could** in dieser Bedeutung demnach mit *könnte* übersetzt.

▶5 Es wird der Wunsch etwas zu können ausgedrückt, daher steht **could**. In dieser Bedeutung wird **could** mit *könnte* übersetzt.

▶6 Es ist zu beachten, dass sich die Verben, die gleiche Stammformen haben, im present tense nur durch das **-s** der 3. Person Singular vom past tense unterscheiden.

Can, could und may, might und ihre Ersatzverben

1 Setzen Sie **can, could,** deren Ersatzverb **to be able to**, oder **may, might** ein.

1. cannot ◀1 2. could ◀2 3. be able to ◀3 4. may ◀4 5. might ◀5 6. could ◀2 7. cannot ◀1 8. may ◀4 9. could ◀6 10. may ◀4 11. might ◀5 12. Can ◀1 13. could ◀2 14. can ◀1 15. could ◀6 16. be able to ◀3 17. might ◀5 18. be able to ◀3 19. be able to ◀3 20. can ◀1/may ◀4 21. might ◀5

Erklärungen und Lernhinweise

▶1 Es wird die Möglichkeit ausgedrückt, daher steht **can**. Das Verb des Hauptsatzes steht im present tense simple, daher wird **can** und nicht **could** verwendet. Es ist zu beachten, dass verneintes **can** zusammengeschrieben wird (**cannot**).

▶2 Es wird die Möglichkeit ausgedrückt, daher steht **could**. Das Verb des Hauptsatzes steht im past tense simple, daher wird **could** und nicht **can** verwendet. Im Deutschen wird **could** in dieser Bedeutung mit *konnte* übersetzt.

▶3 Es wird die Möglichkeit ausgedrückt und es geht ein Verb voraus oder es ist die Verwendung der zusammengesetzten Zeiten erforderlich, daher steht **to be able to**.

▶4 Es wird die Wahrscheinlichkeit, Möglichkeit, die unter gewissen Umständen gegeben ist, ausgedrückt, daher steht **may**. Das Verb des Hauptsatzes steht im present tense simple, daher wird **may** und nicht **might** verwendet.

▶5 Es wird die Wahrscheinlichkeit, Möglichkeit, die unter gewissen Umständen gegeben ist, ausgedrückt, daher steht **might**. Das Verb des Hauptsatzes steht im past tense simple, daher wird **might** und nicht **may** verwendet.

▶6 Es wird der Wunsch etwas möglich zu machen ausgedrückt, daher steht **could**. In dieser Bedeutung wird **could** mit *könnte* übersetzt.

2 Setzen Sie **can, could, may, might** oder ihre Ersatzverben **to be allowed, to be permitted to** ein.

1. cannot ◀1/am not allowed/permitted to ◀5 2. can ◀1/may ◀3 3. could ◀2/might ◀4 4. cannot ◀1 5. are allowed/permitted to ◀5 6. may ◀3 7. could ◀2/might ◀4 8. might ◀4 9. are not allowed/permitted to ◀5 10. can ◀1/may ◀3 11. may ◀3 12. could ◀2/might ◀4 13. can ◀1/may ◀3 14. could ◀2/might ◀4 15. can ◀1/may ◀3 16. are not allowed/permitted to ◀5 17. to be allowed/permitted to ◀5

Erklärungen und Lernhinweise

▶1 Es wird die Erlaubnis ausgedrückt, daher steht **can**. Das Verb des Hauptsatzes steht im present tense simple, daher wird **can** und nicht **could** verwendet. Es ist zu beachten, dass verneintes **can** zusammengeschrieben wird (**cannot**).

▶2 Es wird die Erlaubnis ausgedrückt, daher steht **could**. Das Verb des Hauptsatzes steht im past tense simple, daher wird **could** und nicht **can** verwendet.

▶3 Es wird die förmliche Erlaubnis ausgedrückt, daher steht **may**. Das Verb des Hauptsatzes steht im present tense simple, daher wird **may** und nicht **might** verwendet. **May** und **can** sind häufig austauschbar, **may** klingt jedoch viel förmlicher. Im verneinten Satz steht es meist in Antworten auf Fragen.

▶4 Es wird die förmliche Erlaubnis ausgedrückt, daher steht **might**. Das Verb des Hauptsatzes steht im past tense simple, daher wird **might** und nicht **may** verwendet. **Might** und **could** sind häufig austauschbar, **might** klingt jedoch förmlicher als **could**.

▶5 Es wird eine offizielle Erlaubnis ausgedrückt (z.B. von Behörden, öffentlichen Institutionen), daher steht **to be allowed/permitted to**. Es muss stehen, wenn die Verwendung der zusammengesetzten Zeiten erforderlich ist oder wenn ein anderes Verb oder sonstiger Ausdruck vorausgeht.

Can, could und may, might und will, would

1 Setzen Sie **can, could, may, might, will, would** ein.

1. Can ◄1/could ◄2/will ◄5/would ◄6 2. Can ◄1/could ◄2/would ◄6 3. Can ◄1 /could ◄2/ will ◄5/ would ◄6 4. Can ◄1/could ◄2/may ◄3/might ◄4 5. may ◄3 6. Can ◄1/ could ◄2/ will ◄5/ would ◄6 7. Can ◄1/could ◄2 may ◄3/ might ◄4 8. Will ◄5 9. Can ◄1/could ◄2/may ◄3/might ◄4 10. Will ◄5 11. Would ◄6 12. Can ◄1/ could ◄2/will ◄5/would ◄6 13. Would ◄6 14. Can ◄1/could ◄2/will ◄5/would ◄6 15. Can't ◄1 16. May ◄3/might ◄4 17. Will ◄7/would ◄7 18. Would ◄6 19. Can ◄1/may ◄3/might ◄4

Erklärungen und Lernhinweise

▶1 Es wird eine Bitte in einer Frage ausgedrückt, daher steht **can.** Im Deutschen wird die mit **can** formulierte Bitte mit *können* übersetzt.

▶2 Die Bitte ist sehr höflich, daher steht **could**. Die mit **could** formulierte Bitte ist höflicher als die Bitte mit **can** und wird im Deutschen mit *könnten* übersetzt.

▶3 Die Bitte ist förmlich, daher steht **may.** Die mit **may** formulierte Bitte ist förmlicher als die Bitte mit **can** und wird im Deutschen mit *dürfen* übersetzt.

▶4 Die Bitte ist förmlich, aber sehr höflich, daher steht **might**. Die mit **might** formulierte Bitte ist förmlicher als die Bitte mit **could** und höflicher als die Bitte mit **may** und wird im Deutschen mit *dürfte* übersetzt.

▶5 Die Bitte ist sehr entschieden, daher steht **will.** Die mit **will** formulierte Bitte klingt viel entschiedener als die Bitte mit **can** und wird im Deutschen mit *wirst du ...* übersetzt.

▶6 Die Bitte ist sehr höflich, daher steht **would.** Die mit **would** formulierte Bitte ist viel höflicher als die Bitte mit **will** und steht vor allem in festen Wendungen wie **would you mind**. **Would** wird in dieser Funktion im Deutschen mit *würden* übersetzt.

▶7 Im future tense continuous klingt die mit **will** bzw. **would** formulierte Bitte sehr höflich.

Must, need und ihre Ersatzverben

1 Setzen Sie **must, need** oder deren Ersatzverb **have to** ein.

1. must ◄1/has to ◄3 2. need ◄2 3. has to ◄3 4. need ◄2 5. have to ◄3 6. must not ◄1/don't have to ◄4/haven't got to tell ◄4 7. must ◄1 8. Do drivers have to ◄4 9. need ◄2 10. must ◄1 11. must ◄1 12. must ◄1/have to ◄3 13. need ◄2 14. Have you ever had to ◄5 15. had had to ◄3

Erklärungen und Lernhinweise

▶1 Es wird die Notwendigkeit ausgedrückt, daher steht **must**. Im Deutschen wird **must** mit *müssen* übersetzt, **must not**, und dies ist besonders zu beachten, bedeutet keinesfalls *nicht müssen* sondern *nicht dürfen.*

▶2 Es wird die Notwendigkeit ausgedrückt, daher steht **need**. **Need** steht vor allem in verneinten und fragenden Sätzen. Es ist zu beachten, dass **need** in der Funktion des Modalverbs (es folgt der Infinitiv eines weiteren Verbs) nicht mit **to do** umschrieben wird und in der 3. Person Singular kein **-s** erhält.

Erklärungen und Lernhinweise

▸3 Es wird die Notwendigkeit ausgedrückt, die durch Dritte auferlegt wird, daher steht **to have (got) to** bei allen Personen. Es ist zu beachten, dass bei der 3. Person Singular des present tense simple (hierzu zählen auch Pronomen wie **who, what, which**, **someone** etc.) **has (got) to** steht.
To have got to steht vor allem in der Umgangssprache.

▸4 Es wird die Notwendigkeit ausgedrückt, die durch Dritte auferlegt wird, daher steht **to have (got) to**. Der Satz ist verneint bzw. ist ein Fragesatz, daher wird **to have (got) to** im present und im past tense mit **to do** umschrieben.
To have got to steht vor allem in der Umgangssprache und wird nicht mit **to do** umschreiben.

▸5 Es wird die Notwendigkeit ausgedrückt, die durch Dritte auferlegt wird, daher steht **to have (got) to.** Der Satz ist ein Fragesatz in einer zusammengesetzten Zeit, daher wird **to do** nicht verwendet, sondern das Hilfsverb der zusammengesetzten Zeit. **Have to** wird in der 3. Stammform hinzugefügt.

Should, ought to und ihre Ersatzverben

1 Setzen Sie **should, ought to** oder deren Ersatzverb **to be supposed to** ein.

1. should ◂1/ought to ◂2 2. ought to ◂2/should ◂1 3. are supposed to ◂3 4. are supposed to ◂3 5. should ◂1/ ought to ◂2 6. should ◂1/ought to ◂2 7. should not laugh ◂1/ought not to laugh ◂2 8. are supposed to ◂3 9. should ◂1/ought not to ◂2 10. should ◂1 11. should not have said ◂1/ ought not to have said ◂2 12. Am I supposed to ◂3

Erklärungen und Lernhinweise

▸1 Es wird die (moralische) Verpflichtung ausgedrückt, dass etwas wünschenswert oder ratsam ist, daher steht **should**.

▸2 Es wird die (moralische) Verpflichtung ausgedrückt, dass etwas wünschenswert oder ratsam ist, daher steht **ought to. Ought to** ist stärker als **should**. Es ist zu beachten, dass **not** zwischen **ought** und **to** tritt.

▸3 Es wird die Verpflichtung ausgedrückt, dass etwas erwartet wird, daher steht **to be supposed to**.

2 Setzen Sie **should** oder seine Ersatzverben **to be to, to want s.o. to do s.th., to be supposed to** ein.

1. should ◂1 2. are you supposed to ◂2 3. was supposed to ◂2/was to ◂3 4. should ◂1 5. wants us to ◂4 6. should ◂1/was to ◂3 7. want me to ◂4 8. want me to ◂4 9. should ◂1 10. are supposed to ◂2 11. want you to ◂4 12. should ◂1, are to ◂3 13. should ◂1 14. will not be supposed to ◂2 15. is to ◂3 16. want me to ◂4 17. should ◂1 18. were to ◂3 19. was to ◂3 20. are not supposed to ◂2

Erklärungen und Lernhinweise

▸1 Es wird ein Befehl, eine Aufforderung, die der Sprecher selbst oder ein Dritter ausspricht, ausgedrückt, daher steht **should**.

Erklärungen und Lernhinweise

2 Es wird ein Befehl, eine Aufforderung eines Dritten, die der Sprecher wiedergibt, ausgedrückt, daher steht **to be supposed to.**

3 Es wird ein Befehl, eine Aufforderung eines Dritten, die der Sprecher wiedergibt, ausgedrückt, daher steht **to be to**. **To be to** klingt viel strenger, stärker als **to be supposed to**.

4 Es wird vom Sprecher ein Befehl, eine Aufforderung erteilt, die von anderen, die genannt sind (z.B. **us**), ausgeführt werden soll, daher steht **to want s.o. to do s.th** (z.B. in **he wants us to leave** fordert der Sprecher (**he**) jemanden (**us**) auf, etwas auszuführen, nämlich zu gehen).

Die reflexiven Verben (Reflexive Verbs)

Die Formen des Reflexivpronomens

1 Setzen Sie das entsprechende Reflexivpronomen ein.

1. myself ◀1, themselves ◀5 2. yourself/yourselves ◀2 3. himself ◀3 4. herself ◀3 5. ourselves ◀4 6. himself ◀3 7. itself ◀6 8. itself ◀6 9. themselves ◀5 10. yourself/yourselves ◀2 11. himself ◀7 12. himself ◀7 13. himself ◀7 14. oneself ◀8 15. himself ◀3 16. oneself ◀8 17. oneself ◀8 18. oneself ◀8 19. yourself/yourselves ◀2

Erklärungen und Lernhinweise

▶1 Das Subjekt bezeichnet die 1. Person Singular, daher lautet das Reflexivpronomen **myself.** Das Subjekt kann auch nach dem Reflexivpronomen stehen.

▶2 Das Subjekt bezeichnet die 2. Person Singular bzw. Plural, daher lautet das Reflexivpronomen **yourself** bzw. **yourselves.** Das Subjekt kann auch nach dem Reflexivpronomen stehen.
Yourself, yourselves steht auch beim Imperativ, da der Imperativ die 2. Person bezeichnet.

▶3 Das Subjekt bezeichnet die 3. Person Singular, daher lautet das Reflexivpronomen für männliche Personen **himself** bzw. für weibliche Personen **herself**. Das Subjekt kann auch nach dem Reflexivpronomen stehen.

▶4 Das Subjekt bezeichnet die 1. Person Plural, daher lautet das Reflexivpronomen **ourselves.** Das Subjekt kann auch nach dem Reflexivpronomen stehen.

▶5 Das Subjekt bezeichnet die 3. Person Plural, daher lautet das Reflexivpronomen **themselves**. Das Subjekt kann auch nach dem Reflexivpronomen stehen.

▶6 Das Subjekt bezeichnet eine Sache (**it**), daher lautet das Reflexivpronomen **itself**. **Itself** steht auch bei Tieren, zu denen kein persönliches Verhältnis besteht. Das Subjekt kann auch nach dem Reflexivpronomen stehen.

▶7 Das Subjekt bezeichnet eine unbestimmte, dritte Person (**someone, everyone** etc.), daher lautet das Reflexivpronomen **himself**. Das Subjekt kann auch nach dem Reflexivpronomen stehen.

▶8 Das Subjekt ist ein grammatisches Subjekt (**it is, there is** etc.) oder das Pronomen **one**, daher lautet das Reflexivpronomen **oneself**.

Reflexive und nicht reflexive Verben

1 Setzen Sie das Reflexivpronomen oder den in Klammern gegebenen Ausdruck ein.

1. everybody ◀1 2. ourselves ◀2 3. himself ◀2 4. Ray Williams ◀1 5. himself ◀2 6. your face ◀1 7. this criminal ◀1 8. themselves ◀2 9. the tigers ◀1 10. yourself ◀2 11. yourself ◀2 12. messages ◀1 13. her ◀1 14. themselves ◀2

Erklärungen und Lernhinweise

Das Reflexivpronomen bezeichnet nicht dieselbe Person wie das Subjekt, (z.B. **ourselves** und **you** statt **ourselves** und **we**), daher kann das Reflexivpronomen nicht verwendet werden.

Das Reflexivpronomen bezeichnet dieselbe Person wie das Subjekt, (z.B. **ourselves** und **we**), daher wird das Reflexivpronomen verwendet.

2 Setzen Sie das Reflexivpronomen oder den in Klammern gegebenen Ausdruck ein.

1. - ; Ich werde dich bestrafen, wenn du dich nicht anständig verhältst. ◀ 2. **yourself;** Beherrsche dich! ◀ 3. **himself;** Er legte sich zurück auf das Bett und versuchte sich zu sammeln. ◀ 4. **his next letter;** Tom begann seinen nächsten Brief an sie zu verfassen. ◀ 5. **the dish;** Wir hoffen, dass Ihnen das Gericht schmecken wird. ◀ 6. **yourselves;** Amüsiert euch, Jungs! ◀ 7. **you**; Wer hilft dir bei deinen Hausaufgaben? ◀ 8. **myself;** Er hatte mir gesagt, ich solle mich seiner Krawatten und Jackets bedienen. ◀ 9. **you;** Sagen Sie/Sag/Sagt mir frei heraus. Womit können wir Ihnen/dir/euch dienen? ◀ 10. **ourselves;** Wir können uns selbst bedienen. ◀

Erklärungen und Lernhinweise

Dieses Verb ändert seine Bedeutung, je nachdem ob es mit oder ohne Reflexivpronomen verwendet wird. Die Übersetzung gibt Aufschluss über die Verwendung des Reflexivpronomens.

3 Übersetzen Sie die Verben in Klammern und verwenden Sie das Reflexivpronomen, wenn nötig. Verwenden Sie das present tense simple, wenn keine andere Zeit angegeben ist.

1. approached ◀ 2. imagine ◀ 3. care for ◀ 4. remember ◀ 5. wondered ◀ 6. afford ◀ 7. fell in love with ◀ 8. has changed ◀ 9. amount to ◀ 10. complains of ◀ 11. join ◀ 12. care about ◀ 13. looking forward ◀ 14. rely on ◀

Erklärungen und Lernhinweise

Dieses Verb ist im Deutschen reflexiv, aber im Englischen nicht. Generell werden im Englischen nicht so viele Verben reflexiv verwendet wie im Deutschen. Die deutsche Bedeutung ist also kein Indiz für die reflexive Verwendung eines Verbs im Englischen.

Das Verb und seine Ergänzungen (The Verb and its Complements)

1 Setzen Sie **to** ein wo nötig.

1. give *short answers* **to** all the questions ◀1 2. remember - *me* ◀2 3. gave *some milk* **to** the cat ◀1 4. gave the cat *some milk* ◀3 5. followed - *the man* ◀2 6. thank - *the courageous girl* ◀2 7. help - *the poverty-stricken areas* ◀2 8. send *a messenger* **to** you ◀1 9. send you *a messenger* ◀3 10. wrote *a postcard* **to** the Barton family ◀1 11. told *her story* **to** her friends ◀1 12. was crowned - King of England ◀4 13. handed *the teapot* **to** her mother ◀1 14. handed her mother *the teapot* ◀3 15. anwer - *the judge's question* ◀2 16. introducing the teachers **to** *them* ◀5 17. enter - *Britain* ◀2 18. waved *his hand* **to** me ◀1 19. believe - *those forgeries* ◀2 20. opened *the door* **to** you ◀1 21. trust - *me*, trusts - *me* ◀2 22. dictating *a letter* **to** her ◀5 23. allow - *local communties* ◀2 24. offer *further education* **to** the young workers ◀1 25. spoke **to** you ◀5 26. permit - *any person* ◀2 27. explains *his case* **to** the jury ◀5 28. serve - *two masters* ◀2 29. obeying - *the law* ◀2 30. resented *the courtesy* **to** her ◀1 31. make *this confession* **to** you ◀1 32. fails - *a course* ◀2 33. give *the document* **to** the next person ◀1 34. elected - ◀4 35. join - *groups* ◀2 36. seem *an irrelevancy* **to** us ◀5

Erklärungen und Lernhinweise

▶1 Das Verb schließt 2 Objekte an, ein direktes, hier kursiv dargestellt und ein indirektes Objekt, hier gesperrt dargestellt. Das direkte Objekt (meist eine Sache) steht vor dem indirekten Objekt (meist eine Person), weil das indirekte Objekt besonders betont oder weil es länger ist als das direkte Objekt, daher wird das indirekte Objekt mit **to** angeschlossen.

▶2 Das Verb schließt ein direktes Objekt, hier kursiv dargestellt, an. Dieses wird im Englischen stets ohne **to** angeschlossen.

▶3 Das Verb schließt 2 Objekte an, ein direktes, hier kursiv dargestellt und ein indirektes Objekt, hier gesperrt dargestellt. Das indirekte Objekt (meist eine Person) steht vor dem direkten Objekt (meist eine Sache), daher entfällt **to.**

▶4 Das Verb gehört zu den Verben (des Ernennens, Dafürhaltens), die ein folgendes Substantiv ohne Präposition anschließen (im Deutschen steht hier meist *zum*).

▶5 Das Verb gehört zu den Verben, die ein indirektes Objekt, hier gesperrt dargestellt, mit **to** anschließen.

Die Zeiten (The Tenses)

Die Bildung der Zeiten

1 Setzen Sie die Verben in Klammern ins present tense simple.

1. cries ◀1 2. plays ◀2 3. lies ◀3 4. catches ◀4 5. wash ◀5 6. possesses ◀4 7. occupies ◀6 8. die, resign ◀5 9. reaches ◀4 10. establishes ◀4 11. miss ◀5 12. marries ◀7 13. enjoys ◀2 14. lie ◀5 15. attaches ◀4 16. distinguishes ◀8

Erklärungen und Lernhinweise

▶1 Das Subjekt bezeichnet die 3. Person Singular, daher erhält das Verb ein **-s**.
Das Verb endet auf **-y**, dem ein Konsonant vorausgeht, daher ändert sich das **-y** beim Anhängen von **-s** in **-ie**.

▶2 Das Subjekt bezeichnet die 3. Person Singular, daher erhält das Verb ein **-s**.
Das Verb endet auf **-y**, dem ein Vokal vorausgeht, daher bleibt das **-y** beim Anhängen von **-s** erhalten.

▶3 Das Subjekt bezeichnet ein Substantiv, das trotz des Plural-s als Substantiv im Singular gilt, daher erhält das Verb ein **-s**.
Verben auf **-ie** ändern diese Endung nicht beim Anhängen von **-s**.

▶4 Das Subjekt bezeichnet die 3. Person Singular, daher erhält das Verb ein **-s**.
Das Verb endet auf **-ch, -sh, -ss** oder **-x**, daher hängt es **-es** an.

▶5 Das Subjekt bezeichnet die 1. oder 2. Person Singular oder die 1., 2. oder 3. Person Plural, daher erhält das Verb kein **-s**.

▶6 Das Subjekt ist ein Verb, das in der Funktion eines Subjekts steht, es gilt als 3. Person Singular, daher erhält das Verb ein **-s**.
Das Verb endet auf **-y**, dem ein Konsonant vorausgeht, daher ändert sich das **-y** beim Anhängen von **-s** in **-ie**.

▶7 Das Subjekt ist ein Pronomen, es gilt als 3. Person Singular, daher erhält das Verb ein **-s**. Hierzu zählen Pronomen wie **who, which, what, someone** etc.
Das Verb endet auf **-y**, dem ein Konsonant vorausgeht, daher ändert sich das **-y** beim Anhängen von **-s** in **-ie**.

▶8 Das Subjekt ist ein Pronomen, es gilt als 3. Person Singular, daher erhält das Verb ein **-s**. Hierzu zählen Pronomen wie **who, which, what, someone** etc.
Das Verb endet auf **-sh**, daher hängt es **-es** an.

2 Setzen Sie die Verben in Klammern ins past tense simple.

1. tried ◀1 2. enjoyed ◀2 3. hated ◀3 4. pl<u>a</u>nned ◀4 5. burst ◀5 6. sent ◀6 7. chose ◀7 8. buried ◀1 9. played ◀2 10. tied ◀3 11. agreed ◀3 12. pref<u>e</u>rred ◀4 13. s<u>u</u>ffered ◀8 14. read ◀5 15. bent ◀6 16. lent ◀6 17. sat, drank ◀7 18. taught ◀7 19. thought ◀7 20. studied ◀1 21. obeyed ◀2 22. died ◀3 23. changed ◀3 24. contr<u>o</u>lled ◀4 25. rec<u>o</u>vered ◀8 26. set ◀5 27. laid ◀7 28. wore ◀7

Erklärungen und Lernhinweise

▶1 Das Verb endet auf **-y,** dem ein Konsonant vorausgeht, daher ändert sich das **-y** in **-ie** beim Anhängen von **-ed.** Die Verbform ist in allen Personen gleich.

▶2 Das Verb endet auf **-y,** dem ein Vokal vorausgeht, daher ändert sich das **-y** beim Anhängen von **-ed** nicht. Die Verbform ist in allen Personen gleich.

▶3 Das Verb endet auf **-e,** es verliert die Endung **-e** beim Anhängen von **-ed**. Dies gilt auch für die Verben auf **-ie** und **-ee**. Die Verbform ist in allen Personen gleich.

▶4 Das Verb endet auf Konsonant, dem ein kurzer, betonter Vokal vorausgeht, daher verdoppelt sich der Konsonant beim Anhängen von **-ed.** Der betonte Vokal ist unterstrichen. Die Verbform ist in allen Personen gleich.

▶5 Das Verb hat in allen 3 Stammformen die gleiche Form, es hängt im past tense simple in der 3. Person Singular kein **-s** an. Die Verbform ist in allen Personen gleich.

▶6 Das Verb gehört zu den Verben, die die Endung **-d** im past tense simple in **-t** ändern. Die Verbform ist in allen Personen gleich.

▶7 Das Verb ist unregelmäßig.

▶8 Das Verb endet auf Konsonant, dem ein unbetonter Vokal vorausgeht, daher verdoppelt sich der Konsonant beim Anhängen von **-ed** nicht. Der betonte Vokal ist unterstrichen. Die Verbform ist in allen Personen gleich.

3 Setzen Sie die Verben in Klammern ins present perfect simple.

1. have studied ◄1 2. has played ◄2 3. have received ◄3 4. has dropped ◄4 5. has hit ◄5 6. has built ◄6 7. have become ◄7 8. have tried ◄1 9. has enjoyed ◄2 10. have died ◄3 11. has had ◄5 12. have caused ◄3 13. has slipped ◄4 14. has developed ◄8 15. have put ◄7 16. has sent ◄6 17. have sprung ◄7

Erklärungen und Lernhinweise

▶1 Das Subjekt bezeichnet die 1. oder 2. Person Singular oder die 1., 2. oder 3. Person Plural, daher steht **have** bzw. die Kurzform **'ve** + 3. Stammform. Das Verb endet auf **-y,** dem ein Konsonant vorausgeht, daher ändert sich das **-y** in **-ie** beim Anhängen von **-ed.**

▶2 Das Subjekt bezeichnet die 3. Person Singular, daher steht **has** bzw. die Kurzform **'s** + 3. Stammform. Das Verb endet auf **-y,** dem ein Vokal vorausgeht, daher ändert sich das **-y** beim Anhängen von **-ed** nicht.

▶3 Das Subjekt bezeichnet die 1. oder 2. Person Singular oder die 1., 2. oder 3. Person Plural, daher steht **have** bzw. die Kurzform **'ve** + 3. Stammform. Das Verb endet auf **-e,** es verliert die Endung **-e** beim Anhängen von **-ed**. Dies gilt auch für die Verben auf **-ie** und **-ee**.

▶4 Das Subjekt bezeichnet die 3. Person Singular, daher steht **has** bzw. die Kurzform **'s** + 3. Stammform. Das Verb endet auf Konsonant, dem ein kurzer betonter Vokal vorausgeht, daher verdoppelt sich der Konsonant beim Anhängen von **-ed.** Der betonte Vokal ist unterstrichen.

▶5 Das Subjekt bezeichnet die 3. Person Singular, daher steht **has** bzw. die Kurzform **'s** + 3. Stammform. Das Verb ist unregelmäßig.

▶6 Das Subjekt bezeichnet die 3. Person Singular, daher steht **has** bzw. die Kurzform **'s** + 3. Stammform. Das Verb gehört zu den Verben, die die Endung **-d** in der 3. Stammform in **-t** ändern.

Erklärungen und Lernhinweise

▶7 Das Subjekt bezeichnet die 1. oder 2. Person Singular oder die 1., 2. oder 3. Person Plural, daher steht **have** oder die Kurzform **'ve** + 3. Stammform. Das Verb ist unregelmäßig.

▶8 Das Subjekt bezeichnet die 3. Person Singular, daher steht **has** bzw. die Kurzform **'s** + 3. Stammform. Das Verb endet auf Konsonant, dem ein unbetonter Vokal vorausgeht, daher verdoppelt sich der Konsonant beim Anhängen von **-ed** nicht. Der betonte Vokal ist unterstrichen.

4 Setzen Sie die Verben in Klammern ins past perfect simple.

1. had tried ◀1 2. had played ◀2 3. had died ◀3 4. had liked ◀3 5. had stopped ◀4 6. had travelled ◀4 7. had happened ◀5 8. had hurt ◀6 9. had spent ◀7 10. had felt ◀8 11. had had ◀8 12. had hurried off ◀1, had seen ◀8 13. had stayed ◀2 14. had continued ◀3 15. had agreed ◀3 16. had let ◀6 17. had built ◀7 18. had forgotten ◀8 19. had got ◀8 20. had crept ◀8 21. had mown ◀8 22. had stuck ◀8 23. had struck ◀8

Erklärungen und Lernhinweise

▶1 In allen Personen steht **had** bzw. die Kurzform **'d** + 3. Stammform. Das Verb endet auf **-y,** dem ein Konsonant vorausgeht, daher ändert sich das **-y** in **-ie** beim Anhängen von **-ed.**

▶2 In allen Personen steht **had** bzw. die Kurzform **'d** + 3. Stammform. Das Verb endet auf **-y,** dem ein Vokal vorausgeht, daher ändert sich das **-y** beim Anhängen von **-ed** nicht.

▶3 In allen Personen steht **had** bzw. die Kurzform **'d** + 3. Stammform. Das Verb endet auf **-e,** es verliert die Endung **-e** beim Anhängen von **-ed**. Dies gilt auch für die Verben auf **-ie** und **-ee**.

▶4 In allen Personen steht **had** bzw. die Kurzform **'d** + 3. Stammform. Das Verb endet auf **-l** oder Konsonant, dem ein kurzer, betonter Vokal vorausgeht, daher verdoppelt sich das **-l** oder der Konsonant beim Anhängen von **-ed.** Der betonte Vokal ist unterstrichen.

▶5 In allen Personen steht **had** bzw. die Kurzform **'d** + 3. Stammform. Das Verb endet auf Konsonant, dem ein unbetonter Vokal vorausgeht, daher verdoppelt sich der Konsonant beim Anhängen von **-ed** nicht. Der betonte Vokal ist unterstrichen.

▶6 In allen Personen steht **had** bzw. die Kurzform **'d** + 3. Stammform. Das Verb hat in allen 3 Stammformen die gleiche Form.

▶7 In allen Personen steht **had** bzw. die Kurzform **'d** + 3. Stammform. Das Verb ändert die Endung **-d** in der 3. Stammform in **-t**.

▶8 In allen Personen steht **had** bzw. die Kurzform **'d** + 3. Stammform. Das Verb ist unregelmäßig.

5 Setzen Sie die Verben in Klammern ins future tense simple.

1. will reply ◀1 2. will receive, will obey ◀1 3. will teach ◀1 4. will continue ◀1 5. will produce ◀1 6. will let ◀1 7. will put ◀1 8. will give ◀1 9. will catch ◀1 10. will live ◀1 11. will prove ◀1 12. will admit ◀1 13. will suffer ◀1 14. will see ◀1

Erklärungen und Lernhinweise

1 In allen Personen steht **will** oder die Kurzform **'ll +**, und dies ist besonders zu beachten, der Infinitiv (also **will reply** und nicht **will replied**). Orthografische Besonderheiten sind demnach nicht zu beachten.

6 Setzen Sie die Verben in Klammern ins future perfect simple.

1. will have finished 1 2. will have disappeared 1 3. will have forgotten 2 4. will have chosen 2 5. will have heard 2

Erklärungen und Lernhinweise

1 In allen Personen steht **will have** bzw. die Kurzform **'ll have** + 3. Stammform. Das Verb bildet die 3. Stammform regelmäßig.

2 In allen Personen steht **will have** bzw. die Kurzform **'ll have** + 3. Stammform. Das Verb bildet die 3. Stammform unregelmäßig.

Die Verwendung der Zeiten

1 Setzen Sie die folgenden Zeitbestimmungen in den entsprechenden Satz ein.

1. once 1 2. for a year and then 1 3. since 1 4. yesterday 1 5. that night 1 6. From about 1930 until 1 7. A year ago 1 8. this morning 1 9. after 1945 1 10. In 1972 1 11. Last summer 1 12. At the beginning of the 20th century 1 13. in 1960 1 14. for two years 2 15. since 2 16. this week 2 17. these last 3 months 2 18. in the past few years 2 19. yet 2 20. today 2 21. In recent years 2 22. Since 2 23. Meanwhile 2

Erklärungen und Lernhinweise

1 Der Vorgang ist in der Vergangenheit völlig abgeschlossen, daher steht das past tense. Völlig abgeschlossene Vorgänge werden häufig durch diese Zeitbestimmungen angezeigt oder, anders ausgedrückt, ist eine solche Zeitbestimmung vorhanden, wird häufig das past tense verwendet.

2 Der Vorgang hat in der Vergangenheit begonnen und dauert in der Gegenwart noch an, daher steht das present perfect. Bis in die Gegenwart hineinreichende Vorgänge werden häufig durch diese Zeitbestimmungen angezeigt oder, anders ausgedrückt, ist eine solche Zeitbestimmung vorhanden, wird häufig das present perfect verwendet. Es ist zu beachten, dass manche Zeitbestimmungen sowohl mit dem past tense als auch mit dem present perfect stehen können (z.B. **we have known each other *since* 1984**, d.h. *wir kennen uns seit 1984 (und wir kennen uns heute immer noch)* im Gegensatz zu **it's six weeks now *since* we moved in**, d.h. *es ist sechs Wochen her, seit wir eingezogen sind (der Umzug ist beendet)*).

2 Setzen Sie die Verben in Klammern ins past tense simple oder ins present perfect simple.

1. have known ◀1 2. have never changed ◀1 3. spent ◀3 4. left ◀2 5. have not replied ◀1 6. prepared ◀2 7. has changed ◀4, arrived ◀2 8. lived, died ◀2 9. have become ◀1 10. made ◀2 11. have been married ◀1 12. thought ◀2 13. tried ◀2 14. has taken ◀4 15. ruled, learnt/learned ◀2 16. left ◀2 17. has lived ◀4 18. enjoyed ◀2 19. made ◀2 20. has left ◀4 21. has gone ◀4 22. have borne ◀5, left ◀2

Erklärungen und Lernhinweise

▶1 Der Vorgang hat in der Vergangenheit begonnen und dauert in der Gegenwart noch an, er ist noch nicht vorbei, daher steht das present perfect. Dafür sprechen auch die vorhandenen Zeitbestimmungen (**all his life, in twenty years, for so long, during the 20th century** etc.).
Im Deutschen wird das present perfect häufig mit dem Präsens übersetzt (z.B.: *ich kenne ihn schon sein ganzes Leben*).

▶2 Der Vorgang ist in der Vergangenheit völlig abgeschlossen, daher steht das past tense. Dafür sprechen auch die vorhandenen Zeitbestimmungen (**last**, **the early settlers**, **the Armada, the Pilgrim Fathers, slave trading** etc.)

▶3 Der Vorgang ist in der Vergangenheit völlig abgeschlossen, daher steht das past tense. Es ist zu beachten, dass das Verb die Endung **-d** im past tense in **-t** ändert.

▶4 Der Vorgang hat in der Vergangenheit begonnen und dauert in der Gegenwart noch an, daher steht das present perfect. Das Subjekt bezeichnet die 3. Person Singular, daher steht **has** + 3. Stammform.

▶5 Der Vorgang hat in der Vergangenheit begonnen und dauert in der Gegenwart noch an, daher steht das present perfect. Die 3. Stammform von **bear** (tragen) lautet **borne** und ist nicht zu verwechseln mit **born** (geboren werden).

3 Setzen Sie die Verben in Klammern ins past tense simple oder ins past perfect simple.

1. came ◀1, had left ◀2 2. had met ◀2, was ◀1 3. had named ◀2, could ◀1 4. burst ◀1, had told ◀2 5. gave ◀1, had happened ◀2 6. was ◀1, had acquired ◀2 7. put ◀1, had stuck ◀2 8. did not know, ◀1 had made ◀2 9. had just finished ◀2, found ◀1, had forgotten ◀2 10. had moved ◀2, had ◀1 11. heard ◀1, had had ◀2 12. had become ◀2, had ◀1 13. wondered ◀1, had had ◀2 14. informed ◀1, had invited ◀2 15. struck ◀1, had changed ◀2

Erklärungen und Lernhinweise

▶1 Der Vorgang ist in der Vergangenheit völlig abgeschlossen und findet nach einem weiteren Vorgang statt, daher steht dieser Vorgang im past tense.

▶2 Der Vorgang fand vor dem Vorgang im past tense statt, daher steht ersterer im past perfect. (z.B.: **the burglar came in through a window which someone had left open**, d.h. das Fenster war (zuerst) offen, bevor der Einbrecher einsteigen konnte).

4 Setzen Sie die Verben in Klammern ins future tense, present tense simple oder ins present tense continuous, oder verwenden Sie **to be going**.

1. Are you coming ◂1 2. am ◂2 3. is playing ◂1 4. am flying ◂1 5. will make ◂3 6. will enjoy ◂3 7. will like ◂3 8. will come, will believe ◂3 9. is leaving ◂1 10. am not going to travel ◂4 11. will move ◂3/are going to move ◂4 12. is coming ◂1 13. enters ◂2 14. will take ◂3 15. leaves ◂2/is leaving ◂1 16. Aren't you going to tell ◂4 17. are/is coming ◂5 18. will take ◂3 19. am going ◂1 20. am going to have ◂4 21. will date ◂3 22. will continue ◂3 23. am not going to pretend ◂4 24. will ultimately conquer ◂3 25. will be annoyed ◂4 26. will face ◂3

Erklärungen und Lernhinweise

▸1 Der Vorgang findet in der nahen Zukunft statt und das Verb drückt die Bewegung, den Vorgang aus, daher steht hier das present tense continuous. Dafür sprechen auch die vorhandenen Zeitbestimmungen (**in a few minutes**, **this afternoon** etc.)

▸2 Der Vorgang findet in der näheren Zukunft statt und das Verb drückt den Zustand, die Tatsache aus, daher steht hier das present tense simple.

▸3 Der Vorgang findet in der (ferneren) Zukunft statt, daher steht hier das future tense. Das future tense steht häufig bei in die Zukunft weisenden Verben (**expect, hope** etc.) oder zum Ausdruck, dass es als sicher angesehen wird, dass ein Vorgang eintritt.

▸4 Der Vorgang findet in der nahen Zukunft statt und drückt die Absicht, Entschlossenheit aus, daher steht hier **to be going to**.

▸5 Der Vorgang findet in der nahen Zukunft statt und das Verb drückt die Bewegung, den Vorgang aus, daher steht hier das present tense continuous. **Police** steht mit einem Verb im Singular, wenn die Gruppe als solche gemeint ist, das Verb steht im Plural, wenn jeder einzelne Polizist gemeint ist.

Simple Ordinary und Continuous Progressive Form

Die Bildung der continuous form in den einzelnen Zeiten

1 Setzen Sie die Verben in Klammern ins present tense continuous.

1. is carrying ◄1 2. are flying ◄2 3. are lying ◄3 4. is blaming ◄4 5. is leaving ◄4 6. am seeing ◄5 7. is slipping ◄6 8. is happening ◄7 9. are saying ◄2 10. is obeying ◄1 11. is living ◄4 12. is getting ◄6 13. is running ◄6 14. is occupying ◄1 15. are trying ◄2 16. is enclosing ◄4 17. is developing ◄8

Erklärungen und Lernhinweise

►1 Das Subjekt bezeichnet die 3. Person Singular, daher steht **is** + ing-Form des Verbs. Das Verb endet auf **-y,** es bleibt beim Anhängen von **-ing** erhalten.

►2 Das Subjekt bezeichnet die 2. Person Singular bzw. die 1., 2., 3. Person Plural, daher steht **are** + ing-Form des Verbs. Das Verb endet auf **-y,** es bleibt beim Anhängen von **-ing** erhalten.

►3 Das Subjekt bezeichnet die 2. Person Singular bzw. die 1., 2., 3. Person Plural, daher steht **are** + ing-Form des Verbs. Das Verb endet auf **-ie,** es ändert sich beim Anhängen von **-ing** in **-y**.

►4 Das Subjekt bezeichnet die 3. Person Singular, daher steht **is** + ing-Form des Verbs. Das Verb endet auf **-e,** es entfällt beim Anhängen von **-ing**.

►5 Das Subjekt bezeichnet die 1. Person Singular, daher steht **am** + ing-Form des Verbs. Das Verb ist ein Verb ohne besondere Endung, daher sind keine orthografischen Besonderheiten zu beachten.

►6 Das Subjekt bezeichnet die 3. Person Singular, daher steht **is** + ing-Form des Verbs. Das Verb endet auf Konsonant, dem ein kurzer, betonter Vokal vorausgeht, daher verdoppelt sich der Endkonsonant beim Anhängen von **-ing**. Der betonte Vokal ist unterstrichen.

►7 Das Subjekt bezeichnet die 3. Person Singular, daher steht **is** + ing-Form des Verbs. Das Verb endet auf Konsonant, dem ein unbetonter Vokal vorausgeht, daher verdoppelt sich der Endkonsonant beim Anhängen von **-ing** nicht. Der betonte Vokal ist unterstrichen.

►8 Das Subjekt ist ein Pronomen, es gilt als 3. Person Singular, daher lautet die entsprechende Personalform **is**. Hierzu zählen Pronomen wie **who, which, what, someone** etc. Das Verb endet auf Konsonant, dem ein unbetonter Vokal vorausgeht, daher verdoppelt sich der Endkonsonant beim Anhängen von **-ing** nicht. Der betonte Vokal ist unterstrichen.

2 Setzen Sie die Verben in Klammern ins past tense continuous.

1. was staying ◄1 2. were dying ◄2 3. was lying ◄3 4. was smoking ◄4 5. were dancing ◄5 6. was facing ◄4 7. was getting ◄6 8. was listening ◄7 9. were riding ◄5 10. was hurrying ◄1 11. was trying ◄1 12. was running ◄6 13. was breathing ◄4 14. was playing ◄1 15. was proving ◄4 16. were arguing ◄5 17. were fitting ◄8 18. were running ◄8 19. was stirring up ◄6

Erklärungen und Lernhinweise

►1 Das Subjekt bezeichnet die 1. oder 3. Person Singular, daher steht **was** + ing-Form des Verbs. Das Verb endet auf **-y,** es bleibt beim Anhängen von **-ing** erhalten.

Erklärungen und Lernhinweise

2 Das Subjekt bezeichnet die 2. Person Singular oder die 1., 2. oder 3. Person Plural, daher steht **were** + ing-Form des Verbs. Das Verb endet auf **-ie,** dies ändert sich beim Anhängen von **-ing** in **-y**.

3 Das Subjekt bezeichnet die 1. oder 3. Person Singular, daher steht **was** + ing-Form des Verbs. Das Verb endet auf **-ie,** dies ändert sich beim Anhängen von **-ing** in **-y**.

4 Das Subjekt bezeichnet die 1. oder 3. Person Singular, daher steht **was** + ing-Form des Verbs. Das Verb endet auf **-e**, dieses entfällt beim Anhängen von **-ing**.

5 Das Subjekt bezeichnet die 2. Person Singular oder die 1., 2. oder 3. Person Plural, daher steht **were** + ing-Form des Verbs. Das Verb endet auf **-e**, dieses entfällt beim Anhängen von **-ing**.

6 Das Subjekt bezeichnet die 1. oder 3. Person Singular, daher steht **was** + ing-Form des Verbs. Das Verb endet auf Konsonant, dem ein kurzer, betonter Vokal vorausgeht, daher verdoppelt sich der Endkonsonant beim Anhängen von **-ing**. Der betonte Vokal ist unterstrichen.

7 Das Subjekt bezeichnet die 1. oder 3. Person Singular, daher steht **was** + ing-Form des Verbs. Das Verb endet auf Konsonant, dem ein unbetonter Vokal vorausgeht, daher verdoppelt sich der Endkonsonant beim Anhängen von **-ing** nicht. Der betonte Vokal ist unterstrichen.

8 Das Subjekt bezeichnet die 2. Person Singular oder die 1., 2. oder 3. Person Plural, daher steht **were** + ing-Form des Verbs. Das Verb endet auf Konsonant, dem ein kurzer, betonter Vokal vorausgeht, daher verdoppelt sich der Endkonsonant beim Anhängen von **-ing**. Der betonte Vokal ist unterstrichen.

3 Setzen Sie die Verben in Klammern ins present perfect continuous.

1. have been playing (1) 2. has been writing (2) 3. have been taking place (3) 4. have been rising (3) 5. have been trying (4) 6. has been running (5) 7. has been lying (6) 8. have been trying (1) 9. has been promoting (2) 10. have been sitting (4)

Erklärungen und Lernhinweise

1 Das Verb endet auf **-y,** dieses bleibt beim Anhängen von **-ing** erhalten. Vor der ing-Form steht **have been** für alle Personen, außer der 3. Person Singular.

2 Das Verb endet auf **-e**, dieses entfällt beim Anhängen von **-ing**. Das Subjekt steht in der 3. Person Singular, daher steht **has been** vor der ing-Form.

3 Das Verb endet auf **-e**, dieses entfällt beim Anhängen von **-ing**. Vor der ing-Form steht **have been** für alle Personen, außer der 3. Person Singular.

4 Das Subjekt ist nicht das Pronomen **who**, sondern der gesamte Ausdruck **to these of us who** bzw. **two Justices of the Peace who**, da es sich um mehrere Personen handelt, steht **have been + -ing** und nicht **has been + -ing**.

5 Das Verb endet auf Konsonant, dem ein kurzer, betonter Vokal vorausgeht, daher verdoppelt sich der Endkonsonant beim Anhängen von **-ing**. Der betonte Vokal ist unterstrichen. Das Subjekt steht in der 3. Person Singular, daher steht **has been** vor der ing-Form.

6 Das Verb endet auf **-ie,** dieses wird beim Anhängen von **-ing** in **-y** geändert. Das Subjekt steht in der 3. Person Singular, daher steht **has been** vor der ing-Form.

4 Setzen Sie die Verben in Klammern ins past perfect continuous.

1. had been lying ◀1 2. had been living ◀2 3. had been going ◀3 4. had been happening ◀4 5. had been knitting ◀5 6. had been worrying ◀6 7. had been celebrating ◀2 8. had been tapping ◀5 9. had been staying ◀6 10. had been bathing ◀2

Erklärungen und Lernhinweise

▶1 Das Verb endet auf **-ie**, es wird beim Anhängen von **-ing** in **-y** geändert. Vor der ing-Form steht **had been** für alle Personen.

▶2 Das Verb endet auf **-e**, dieses entfällt beim Anhängen von **-ing**. Vor der ing-Form steht **had been** für alle Personen.

▶3 Das Verb ist ein Verb ohne besondere Endung, daher wird die Endung **-ing** einfach am Verbende angehängt. Vor der ing-Form steht **had been** für alle Personen.

▶4 Das Verb endet auf Konsonant, dem ein unbetonter Vokal vorausgeht, daher verdoppelt sich der Endkonsonant beim Anhängen von **-ing** nicht. Der betonte Vokal ist unterstrichen. Vor der ing-Form steht **had been** für alle Personen.

▶5 Das Verb endet auf Konsonant, dem ein kurzer, betonter Vokal vorausgeht, daher verdoppelt sich der Endkonsonant beim Anhängen von **-ing**. Der betonte Vokal ist unterstrichen. Vor der ing-Form steht **had been** für alle Personen.

▶6 Das Verb endet auf **-y**, es bleibt beim Anhängen von **-ing** erhalten. Vor der ing-Form steht **had been** für alle Personen.

Die Verwendung der continuous form

1 Setzen Sie die folgenden Ausdrücke in den entsprechenden Satz ein.

1. now ◀1 2. denser and denser, more and more ◀2 3. day by day, minute by minute ◀2 4. while ◀3 5. When ◀4 6. As ◀4 7. Suddenly ◀5 8. At present ◀1 9. worse and worse ◀2 10. when ◀4 11. at the same time ◀3 12. while ◀3 13. while ◀3 14. as ◀4 15. increasingly ◀2 16. while ◀3 17. Suddenly ◀5 18. when ◀4

Erklärungen und Lernhinweise

▶1 Der Vorgang findet gerade, im Moment des Sprechens statt, daher steht die continuous form. Diese Vorgänge werden häufig durch diese Zeitbestimmungen eingeleitet oder, anders ausgedrückt, ist diese Zeitbestimmung vorhanden, wird häufig die continuous form verwendet.

▶2 Der Vorgang bezeichnet die allmähliche Entwicklung, daher steht die continuous form. Diese Vorgänge werden häufig durch Komparative oder diese Zeitbestimmungen gekennzeichnet oder, anders ausgedrückt, ist diese Zeitbestimmung vorhanden, wird häufig die continuous form verwendet.

▶3 Die Vorgänge finden zur gleichen Zeit statt, daher steht die continuous form (z.B. bei **I came in while you were watching the film**, findet das Hereinkommen und das Sehen des Films gleichzeitig statt). Diese Vorgänge werden häufig durch diese Zeitbestimmungen eingeleitet oder, anders ausgedrückt, ist diese Zeitbestimmung vorhanden, wird häufig die continuous form verwendet.

Erklärungen und Lernhinweise

▶4 Der eine Vorgang tritt neu ein, während der andere Vorgang andauert, daher steht die simple form für den neu eintretenden Vorgang und die continuous form für den noch andauernden Vorgang (z.B. bei **when he came in, Linda was making the beds**, ist das Hereinkommen der neu eintretende Vorgang, das Machen der Betten hat schon vor dem Hereinkommen stattgefunden und findet auch beim Hereinkommen noch statt). Diese Vorgänge werden häufig durch diese Zeitbestimmungen eingeleitet oder, anders ausgedrückt, ist diese Zeitbestimmung vorhanden, wird häufig die simple und die continuous form verwendet.

▶5 Der Vorgang findet plötzlich statt, dauert nur einen Augenblick, daher steht die continuous form. Diese Vorgänge werden häufig durch diese Zeitbestimmungen eingeleitet oder, anders ausgedrückt, ist diese Zeitbestimmung vorhanden, wird häufig die continuous form verwendet.

2 Setzen Sie die Verben in Klammern in die simple oder continuous form im past tense.

1. was rising, were getting ◀1 2. jumped, tried ◀2 3. worked ◀3 4. was staying ◀1 5. stayed ◀4 6. were playing, were sitting, were drinking ◀5 7. asked, tried ◀6 8. led, was playing ◀7 9. left, returned ◀3 10. are talking ◀1 11. was waiting ◀1 12. heard, changed ◀6 13. were having, was talking ◀5 14. felt, tried ◀6 15. reached, was lying, sat up ◀7 16. are talking ◀1 17. continued ◀2 18. sank, revived ◀3 19. were lit ◀4 20. was steering, were going, was looking ◀5 21. went, tried ◀2 22. was sweating, took off ◀7 23. were always asking ◀8 24. was always picking ◀8

Erklärungen und Lernhinweise

▶1 Der Vorgang bezeichnet die allmähliche Entwicklung, den Verlauf aus, er dauert nur eine Zeit lang, daher steht die continuous form.

▶2 Der Vorgang findet plötzlich statt, dauert nur einen Augenbilick, daher steht die simple form. Dafür sprechen auch die vorhandenen Zeitbestimmungen (**quickly**).

▶3 Der Vorgang drückt die Gewohnheit aus, daher steht die simple form. Dafür sprechen auch die vorhandenen Zeitbestimmungen (**every evening, every week, every morning**).

▶4 Der Vorgang drückt die Dauer aus, daher steht die simple form. Dafür sprechen auch die vorhandenen Zeitbestimmungen (**all the time**).

▶5 Die Vorgänge finden zur gleichen Zeit statt, daher steht die continuous form.

▶6 Die Vorgänge finden nacheinander statt, daher steht die simple form. Dafür sprechen auch die vorhandenen Zeitbestimmungen (**when, from time to time**).

▶7 Der eine Vorgang tritt ein, während der andere Vorgang andauert, daher steht die simple form für den neu eintretenden Vorgang und die continuous form für den noch andauernden Vorgang (z.B.: bei **Mr Jackson led him to the living-room where Billy was playing cards with his mother** ist das Führen zum Wohnzimmer der neu eintretende Vorgang, während das Kartenspielen schon vorher stattgefunden hat und währenddessen noch andauert).

▶8 Der Vorgang bringt die besondere Nachdrücklichkeit, Gefühlsbetontheit zum Ausdruck, daher steht die continuous form (z.B.: in **he was always picking on me** beklagt "er" sich darüber, dass ständig auf ihm herumgehackt wird). Vorgänge in der simple form haben neutrale, sachliche Bedeutung.

3 Setzen Sie die Verben in Klammern in die simple oder continuous form. Beachten Sie die Zeit.

1. is repairing ◀1 2. am flying ◀2 3. was walking ◀3 4. has been sleeping ◀4 5. has been speaking ◀4 6. did not know, had been looking ◀5 7. loves, loves ◀6 8. married, started ◀7 9. is growing ◀8 10. have been doing ◀4 11. are/is coming ◀2 12. stayed, came ◀7

Erklärungen und Lernhinweise

▶1 Der Vorgang findet gerade, im Moment des Sprechens statt, daher steht die continuous form. Er findet in der Gegenwart statt, daher steht das present tense.

▶2 Der Vorgang bezeichnet die nahe Zukunft statt, daher steht das present tense continuous. Dafür sprechen auch die vorhandenen Zeitbestimmungen (**this afternoon, in about an hour**).
Police steht mit **is**, wenn die Gruppe als solche gemeint ist, **are** steht , wenn jeder einzelne Polizist bezeichnet werden soll.

▶3 Der Vorgang bezeichnet den Verlauf, eine gewisse Zeitdauer, daher steht die continuous form. Er ist in der Vergangenheit völlig abgeschlossen, daher steht das past tense. Dafür sprechen auch die vorhandenen Zeitbestimmungen (**one evening**).

▶4 Der Vorgang bezeichnet den Verlauf, eine gewisse Zeitdauer, daher steht die continuous form. Er hat in der Vergangenheit begonnen und dauert in der Gegenwart noch an, daher steht das present perfect. Dafür sprechen auch die vorhandenen Zeitbestimmungen (**still, ever since**).
Steht das Subjekt in der 3. Person Singular, steht **has**.

▶5 Der erste Vorgang tritt neu ein, daher steht die simple form, während der zweite Vorgang schon andauert, daher steht die continuous form. Der zweite Vorgang findet vor dem ersten statt, daher steht der zweite Vorgang im past perfect, der erste Vorgang steht im past tense.

▶6 Der Vorgang bezeichnet die Tatsache, daher steht das present tense simple. Das Subjekt steht in der 3. Person Singular, daher erhält das Verb ein **-s**.

▶7 Die Vorgänge finden nacheinander statt, daher steht die simple form. Die Vorgänge sind in der Vergangenheit völlig abgeschlossen, daher steht das past tense.

▶8 Der Vorgang bezeichnet die allmähliche Entwicklung, daher steht die continuous form. Es wird von der Gegenwart aus in Zukunft geblickt, daher steht present tense.

Das Passiv (The Passive Voice)

Die Bildung des Passivs in den einzelnen Zeiten

1 Setzen Sie die Verben in Klammern ins Passiv im present tense simple.

1. are set 2. are built 3. is occupied 4. is planned 5. is laid out 6. is estimated 7. is controlled 8. is put 9. are sent 10. are required 11. are born 12. are borne 13. is judged 14. are bound 15. is tied

Erklärungen und Lernhinweise

Das Verb wird in die 3. Stammform gesetzt, die entsprechende Personal- und Zeitform von **to be** tritt davor, d.h. steht das Subjekt in der 1. Person Singular, lautet die korrekte Verbform von **to be** im present tense simple **am** bzw. **'m,** bei der 3. Person Singular steht **is** bzw. **'s**, bei allen andern Personen steht **are** bzw. **'re**. Es sind die Besonderheiten bei der Bildung der 3. Stammform zu beachten (z.B. **-y** wird zu **-ie** etc.).

Das Verb gehört zu den Verben, die die Endung **-d** in der 3. Stammform in **-t** ändern.

Das Subjekt besteht aus mehreren Substantiven (**consent and approval**), daher steht **are** + 3. Stammform, auch wenn es sich dabei um Substantive im Singular handelt.

Die 3. Stammform von **bear** (tragen) lautet **borne** und ist nicht zu verwechseln mit **born** (geboren werden).

2 Setzen Sie die Verben in Klammern ins Passiv im past tense simple.

1. were destroyed 2. was promised 3. was admitted 4. was hit, was knocked over 5. was shot 6. was hurt 7. was left 8. was she taken, was taken 9. was accompanied 10. was thoroughly and carefully worked out, was judged 11. was raised 12. were permitted 13. was tied 14. was received 15. were referred to

Erklärungen und Lernhinweise

Das Verb wird in die 3. Stammform gesetzt, die entsprechende Personal- und Zeitform von **to be** tritt davor, d.h. steht das Subjekt in der 1. oder 3. Person Singular, lautet die korrekte Verbform von **to be** im past tense simple **was,** in allen anderen Personen steht **were**. Es sind die Besonderheiten bei der Bildung der 3. Stammform zu beachten (z.B. **-y** wird zu **-ie** etc.).

Das Subjekt ist ein Substantiv, das trotz des Plural-s als Substantiv im Singular gilt, daher steht **was** + 3. Stammform.

3 Setzen Sie die Verben in Klammern ins Passiv im present perfect simple.

1. have been carried 2. have been admitted 3. have been spent 4. has been said 5. has been improved 6. has been divided 7. have been accompanied 8. have been built 9. have been used 10. has been told

Erklärungen und Lernhinweise

1. Das Verb wird in die 3. Stammform gesetzt, vor der Stammform steht für alle Personen, außer für die 3. Person Singular, **have been** bzw. die Kurzform **'ve been**. Es sind die Besonderheiten bei der Bildung der 3. Stammform zu beachten (z.B. **-y** wird zu **-ie** etc.).
2. Das Subjekt steht in der 3. Person Singular, daher steht **has been** bzw. die Kurzform **'s been** + 3. Stammform.
3. Das Verb gehört zu den Verben, die die Endung **-d** in der 3. Stammform in **-t** ändern.
4. Das Subjekt ist ein Adjektiv, das als 3. Person Singular gilt, daher steht **has been** + 3. Stammform.
5. Das Subjekt besteht aus mehreren Substantiven (**scientific and economic advance** und **rising material prosperity**), daher steht **have been** bzw. die Kurzform **'ve been** + 3. Stammform, auch wenn es sich dabei um Substantive im Singular handelt.

4 Setzen Sie die Verben in Klammern ins Passiv im past perfect simple.

1. had been laid ◀1 2. had been served ◀1 3. had been done ◀1 4. had been invented ◀1, had been built ◀2 5. had been destroyed ◀1 6. had been committed ◀1 7. had been involved ◀1 8. had been sent ◀2 9. had been seen ◀1 10. had been emptied ◀1 11. had been conferred ◀1 12. had been taken ◀1

Erklärungen und Lernhinweise

1. Das Verb wird in die 3. Stammform gesetzt, vor der Stammform steht für alle Personen **had been** bzw. die Kurzform **'d been**. Es sind die Besonderheiten bei der Bildung der 3. Stammform zu beachten (z.B. **-y** wird zu **-ie** etc.).
2. Das Verb gehört zu den Verben, die die Endung **-d** in der 3. Stammform in **-t** ändern.

5 Setzen Sie die Verben in Klammern ins Passiv im future tense simple.

1. will be carried ◀1 2. will be proposed ◀1 3. will be held ◀1 4. will be hurt ◀1 5. will be required ◀1 6. will be sent ◀2 7. will be given ◀1 8. will be met ◀1 9. will be cut off ◀1 10. will be made ◀1

Erklärungen und Lernhinweise

1. Das Verb wird in die 3. Stammform gesetzt, vor der Stammform steht für alle Personen **will be** bzw. die Kurzform **'ll be**. Auf **will** folgt der Infinitiv von **be** (also **will be** nicht **will been**). Es sind die Besonderheiten bei der Bildung der 3. Stammform zu beachten (z.B. **-y** wird zu **-ie** etc.).
2. Das Verb gehört zu den Verben, die die Endung **-d** in der 3. Stammform in **-t** ändern.

6 Setzen Sie die Verben in Klammern ins Passiv im present tense continuous.

1. are being changed ◀1 2. are being controlled ◀1 3. is being developed ◀1 4. is being driven ◀1 5. is being built ◀2 6. is being taught ◀1 7. is being spoken ◀1 8. is being urbanized ◀1 9. is being done ◀3 10. is being revived ◀1

Erklärungen und Lernhinweise

- Das Verb wird in die 3. Stammform gesetzt, vor der Stammform steht für alle Personen, außer für die 1. und 3. Person Singular, **are being**, in der 1. Person Singular steht **am being**, in der 3. Person Singular steht **is being**. Es sind die Besonderheiten bei der Bildung der 3. Stammform zu beachten (z.B. **-y** wird zu **-ie** etc.).
- Das Verb gehört zu den Verben, die die Endung **-d** in der 3. Stammform in **-t** ändern.
- Das Subjekt ist ein Pronomen. Pronomen gelten als 3. Person Singular, daher steht **is** + 3. Stammform.

7 Setzen Sie die Verben in Klammern ins Passiv im past tense continuous.

1. was being tossed 2. was being said 3. were being brought 4. was being waited for 5. was being looked for 6. were being watched

Erklärungen und Lernhinweise

- Das Verb wird in die 3. Stammform gesetzt, vor der Stammform steht für alle Personen, außer für die 1. und 3. Person Singular, **were being**, in der 1. und 3. Person Singular steht **was being**.
- Das Subjekt ist ein Pronomen, dieses gilt als 3. Person Singular, daher steht **was being** + 3. Stammform.

Die Umwandlung aktiver Sätze in passive Sätze

1 Setzen Sie die folgenden Sätze, die ein Objekt enthalten, ins Passiv.

1. All the team obeyed the trainer's orders without any protest.
   The trainer's orders were obeyed by all the team without any protest.

2. By the next afternoon some people had invited him to a party.
   By the next afternoon he had been invited to a party (by some people).

3. He delivered the parcel next door by mistake.
   The parcel was delivered (by him) next door by mistake.

4. Several first-class orchestras regularly give orchestral concerts in London.
   Orchestral concerts are regularly given by several first-class orchestras in London.

5. The afternoon train will take him there on Wednesday.
   He will be taken there by the afternoon train on Wednesday.

6. Their Clerks advise the Justices of the Peace on points of law.
   The Justices of the Peace are advised by their Clerks on points of law.

7. They planned new industrial estates around the city.
   New industrial estates are planned (by them) around the city.

8. They will help them on and off every bus and across every street.
They will be helped (by them) on and off every bus and across every street.

9. We told Susan to come too, and she was the first to arrive.
Susan was told (by us) to come too, and she was the first to arrive.

10. We will do everything to make your flight comfortable.
Everything will be done (by us) to make your flight comfortable.

11. They had set the table on the terrace for three.
The table had been set (by them) on the terrace for three.

12. We will find radioactive pollutants on the earth's surface for generations.
Radioactive pollutants will be found (by us) on the earth's surface for generations.

13. Her sister will join her.
She will be joined by her sister.

14. We are making great efforts to ensure that poor people are helped.
Great efforts are being made (by us) to ensure that poor people are helped.

15. We consider only 16.7 million out of Kenya's 140 million acres good enough for high potential farming.
Only 16.7 million out of Kenya's 140 million acres are considered (by us) good enough for high potential farming.

16. Do not enter the studio, we are filming a play for today's programme.
Do not enter the studio, a play for today's programme is being filmed (by us).

17. Bob had the feeling that somebody was following him.
Bob had the feeling that he was being followed (by somebody).

18. They put the growth in average earnings at 7 3/4 %, a fraction higher than last summer.
The growth in average earnings was/is put at 7 3/4 % (by them), a fraction higher than last summer.

19. If I hadn't fled and changed my name, they should have put me into prison.
If I hadn't fled and changed my name, I should have been put into prison (by them).

20. There a friend will meet you.
You will be met by a friend there.

21. As soon as they discovered the crime search parties combed the whole forest.
As soon as the crime was discovered (by them) the whole forest was combed by search parties.

22. In 1968 new laws enabled courts to take away the driving licence of a driver whom they found to have more than 80 ml of alcohol.
In 1968 courts were enabled (by new laws) to take away the driving licence of a driver who was found to have more than 80 ml of alcohol (by them). ◀3

23. The Justices of the Peace are ordinary but worthy citizens whom the Lord Chancellor has appointed to their positions.
The Justices of the Peace are ordinary but worthy citizens who have been appointed to their positions by the Lord Chancellor. ◀3

Erklärungen und Lernhinweise

▶1 Das direkte Objekt (dunkelgrau) des Aktivsatzes, wird zum Subjekt des Passivsatzes. Ist das Objekt ein Pronomen (z.B. **him**) wird es im Passivsatz ein Pronomen im Subjektfall (z.B. **he**).
Das Subjekt des Aktivsatzes (hellgrau) wird zum Objekt des Passivsatzes und wird mit **by** angeschlossen oder weggelassen, wenn es unwichtig ist. Ist das Subjekt ein Pronomen (z.B. **he**) wird es im Passivsatz ein Pronomen im Objektfall (z.B. **him**).
Die Zeit, in der das Verb (weiß) steht, wird in die richtige Zeit und Form im Passiv übertragen.
Zum besseren Verständnis ist der jeweilige Aktivsatz ebenfalls dargestellt.

▶2 Das Verb hat in allen 3 Stammformen dieselbe Form, daher ist im Aktivsatz nur in der 3. Person Singular an der Endung -s zu erkennen, dass es sich um das present tense simple handelt. In allen anderen Personen unterscheidet sich die Verbform im present und past tense simple nicht.

▶3 Das direkte Objekt ist das Objektpronomen **whom,** das dann regelgemäß zum Pronomen im Subjektfall wird, **who**.

2 Setzen Sie die folgenden Sätze mit zwei Objekten ins Passiv und verwenden Sie das richtige Objekt als Subjekt des Passivsatzes.

1. He realized too late that the letter was addressed to Mr Harrison. ◀1 2. I was recommended another doctor. ◀2 3. Here vagabonds are offered warm food and dry beds. ◀2 4. In the ante-chapel, next the hall where we were, petitions were presented to the queen. ◀1 5. On Christmas Day, 1066, William the Conqueror was crowned King of England in Westminster Abbey. ◀3 6. There you will be given all the instructions you need. ◀2 7. He is allowed five marks pocket money a week. ◀2 8. The event was announced to everybody. ◀1 9. He was considered a prudent man. ◀3 10. She was granted a small pension. ◀2 11. George Washington was made the first President of the United States of America. ◀3 12. A reward was promised to anyone who would write a good article for the school magazine. ◀1 13. He was saved a lot of trouble. ◀2 14. We shall be asked several questions. ◀4 15. He was shown all the books. ◀2 16. He will be appointed director general. ◀3 17. The computer was explained to us by a top-level expert. ◀1 18. At the airport duty-free cigarettes, spirits and perfume can be bought ◀5 by passengers and during the flight they may be served dinner or a snack, depending on the time of the day. ◀4 19. At today's press conference at the Yard the journalists were handed photographs of the stolen paintings. ◀2 20. I hope he may be spared this ordeal. ◀4 21. In general the Bachelor's degree is given to students who pass examinations at the end of three or four years of study. ◀1 22. Should they be given the chance? ◀4 23. This assistance was offered to anyone who cared

to take it. ◀1 24. Most full-time directors of large companies are paid salaries between £ 20,000 and £ 30,000 a year. ◀2 25. All things possible should be made reality. ◀4 26. At the cocktail party the famous professor was taken ◀5 no notice of, but his lovely young wife was made a fuss of ◀5 from the moment she was introduced to the guests. ◀1 27. He was so stupid that he was made the laughing stack. ◀2 28. The beggar was given an alms. ◀2 29. Workers who lose their jobs through labour-saving techniques will have to be offered another job of similar status and pay. ◀6 30. Every question must be handed to the officials ◀7 of the house in writing at least 48 hours before the answer is to be given. ◀5

Erklärungen und Lernhinweise

▶1 Das indirekte Objekt (hellgrau) wird mit **to** angeschlossen, daher kann nur das direkte Objekt (dunkelgrau) zum Subjekt des Passivsatzes werden.

▶2 Das indirekte Objekt (hellgrau) wird nicht mit **to** angeschlossen, daher kann das indirekte Objekt zum Subjekt des Passivsatzes werden.

▶3 Die pädikative Ergänzung (hellgrau) wird ohne Präposition an die Verben des Ernennens, Dafürhaltens angeschlossen, sie bleibt im Passivsatz Objekt.

▶4 Das indirekte Objekt (hellgrau) wird nicht mit **to** angeschlossen, daher kann das indirekte Objekt zum Subjekt des Passivsatzes werden. Das Verb besteht aus Modalverb und Vollverb, dies wird im Passivsatz zu Modalverb + **be** + 3. Stammform (z.B.: **can buy** wird zu **can be bought**).

▶5 Es ist nur ein Objekt vorhanden, es wird daher dieses Objekt zum Subjekt des Passivsatzes.

▶6 Das indirekte Objekt (hellgrau) wird nicht mit **to** angeschlossen, daher kann das indirekte Objekt zum Subjekt des Passivsatzes werden. Das Verb besteht aus dem Ersatzverb **have to** und **will** zum Ausdruck des future tense, dies wird im Passivsatz regelgemäß zu **will + have to** + **be** + 3. Stammform.

▶7 Das indirekte Objekt (hellgrau) wird mit **to** angeschlossen, daher wird das direkte Objekt (dunkelgrau) zum Subjekt des Passivsatzes. Das Verb besteht aus Modalverb und Vollverb, dies wird im Passivsatz zu Modalverb + **be** + 3. Stammform.

3 Setzen Sie die folgenden Sätze ins Passiv.

1. This question **has been dealt *with*** by an expert. ◀ 2. He **has** never **been heard *of*** since. ◀ 3. He **has** always **been laughed *at*.** ◀ 4. He **was listened *to*** with pleasure. ◀ 5. When Mrs Douglas came home from hospital, she found that the cat **had been looked *after*.** ◀ 6. He **was looked *upon*** as a sportive man. ◀ 7. The solution **was arrived *at*** by chance. ◀ 8. People **have** often **been discriminated *against*** because of race, religion, or colour. ◀ 9. **Has** any decision **been come *to*?** ◀ 10. You can rely on it that your orders **will be attended *to*** without delay. ◀ 11. Charles hardly knew Parker, and had no idea what work he **was employed *on*.** ◀ 12. Nothing seems to have been disarranged and the drawers **have not been interfered *with*.** ◀ 13. My hat **has been sat *on*.** ◀ 14. The bed **has been slept *in*.** ◀ 15. They forgot their quarrels on seeing that their right **was infringed *upon*.** ◀ 16. But in among all this terrible poverty there were just a few great big beautiful houses which **were lived *in*** by rich men who had as many as thirty servants to look after them. ◀ 17. Oxford, like Rome, abounds in beauty, but it is a hidden beauty that **must be sought *for*.** ◀

Erklärungen und Lernhinweise

Die Präposition gehört zum Verb (nicht zum Objekt), daher muss diese im Passivsatz auch beim Verb verbleiben. Zur Veranschaulichung ist die Präposition fett und kursiv dargestellt.

Die Umwandlung passiver Sätze in aktive Sätze

1 Setzen Sie die folgenden Passivsätze ins Aktiv.

1. More than 800 million people speak English in many different countries all over the world. 1 2. Bob checked in at the hotel Miramare which some Americans had recommended to him. 1 3. They closed that pat of the road for resurfacing. 2 4. They have carried through several reforms in recent years. 2 5. He had run away at seventeen but they had brought him back. 2 6. I will finish my business in a few seconds. 2 7. They gave him another 1,500 dollars. 2 8. They had long dealt with the matter. 2 9. You needn't look after boys and girls of 16 all the time. 2 10. They estimate the total loss resulting from all thefts at $ 6 million. 2 11. We use disposable dishware for everyday occasions. 2 12. A judge presides over the court, but a jury makes the decision on guilt or innocence. 1 13. They warned the public of the dangers of drinking. 2 14. Somebody is following us. 2 15. They were doing something. 2 16. Some women with small children would like to work, if somebody could care for the children during mothers' working hours. 2 17. They hoped that the Health Service would improve health in general. 3 18. It is a shame that they should have treated him like that. 2 19. We are turning over the trivial tasks to the machines. 2 20. They may well pay a person in a middle-class salaried job his full salary for long periods of absence through sickness. 2 21. What advances have we made in the last few years in computer technology? 2 22. In 1961 they decided that we would need a third new airport for London by the early 1970s. 2 23. First, the Cabinet has approved every bill 1 that the Government brought in. 1 24. What are they doing about the situation? 2 25. I don't want you to see me off. 4

Erklärungen und Lernhinweise

1 Das Objekt des Passivsatzes (dunkelgrau) (oft mit **by** angeschlossen), wird zum Subjekt des Aktivsatzes. Ist das Objekt ein Pronomen (z.B. **him**) wird es im Aktivsatz ein Pronomen im Subjektfall (z.B. **he**).
Das Subjekt (hellgrau) des Passivsatzes wird zum Objekt des Aktivsatzes. Ist das Subjekt ein Pronomen (z.B. **he**) wird es im Aktivsatz ein Pronomen im Objektfall (z.B. **him**).
Die Zeit, in der das Verb steht, wird in die richtige Zeit und Form im Aktiv übertragen.

2 Es ist kein Objekt, das zum Subjekt des Aktivsatzes werden kann, vorhanden. Daher wird eines, das in den Sinnzusammenhang passt, erfunden. Hier wurde meist **they** gewählt, es sind aber, je nach Sinn des Satzes, auch andere Subjekte möglich (z.B. **people, someone, Peter** etc.).

3 Grammatische Subjekte (**it, there**) im Passivsatz entfallen im Aktivsatz.

4 Der passive infinitive **to be seen** wird in den active infinitive **to see** umgewandelt. Das im Passivsatz **I don't want to be seen off** (ich möchte nicht fortbegleitet werden) fehlende Subjekt und Objekt wird im Aktivsatz **I don't want *you* to see *me* off** (ich möchte nicht, dass **Sie mich** fortbegleiten) hinzugefügt.

Die indirekte Rede (Reported, Indirect Speech)

Die Umwandlung von Aussagesätzen

1 Ändern Sie die Verben im present tense in die richtige Zeit in der indirekten Rede.

1. was ◀ 2. needed ◀ 3. didn't/did not need ◀ 4. made, were ◀ 5. was going ◀ 6. did not use, liked ◀ 7. swore, was ◀ 8. were to integrate ◀ 9. were to do ◀ 10. happened, wanted ◀

Erklärungen und Lernhinweise

Das Verb steht im present tense, in indirekter Rede wird es ins past tense gesetzt.

2 Ändern Sie die Verben im past tense in die richtige Zeit in indirekter Rede.

1. hadn't/had not done ◀ 2. had been ◀ 3. had not been ◀ 4. had still been ◀ 5. had apparently had ◀ 6. had died ◀ 7. had thought, had been ◀ 8. had been, had seen, had given ◀ 9. had had ◀ 10. had taken, had had ◀

Erklärungen und Lernhinweise

Das Verb steht im past tense, in indirekter Rede wird es ins past perfect gesetzt.
Adverbien stehen in der Regel nach dem ersten Hilfsverb (z.B. **had *still* been**).

3 Ändern Sie die Verben im present perfect in die richtige Zeit in indirekter Rede.

1. had just left ◀ 2. had torn ◀ 3. had been ◀ 4. had not/hadn't found ◀ 5. had been ◀ 6. had been ◀ 7. had been given ◀ 8. had had ◀ 9. had just been requested ◀ 10. had lost ◀

Erklärungen und Lernhinweise

Das Verb steht im present perfect, es wird in indirekter Rede ins past perfect gesetzt.
Adverbien stehen in der Regel nach dem ersten Hilfsverb (z.B. **had *just* left**).

4 Ändern Sie die Verben im past perfect in die richtige Zeit in indirekter Rede.

1. had guaranteed ◀ 2. had been collected ◀ 3. had been ◀ 4. had been ◀ 5. had been ◀ 6. had failed ◀ 7. had seen ◀ 8. had been ◀ 9. had been led away ◀ 10. had been ◀

Erklärungen und Lernhinweise

Das Verb steht im past perfect, es bleibt in indirekter Rede unverändert, also im past perfect.

5 Ändern Sie die folgenden Verben im future tense, future perfect tense oder im conditional I in die korrekte Zeit in indirekter Rede.

1. would be ◀1 2. would make ◀1 3. wouldn't/would not drink ◀1 4. would never end ◀1 5. would have been ◀2 6. wouldn't/would not like ◀3 7. would like ◀3 8. would be ◀1 9. would have ◀1 10. would have ◀1 11. would have left ◀2 12. would ultimately conquer ◀1

Erklärungen und Lernhinweise

▶1 Das Verb steht im future tense, es wird in indirekter Rede ins conditional gesetzt. Adverbien stehen in der Regel nach dem ersten Hilfsverb (z.B. **would *never* end**).

▶2 Das Verb steht im future perfect, es wird in indirekter Rede ins conditional perfect gesetzt.

▶3 Das Verb steht im conditional, es bleibt in indirekter Rede unverändert, also im conditional.

6 Setzen Sie die folgenden Modalverben in die indirekte Rede.

1. couldn't ◀1 2. couldn't ◀2 3. might ◀3 4. might ◀2 5. ought to ◀2 6. might ◀2 7. must ◀2 8. should ◀4 9. should ◀2 10. ought to ◀2 11. had to ◀5 12. were to ◀6

Erklärungen und Lernhinweise

▶1 **Can** wird in indirekter Rede zu **could**.

▶2 **Could, might, must, ought to, should** und **would** bleiben in indirekter Rede unverändert, also **could, might, must, ought to, should** und **would.**

▶3 **May** wird in indirekter Rede zu **might**.

▶4 **Shall** wird in indirekter Rede zu **should**.

▶5 Das Ersatzverb **have to** wird in indirekter Rede zu **had to**.

▶6 In der 3. Person Singular wird **is to** (von **to be to**) in indirekter Rede zu **were to** (nicht **was to**).

7 Setzen Sie die folgenden Personalpronomen in die indirekte Rede und fügen Sie diese in die Tabelle auf der rechten Seite ein.

1. I, we ◀1 2. he, they ◀1 3. you ◀1 4. you ◀2 5. he, they ◀2 6. we, I ◀2 7. he, they ◀3 8. he, they ◀3 9. I, we, you ◀3 10. we ◀4 11. he, they ◀4 12. you ◀4 13. they ◀5 14. they, he ◀5 15. you, I, we ◀5

Erklärungen und Lernhinweise

▶ 1. Ich sage, was ich/wir selbst getan oder gesagt habe/haben;
2. ich sage, was er/sie getan oder gesagt hat/haben;
3. ich sage, was du/ihr getan oder gesagt hast/habt.

Erklärungen und Lernhinweise

▶2 1. Du sagst, was du/ihr selbst getan oder gesagt hast/habt;
2. du sagst, was er/sie getan oder gesagt hat/haben;
3. du sagst, was ich/wir getan oder gesagt habe/haben.

▶3 1. Er sagt, was er/sie selbst getan oder gesagt hat/haben;
2. er sagt, was er/sie (Dritte, nicht er selbst) getan oder gesagt hat/haben;
3. er sagt, was ich/wir getan oder gesagt habe/haben oder was du/ihr getan oder gesagt hast/habt.

▶4 1. Wir sagen, was wir selbst getan oder gesagt haben;
2. wir sagen, was er/sie getan oder gesagt hat/haben;
3. wir sagen, was du/ihr getan oder gesagt hast/habt.

▶5 1. Sie sagen, was sie selbst getan oder gesagt haben;
2. sie sagen, was er/sie (Dritte, nicht sie selbst) getan oder gesagt haben;
3. sie sagen, was du/ihr getan oder gesagt hast/habt oder was ich/wir getan oder gesagt habe/haben.

8 Setzen Sie die folgenden Zeit- und Ortsangaben in die indirekte Rede.

1. that day 2. the day before/the previous day 3. two days before 4. the next day/the following day 5. the following week 6. the week before/the previous week 7. before 8. then 9. there

9 Setzen Sie die folgenden Sätze in die indirekte Rede.

1. I said **that I thought he was** wrong. ◀1 2. He said **that Andrew Johnson was** innocent. ◀1 3. You said **that she didn't admit** anything. ◀1 4. They said **that this would** have only negative consequences. ◀2 5. The Speaker said **that it was** time to go on to the next question. ◀1 6. The doctors said **that he had been** dead at least twelve hours. ◀6 7. We said **that the burglar had entered** the garden from the back. ◀3 8. He said **that there had been** no risk of an accident. ◀4 9. The captain **said that it had been** no use arguing with the angry crew. ◀3 10. They said **that they would disarm** and **they would arrange** to have a conference to settle the matter. ◀5 11. He told us **that he would receive** the Burtons on Sunday out of doors and give them tea in the garden. ◀2 12. He said **that these two moves** between them **would lay** a basis for future cooperation. ◀2 13. They said **that man's lot could** no more be improved by violent and doctrinaire assaults. ◀7 14. She said **that there should be** redistribution of the male and female roles in society. ◀7 15. I said **that he had set out** with the idea of calling upon Clayton. ◀8 16. I said **that he set out** with the idea of calling upon Clayton. ◀8 17. He said **that** before taking a decision on some bill **it ought to** make thorough enquiries into the background and the desirability of the new proposals. ◀7 18. They said **that marriages should hold** ◀7 all kinds of work combinations without society attaching any stigma to the man who **stayed** ◀1 at home or the mother who **opted** ◀1 for a fulltime career.

Erklärungen und Lernhinweise

Die indirekte Rede wird durch **that**, das weggelassen werden kann, eingeleitet, die Anführungszeichen der direkten Rede entfallen. Zum besseren Verständnis sind die vorzunehmenden Änderungen in den oben aufgeführten Lösungssätzen fett gedruckt.

Erklärungen und Lernhinweise

▶1 Das Verb steht im present tense, es wird daher ins past tense gesetzt. Es wird mitgeteilt, was der Sprecher selbst oder ein Dritter getan oder gesagt hat, daher werden die Personenangaben nicht verändert.

▶2 Das Verb steht im future tense, es wird daher ins conditional gesetzt. Es wird mitgeteilt, was ein Dritter getan oder gesagt hat, daher werden die Personenangaben nicht verändert.

▶3 Das Verb steht im past tense, es wird daher ins past perfect gesetzt. Es wird mitgeteilt, was ein Dritter getan oder gesagt hat, daher werden die Personenangaben nicht verändert.

▶4 Das Verb steht im present perfect, es wird daher ins past perfect gesetzt. Es wird mitgeteilt, was ein Dritter getan oder gesagt hat, daher werden die Personenangaben nicht verändert.

▶5 Das Verb steht im future tense, es wird daher ins conditional gesetzt. Die Sprecher geben ihre eigenen Worte wieder, daher ändern sich die Personalpronomen von **we** in **they**.

▶6 Das Verb steht im past perfect, es bleibt daher unverändert. Es wird mitgeteilt, was ein Dritter getan oder gesagt hat, daher werden die Personenangaben nicht verändert.

▶7 Das Verb ist das Modalverb **can** bzw. **should, ought to**, sie werden daher in **could** geändert bzw. bleiben unverändert **should, ought to**. Es wird mitgeteilt, was ein Dritter getan oder gesagt hat, daher werden die Personenangaben nicht verändert.

▶8 Das Verb steht im past tense, es wird daher ins past perfect gesetzt. Das Verb gehört zu den Verben, die in allen 3 Stammformen die gleiche Form haben, sie unterscheiden sich daher nur in der 3. Person Singular des present tense simple und des past tense simple (z.B. **he sets** und **he set**). Es wird mitgeteilt, was ein Dritter getan oder gesagt hat, daher werden die Personenangaben nicht verändert.

Die Umwandlung von Fragesätzen

1 Setzen Sie die folgenden Fragesätze ohne Fragewort in die indirekte Rede.

1. I wanted to ask you **whether/if you had got** any razor blades. ◀3 2. He asked **whether/if I could** bring Carol over for a drink around five o'clock. ◀2 3. Our teacher asked us **whether/if we would** like to form a pen-club. ◀2 4. I wondered **whether/if** that sweet little cat **was** still **sitting** on the roof. ◀3 5. I wondered **whether/if he would** make it. ◀4 6. I wondered **whether/if I should** ever have time to see London. ◀5 7. I wondered **whether/if** any strangers **had been seen** round **there.** ◀1 8. I wondered **whether/if you would** like to come to our house and see the President from our balcony. ◀2 9. The Clerk read the indictment and asked the prisoner **whether/if he was** guilty or not guilty. ◀3 10. He wondered **whether/if they would** ◀2 necessarily inform him if any radio messages **had come** ◀6 about him. 11. She wondered **whether/if she would** ever get married. ◀2 12. He wondered **whether/if** there **was** a microphone **hidden** somewhere near. ◀3 13. Bob wondered **whether/if** Daniel **had had** friends with him at his hotel or wherever he **had been staying.** ◀6 14. He wondered **whether/if** Daniel **had** people **waiting** for him anywhere. ◀1 15. I hesitated with my hand on the door handle, looking back and wondering **whether/if** there **was** ◀3 anything I **had left** undone. ◀6 16. My wife asked me **whether/if I had happened to** see **her** passport lying about. ◀8 17. I wondered **whether/if we regarded** ◀3 the machine not as an adjunct to our powers, but as something to extend our powers, **whether/if we could keep** it controlled. ◀5

18. At the end of every debate the Speaker put the question **whether/if we would accept** ◄4 the motion that **had been debated.** ◄1 19. The Government decided to put to the people the question **whether/if Britain should** remain within the E.E.C. or not. ◄2 20. He wondered **whether/if she took** ◄8 in washing for a living, or **whether/if she had** merely **been** the slave of her grandchildren. ◄7

Erklärungen und Lernhinweise

Der indirekte Fragesatz wird durch **whether** oder **if** eingeleitet, die Anführungszeichen entfallen, das Fragezeichen wird durch Punkt ersetzt.
Die Worstellung wird in die des Aussagesatzes geändert, d.h. das Subjekt steht nicht hinter sondern vor dem Verb, Hilfs- oder Modalverb.
Die Personalpronomen bleiben unverändert, wenn der Sprecher seine eigenen Worte wiedergibt, betrifft die Frage den Angesprochenen, dann stehen die Personalpronomen in der 2. Person, betrifft die Frage eine dritte Person, dann stehen die Personalpronomen in der 3. Person.
Zum besseren Verständnis sind die vorzunehmenden Änderungen in den oben aufgeführten Lösungssätzen fett gedruckt.

►1 Das Verb steht im present perfect, es wird daher ins past perfect gesetzt.

►2 Das Verb ist das Modalverb **could, would** oder **should**, sie werden daher nicht verändert.

►3 Das Verb steht im present tense, es wird daher ins past tense gesetzt.

►4 Das Verb steht im future tense, es wird daher ins conditional gesetzt.

►5 Das Verb ist das Modalverb **shall** bzw. **can**, sie werden daher in **should** bzw. **could** geändert.

►6 Das Verb steht im past perfect, es wird daher nicht geändert.

►7 Das Verb steht im past tense, es wird daher ins past perfect gesetzt.

►8 Fragesätze werden in indirekter Rede in Aussagesätze umgewandelt, daher entfällt **to do** des direkten Fragesatzes. Es ist zu beachten, dass die Verbform von **to do** die Zeit angibt (z.B.: **did** steht im past tense, daher steht das Verb (nicht mehr **to do**) in der indirekten Rede im past perfect).

2 Setzen Sie die folgenden Fragesätze mit Fragewort in die indirekte Rede.

1. I wondered **why Mike hadn't turned** up yet. ◄1 2. I wondered **how often the old lady left** her house. ◄2 3. I wondered **why he didn't come.** ◄3 4. I wondered **what Gerald and Caroline were doing.** ◄4 5. I wondered **whose dog this was.** ◄4 6. He wondered **what they had done** to the woman in the yard. ◄5 7. The king wondered **what he might give** the queen for her birthday. ◄6 8. They asked **what people had done** ◄2 with their leisure before there **had been** television. ◄7 9. Now that he has been in America for three years, I asked him **what his first impression had been.** ◄7 10. The theft once again raised the question **what happened** to stolen paintings. ◄4 11. Much had been written on the question **how a teacher should** try to gain the positive interest of unco-operative pupils. ◄6 12. She stood before him very upright as though she was wondering **why he had been** so slow to act. ◄7 13. The police were going to wonder **where the hell he went to.** ◄2 14. As he was curiously watching a gang of workmen putting in long pipes, he began to wonder **what this was** all about. ◄4 15. I wondered **why he had had** that idea. ◄2 16. I do not know how long I waited and I rather wondered **what I could** possibly have looked like. ◄6 17. I was always asking him **how he spent**

his time. ◄2 18. Daniel wondered **what the Germans and Dutch would think** ◄8 if they **saw** ◄4 his father sailing his boat down their busy canals. 19. If you asked them **what they did** ◄2 for a living, they said **that they worked** for standard. ◄4

Erklärungen und Lernhinweise

Direkte Fragesätze mit Fragewort werden in indirekter Rede durch dieses Fragewort eingeleitet und mit Punkt (nicht mit Fragezeichen) abgeschlossen. Die Anführungszeichen entfallen.
Die Worstellung wird in die des Aussagesatzes geändert, d.h. das Subjekt steht nicht hinter sondern vor dem Verb, Hilfs- oder Modalverb.
Die Personalpronomen bleiben unverändert, wenn der Sprecher seine eigenen Worte wiedergibt, betrifft die Frage den Angesprochenen, dann stehen die Personalpronomen in der 2. Person, betrifft die Frage eine dritte Person, dann stehen die Personalpronomen in der 3. Person.
Zum besseren Verständnis sind die vorzunehmenden Änderungen in den oben aufgeführten Lösungssätzen fett gedruckt.

▶1 Das Verb steht im present perfect, es wird daher ins past perfect gesetzt.

▶2 Fragesätze werden in indirekter Rede in Aussagesätze umgewandelt, daher entfällt **to do** des direkten Fragesatzes. Es ist zu beachten, dass die Verbform von **to do** die Zeit angibt (z.B.: **does** steht im present tense, daher steht das Verb (nicht mehr **to do**) in der indirekten Rede im past tense).
Dabei sind die Verben, die im past tense die Endung **-d** in **-t** ändern, besonders zu beachten.

▶3 Verneinte Fragesätze werden in indirekter Rede in verneinte Aussagesätze, umgewandelt, d.h. **to do** bleibt erhalten. Es ist zu beachten, dass die Verbform von **to do** die Zeit angibt (z.B.: **doesn't** steht im present tense, daher steht in der indirekten Rede das past tense, **didn't**).

▶4 Das Verb steht im present tense, es wird daher ins past tense gesetzt.

▶5 Das Verb steht im past perfect, es wird daher nicht geändert.

▶6 Das Verb ist das Modalverb **might, should** oder **could**, sie werden daher nicht verändert.

▶7 Das Verb steht im past tense, es wird daher ins past perfect gesetzt.

▶8 Das Verb steht im future tense, es wird daher ins conditional gesetzt.

Die Umwandlung von Befehlen, Aufforderungen

1 Setzen Sie die folgenden Befehle in die indirekte Rede.

1. He said **that I/we/they/he/you should write** neatly. ◄1 2. He proposed **to try** the examination again. ◄2 3. The officer told them **to lower** the flag. ◄2 4. I proposed **to give** me six hundred dollars in traveller's cheques. ◄2 5. They were told **to lie** ◄2 on the grass beside the line and **not to look up** ◄3 at any cost. 6. They told me **to go** to the information desk. ◄2 7. I told them **not to forget** to lock the door. ◄3 8. His wife told him **not to drive** too fast. ◄3 9. His mother told them **not to be** greedy. ◄3 10. My father said **that we should go up** to the restaurant to have a good look at the planes taking off. ◄4 11. People exerted pressure on the state **to take** action to eliminate unhappiness and discomfort. ◄2 12. I told them **not to let** him go just yet. ◄3 13. I proposed **to have** a conversation this evening. ◄2 14. I said **that they should not do** so. ◄5 15. I told him **not to bother** about having failed. ◄3 16. He said **that he shouldn't have said** this. ◄1 17. The judge ordered **the juvenile delinquent to be sent** to a home. ◄6

Erklärungen und Lernhinweise

1 Direkte Befehle werden in indirekter Rede mit Punkt (nicht mit Ausrufezeichen) abgeschlossen. Die Anführungszeichen entfallen.
Die Personalpronomen bleiben unverändert, wenn der Sprecher seine eigenen Worte wiedergibt, betrifft die Frage den Angesprochenen, dann stehen die Personalpronomen in der 2. Person, betrifft die Frage eine dritte Person, dann stehen die Personalpronomen in der 3. Person.
Zum besseren Verständnis sind die vorzunehmenden Änderungen in den oben aufgeführten Lösungssätzen fett gedruckt.

►1 Das einleitende Verb schließt einen Nebensatz mit **that** an (nicht den Infinitiv mit **to**), daher steht **should** + der Infinitiv der direkten Rede. Die Person bzw. die Personen, denen der Befehl erteilt wird, stehen vor **should**.

►2 Das einleitende Verb kann einen Infinitiv anschließen, daher steht **to** + der Infinitiv der direkten Rede.

►3 Der direkte Befehl ist verneint und wird durch ein Verb, das einen Infinitiv anschließen kann eingeleitet, daher steht **not + to** + Infinitiv der direkten Rede, **to do** der direkten Rede entfällt.

►4 Das einleitende Verb schließt einen Nebensatz mit **that** an (nicht den Infinitiv mit **to**), daher steht **should** + der Infinitiv der direkten Rede**. Let's** der direkten Rede entfällt. Die Personen, denen der Befehl erteilt wird, ist **we** und steht vor **should**.

►5 Der direkte Befehl ist verneint und wird durch ein Verb, das einen Nebensatz mit **that** anschließt, eingeleitet, daher steht **should not** + der Infinitiv der direkten Rede, **to do** der direkten Rede entfällt. Die Person bzw. die Personen, denen der Befehl erteilt wird, stehen vor **should**.

►6 Das einleitende Verb kann einen Infinitiv anschließen, daher steht **to** + der Infinitiv der direkten Rede. Subjekt (**the judge**) und Objekt (**the juvenile delinquent**) bezeichnen verschiedene Personen, daher muss das Objekt dem Infinitiv + **to** vorangestellt werden. Der Satz steht im Passiv, daher muss auch der passive infinitive verwendet werden.
Es ist zu beachten, dass **send** zu den Verben gehört, die die Endung **-d** in der 3. Stammform in **-t** ändern.

Die Umwandlung von indirekter Rede in direkte Rede

1 Setzen Sie die folgenden Sätze in die direkte Rede.

1. We thought: <<There **are** very fundamental problems in their family.>> ◄1 2. Some experts believed: << Prices **will** eventually **drop.**>> ◄1 3. He cried: <<**I am going** to save **you.** >> ◄1 4. He suggested: <<**Let's go** up to the restaurant.>> ◄2 5. I told him: <<**Don't be** a fool.>> ◄3 6. He asked: <<**What has gone/went** wrong?>> ◄4 7. They were whispering. I wondered: <<**What are they saying?**>> ◄4 8. He asked him: <<**Have you read/Did you read** a book by a certain Harry Williams?>> ◄5 9. I wondered: <<**Has she been out**, for she **is breathing** hard as though she **has been running.**>> ◄5 10. He said: <<They **make** heavy complaints of ill treatment on the part of the government.>> ◄1 11. He saw himself confronted by a dozen policemen asking him: <<**Where is David Adams?**>> ◄4 12. I thought: <<Swift motion across a countryside **does not** necessarily take away all appreciation of its charm.>> ◄1 13. We believed: <<In some marriages the roles **should** be reversed, with the wife as breadwinner and the husband as household manager.>> ◄6 14. Some critics argued: <<Parliament **could/can contribute** to the processes of government and administration more effectively if it **strengthened/strengthens** its system of

'select committees'.>> ◀7 15. Egypt demanded**:** <<Britain **should withdraw** its forces, and the Sudan **should be incorporated** in Egypt.>> ◀8

Erklärungen und Lernhinweise

▶1 Der Satz ist ein Aussagesatz, er wird daher durch Doppelpunkt eingeleitet, durch Punkt abgeschlossen und in Anführungszeichen gesetzt. Das einleitende **that** der indirekten Rede entfällt. Das Verb steht im past tense bzw. conditional, es wird daher ins present tense bzw. future tense gesetzt.

▶2 Der Satz ist ein Befehlssatz, er wird daher durch Doppelpunkt eingeleitet, durch Punkt abgeschlossen und in Anführungszeichen gesetzt. Das einleitende Verb drückt einen Vorschlag aus, es wird daher **let's** + der Infinitiv der indirekten Rede verwendet. **Should** und das einleitende **that** der indirekten Rede entfallen.

▶3 Der Befehlssatz ist verneint, es wird daher **to do** benötigt, der Infinitiv wird ohne **to** angefügt. Der direkte Befehl wird durch Doppelpunkt eingeleitet, durch Punkt abgeschlossen und in Anführungszeichen gesetzt.

▶4 Der Satz ist ein Fragesatz mit Fragepronomen, der direkte Fragesatz wird daher mit diesem Fragepronomen eingeleitet, durch Fragezeichen abgeschlossen und in Anführungszeichen gesetzt. Das Subjekt tritt im Fragesatz hinter das Verb bzw. Hilfsverb.
Steht das Verb im past tense wird es ins present tense gesetzt. Steht das Verb im past perfect wird es ins present perfect gesetzt, wenn aus dem Zusammenhang eindeutig hervorgeht, dass der Vorgang bis in die Gegenwart reicht, ist der Vorgang völlig abgeschlossen, wird das Verb ins past tense gesetzt.

▶5 Der Satz ist ein Fragesatz ohne Fragepronomen, er ist durch **whether** oder **if** eingeleitet. Im direkten Fragesatz entfällt **whether** bzw. **if**, er wird durch Fragezeichen abgeschlossen und in Anführungszeichen gesetzt.
Das Verb steht im past perfect, es wird daher in past tense wenn aus dem Zusammenhang eindeutig hervorgeht, dass der Vorgang völlig abgeschlossen ist, reicht der Vorgang bis in die Gegenwart wird das Verb ins present perfect gesetzt. Fragesätze ohne Fragewort werden im past tense mit **did** gebildet, wenn das Verb ein Vollverb ist. Es ist zu beachten, dass auf **did** der Infinitiv folgt (also z.B. **did he look** und nicht **did he looked**). Im present perfect ist das Hilfsverb **have** vorhanden, die Frage wird daher nicht mit **to do** sondern mit diesem Hilfsverb gebildet. Das Subjekt tritt im Fragesatz hinter das Verb bzw. Hilfsverb.
Bei **to be** wird **to do** nicht benötigt.

▶6 Der Satz ist ein Aussagesatz, er wird daher durch Doppelpunkt eingeleitet, durch Punkt abgeschlossen und in Anführungszeichen gesetzt. Das einleitende **that** der indirekten Rede entfällt. Das Verb ist das Modalverb **should** und drückt aus, dass etwas wünschenswert ist, es bleibt daher unverändert und wird nicht durch **shall** ersetzt, da **shall** als Modalverb die Vermutung ausdrückt.

▶7 Der Satz ist ein Aussagesatz und zwar ein Bedingungssatz, er drückt aus, was unter bestimmten Voraussetzungen sein könnte (if-clause, type II), die Verben bleiben daher unverändert (also: *das Parlament könnte beitragen...,wenn es das System stärken würde...*).
Zur Beschreibung der Tatsachen, d.h. was eintritt, wenn die Handlung ausgeführt wird (if-clause, type I), können **could** und **strengthened** regelgemäß in **can** und **strengthens** umgewandelt werden. (also: *das Parlament kann beitragen...,wenn es das System stärkt...*).

▶8 Die Verben **withdraw** und **be** stehen im subjunctive (im subjunctive erhält das Verb in der 3. Person Singular z.B. kein -s). Es wird ausgedrückt, was gewünscht bzw. verlangt wird, dies wird in direkter Rede durch das Modalverb **should** ausgedrückt.

Das Konditional (The Conditional)

1 Setzen Sie die Verben in Klammern in die richtige Zeit (Typ I).

1. will/'ll kill ◀1 2. will have ◀1 3. will not/won't take place ◀1 4. will you do ◀1 5. pulls ◀2 6. does not behave ◀2 7. rains ◀2 8. can ◀3 9. has ◀2 10. does not like ◀2 11. will soon be able to ◀1 12. will be ◀1 13. will be ◀1 14. will be ◀1 15. does ◀2 16. can ◀3 17. will have ◀1 18. is ◀2 19. will not answer ◀1 20. will ◀4

Erklärungen und Lernhinweise

▶1 Das Verb im Bedingungssatz steht im present tense, daher steht das Verb im Hauptsatz im future tense. Es ist zu beachten, dass auf **will** der Infinitiv des Verbs folgt (also z.B.: **will kill** und nicht **will killed**).
Statt **will** kann auch die Kurzform **'ll**, die hier nicht jedesmal aufgeführt ist, verwendet werden. Die verneinte Kurzform von **will** heißt **won't**.

▶2 Das Verb im Hauptsatz steht im future tense, daher steht das Verb im Bedingungssatz im present tense.
Merke: In der Regel kein future tense im Bedingungssatz!

▶3 Das Verb ist ein Modalverb, daher entfällt **will**, da ein Modalverb keine zusammengesetzten Zeiten bilden und somit auch kein future tense bilden kann.

▶4 Das Verb ist **will** selbst, daher entfällt das Hilfsverb **will** des future tense.

2 Setzen Sie die Verben in Klammern in die richtige Zeit (Typ II).

1. left ◀1 2. rang ◀1 3. were ◀1 4. had ◀1 5. did not mention ◀1 6. would/'d come ◀2 7. would be ◀2 8. would be ◀2 9. stung ◀1 10. could ◀1 11. stayed ◀1 12. would be ◀2 13. would have to leave ◀3 14. did not have to ◀1 15. were ◀4 16. were ◀4 17. were attacked ◀4 18. were to ◀1 19. were not given ◀1 20. would not be used ◀2 21. would he be likely to ◀2

Erklärungen und Lernhinweise

▶1 Das Verb im Hauptsatz steht im conditional I, daher steht das Verb im Bedingungssatz im past tense.
Merke: In der Regel kein conditional im Bedingungssatz!

▶2 Das Verb im Bedingungssatz steht im past tense, daher steht das Verb im Hauptsatz im conditional I. Es ist zu beachten, dass auf **would** der Infinitiv des Verbs folgt (also z.B.: **would help** und nicht **would helped**).
Statt **would** kann auch die Kurzform **'d**, die hier nicht jedesmal aufgeführt ist, verwendet werden.

▶3 Das Verb ist das Ersatzverb **have to** (müssen), das ja zusammengesetzte Zeiten und somit auch das conditional bilden kann.

▶4 In der 1. und 3. Person Singular steht in Bedingungssätzen **were** statt **was**.

3 Setzen Sie die Verben in Klammern in die richtige Zeit (Typ III).

1. would have run away or caught ◀1 2. would not have gone back ◀1 3. would not have got ◀1 4. had not tried ◀2 5. had not carried ◀2 6. had not hit ◀2 7. had not held ◀2 8. would Mr Palmer have taken ◀1 9. Would it not have been/wouldn't it have been ◀1 10. would have been ◀1 11. would have had ◀1 12. would have died out ◀1 13. would have had ◀1 14. had bought ◀2 15. had been ◀2 16. could have moved ◀2 17. had been possible ◀2 18. would have been ◀1 19. would have had ◀1 20. would have been taken ◀1 21. would he have said ◀1 22. would most inevitably have been killed ◀1 23. had not happened ◀2

Erklärungen und Lernhinweise

▶1 Das Verb im Bedingungssatz steht im past perfect, daher steht das Verb im Hauptsatz im conditional perfect.
Statt **would** kann auch die Kurzform **'d**, die hier nicht jedesmal aufgeführt ist, verwendet werden.

▶2 Das Verb im Hauptsatz steht im conditional perfect, daher steht das Verb im Bedingungssatz im past perfect.
Merke: In der Regel kein conditional im Bedingungssatz!

4 Bilden Sie drei Sätze und verwenden Sie die Zeiten von Typ 1 - 3.

1. **Will you help, need**; Hilfst du mir/wirst du mir helfen, wenn ich dich brauche?◀1 **Would you help, needed**; Würdest du mir helfen, wenn ich dich bräuchte?◀2 **Would you have helped, had needed**; Hättest du mir geholfen, wenn ich dich gebraucht hätte?◀3
2. **will not be enough, goes**; Es wird nicht genug Sauerstoff zum Atmen geben, wenn die gegenwärtige Entwicklung so weiter geht.◀1 **would not be enough, went**; Es würde nicht genug Sauerstoff zum Atmen geben, wenn die gegenwärtige Entwicklung so weiter ginge.◀2 **would not have been enough, had gone**; Es hätte nicht genug Sauerstoff zum Atmen gegeben, wenn die gegenwärtige Entwicklung so weiter gegangen wäre.◀3
3. **will catch, take**; Du wirst den Zug erreichen/du erreichst den Zug, wenn du ein Taxi nimmst.◀1 **would catch, took**; Du würdest den Zug erreichen, wenn du ein Taxi nehmen würdest.◀2 **would have caught, had taken**; Du hättest den Zug erreicht, wenn du ein Taxi genommen hättest◀3
4. **does not calm down, will faint**; Wenn sie sich nicht beruhigt, wird sie ohnmächtig.◀1 **did not calm down, would faint**; Wenn sie sich nicht beruhigen würde, würde sie ohnmächtig.◀2 **had not calmed down, would have fainted**: wenn sie sich nicht beruhigt hätte, wäre sie ohnmächtig geworden.◀3
5. **lose, will ask**; wenn ich mich in London verirre, frage ich einen Polizisten,◀1 **lost, would ask**; wenn ich mich in London verirren würde, würde ich einen Polizisten fragen,◀2 **had lost, would have asked**; wenn ich mich in London verirrt hätte, hätte ich einen Polizisten gefragt.◀3
6. **will pay, agrees**; Bob bezahlt die Hotelrechnung, wenn Simon zustimmt über Nacht zu bleiben,◀1 **would pay, agreed**; Bob würde die Hotelrechnung bezahlen, wenn Simon zustimmen würde über Nacht zu bleiben ◀2 **would have paid, had agreed**; Bob hätte die Hotelrechnung bezahlt, wenn Simon zugestimmt hätte über Nacht zu bleiben ◀3

7. **runs away, will get away**; wenn sie wegläuft, werden die Einbrecher mit den Sachen entkommen, **ran away, would get away**; wenn sie weglaufen würde, würden die Einbrecher mit den Sachen entkommen, **had run away, would have got away**; wenn sie weggelaufen wäre, wären die Einbrecher mit den Sachen entkommen.
8. **will come, ring**; er kommt/wird kommen, wenn du anrufst, **would come, rang**; er würde kommen, wenn du anrufen würdest, **would have come, had rung**; er wäre gekommen, wenn du angerufen hättest.
9. **intervene, will be better equipped**; wir können uns mit dem Gedanken trösten, dass, wenn ein Krieg oder eine Umweltkatastrophe über uns hereinbricht, wir besser ausgerüstet sind, sie zu überleben, **intervened, would be better equipped**; wir können uns mit dem Gedanken trösten, dass, wenn ein Krieg oder eine Umweltkatastrophe über uns hereinbrechen würde, wir besser ausgerüstet wären, sie zu überleben, **had intervened, would have been better equipped**; wir können uns mit dem Gedanken trösten, dass, wenn ein Krieg oder eine Umweltkatastrophe über uns hereingebrochen wäre, wir besser ausgerüstet gewesen wären, sie zu überleben.
10. **is invented, will become**; wenn ein sauberer Motor erfunden wird, wird die Luftverschmutzung weniger gefährlich, **was invented, would become**; wenn ein sauberer Motor erfunden würde, wäre die Luftverschmutzung weniger gefährlich, **had been invented, would have become**; wenn ein sauberer Motor erfunden worden wäre, wäre die Luftverschmutzung weniger gefährlich gewesen.
11. **will you do, lend**; was wirst du tun/tust du, wenn ich dir mein Fahrrad leihe, **would you do, lent**; was würdest du tun, wenn ich dir mein Fahrrad leihen würde, **would you have done; had lent**; was hättest du getan, wenn ich dir mein Fahrrad geliehen hätte
12. **can, like**; du kannst Pamela fragen, wenn du willst, **could, liked**; du könntest Pamela fragen, wenn du wolltest, **could have, had liked**; du hättest Pamela fragen können, wenn du gewollt hättest
13. **have, will be able**; wenn sie eine Expertenkommission haben, können sie wahrscheinlich sagen, dass drei Unterschriften Fälschungen waren, **had, would be able**; wenn sie eine Expertenkommission hätten, könnten sie wahrscheinlich sagen, dass drei Unterschriften Fälschungen waren, **had had, would have been able**; wenn sie eine Expertenkommission gehabt hätten, hätten sie wahrscheinlich sagen können, dass drei Unterschriften Fälschungen waren.
14. **discover, will have**; wenn sie herausfinden, dass das Testament eine Fälschung ist, haben sie kein Erbarmen mit ihm, **discovered, would have**; wenn sie herausfinden würden, dass das Testament eine Fälschung ist, hätten sie kein Erbarmen mit ihm, **had discovered, would have had**; wenn sie herausgefunden hätten, dass das Testament eine Fälschung ist, hätten sie kein Erbarmen mit ihm gehabt.
15. **will it be, just sits down**; wie viel besser ist es, wenn er sich einfach in eines der Cafés unten am Strand setzt, **would it be, just sat down**; wie viel besser wäre es, wenn er sich einfach in eines der Cafés unten am Strand setzen würde, **would it have been, just had sat down**; wie viel besser wäre es gewesen, wenn er sich einfach in eines der Cafés unten am Strand gesetzt hätte.
16. **read, will understand**; wenn sie das Kleingedruckte lesen, verstehen sie den Unterschied/ werden sie den Unterschied verstehen, **read, would understand**; wenn sie das Kleingedruckte lesen würden, würden sie den Unterschied verstehen, **had read, would have understood;** wenn sie das Kleingedruckte gelesen hätten, hätten sie den Unterschied verstanden.

17. **is, will be paid**; wenn weder eine Versetzung noch eine Umschulung möglich ist, erhalten die Arbeiter, die eine Arbeit mit geringerem Ansehen und geringerer Bezahlung akzeptieren eine Ausgleichszahlung,◀1 **was, would be paid**; wenn weder eine Versetzung noch eine Umschulung möglich wäre, würden die Arbeiter, die eine Arbeit mit geringerem Ansehen und geringerer Bezahlung akzeptieren eine Ausgleichszahlung erhalten,◀2 **had been, would have been paid**; wenn weder eine Versetzung noch eine Umschulung möglich gewesen wäre, hätten die Arbeiter, die eine Arbeit mit geringerem Ansehen und geringerer Bezahlung akzeptieren eine Ausgleichszahlung erhalten.◀3
18. **is built, will hinder**; wenn eine Pipeline oberirdisch gebaut wird, verhindert dies die Wanderung von Tieren, die normalerweise den geplanten Verlauf kreuzen,◀4 **was built, would hinder**; wenn eine Pipeline oberirdisch gebaut würde, würde dies die Wanderung von Tieren, die normalerweise den geplanten Verlauf kreuzen, verhindern,◀4 **had been built, would have hindered**; wenn eine Pipeline oberirdisch gebaut worden wäre, hätte dies die Wanderung von Tieren, die normalerweise den geplanten Verlauf kreuzen, verhindert.◀4

Erklärungen und Lernhinweise

▶1 Die Bedingung ist erfüllbar, die Handlung wird ausgeführt, daher steht im Bedingungssatz present tense und im Hauptsatz future tense (type I). Dies wird durch die gegebene Übersetzung deutlich.

▶2 Die Bedingung wäre erfüllbar, wenn die Handlung ausgeführt würde, was nicht sicher oder bekannt ist, daher steht im Bedingungssatz past tense und im Hauptsatz conditional I (type II). Dies wird durch die gegebene Übersetzung deutlich.

▶3 Die Bedingung wäre erfüllbar gewesen, wenn die Handlung ausgeführt worden wäre, was nicht der Fall ist, daher steht im Bedingungssatz past perfect und im Hauptsatz conditional perfect (type III). Dies wird durch die gegebene Übersetzung deutlich.

▶4 **Lend** und **build** gehören zu den Verben, die in der 2. und 3. Stammform die Endung **-d** in **-t** ändern. Inhaltlich gelten die Bestimmungen von Typ 1 - 3.

5 Setzen Sie die Verben in Klammern in die richtige Zeit und verwenden Sie Typ 1 oder 2 oder 3.

1. rains, will be ◀1/rained, would be ◀2 2. will be, don't cease ◀1/ would be, didn't cease ◀2/ would have been, had not ceased ◀3 3. would like, could be cared for ◀2 4. would you choose, were ◀2 5. had not gone back, would not have caught ◀3 6. had known, would never have taken ◀3 7. will be exhausted, are preserved ◀1/would be exhausted, were preserved ◀2 8. continue, will add ◀1 9. were, would build ◀4 10. would not have escaped, had not come ◀3 11. is to recover, will have to be ◀1 12. is given, will have ◀1

Erklärungen und Lernhinweise

▶1 Die Bedingung ist erfüllbar, die Handlung wird ausgeführt, daher steht das present tense im if-Satz und das future tense im Hauptsatz.

▶2 Die Bedingung wäre erfüllbar, wenn die Handlung ausgeführt würde, was nicht sicher oder bekannt ist, daher steht das past tense im if-Satz und das conditional im Hauptsatz.

▶3 Die Bedingung wäre erfüllbar gewesen, wenn die Handlung ausgeführt worden wäre, was nicht der Fall ist, daher steht das past perfect im if-Satz und das conditional perfect im Hauptsatz.

▶4 In der 1. und 3. Person Singular steht in Bedingungssätzen im past tense **were** statt **was**.

Der Infinitiv (The Infinitive)

Der Present Infinitive Active

1 Setzen Sie **to** ein wo nötig.

1. to ◀1 2. - ◀2 3. - ◀3 4. - ◀3 5. - ◀4 6. - ◀4 7. - ◀4 8. to ◀1 9. - ◀2 10. - ◀3 11. - ◀3 12. - ◀4 13. to ◀5 14. - ◀4 15. - ◀4 16. to ◀1 17. - ◀2, to ◀6 18. - ◀3 19. -, - ◀3 20. - ◀3 21. to ◀5 22. - ◀4

Erklärungen und Lernhinweise

▶1 **To make** steht im Passiv, daher wird der Infinitiv mit **to** angeschlossen.

▶2 **To make** steht im Aktiv, daher wird der Infinitiv nicht mit **to** angeschlossen.

▶3 **To let, to have** (veranlassen), **had better** stehen immer mit dem Infinitiv ohne **to**.

▶4 Das Verb ist ein Verb der Sinneswahrnehmung und es steht im Aktiv, daher steht der Infinitiv ohne **to**.

▶5 Das Verb ist ein Verb der Sinneswahrnehmung und es steht im Passiv, daher steht der Infinitiv mit **to**.

▶6 Nach **not** steht der Infinitiv mit **to**.

2 Ersetzen Sie die fett gedruckten Sätze durch eine Infinitivkonstruktion und formulieren Sie die Sätze neu.

1. I want **you to say** something. ◀1 2. Would you like **me to help** you. ◀2 3. Peter wanted **you to go home** now. ◀1 4. He wanted **me to leave** in the morning. ◀1 5. We consider **it to go** over 13%. ◀2 6. People think **Mr Templeton to be** a very cautious man all his life. ◀2 7. I should hate **you to ask** him a favour. ◀2 8. Not for an instant did he believe **Daniel to speak** the truth. ◀2 9. The natives of these islands **are said to be** cannibals. ◀3 10. She **was believed to lie**. ◀3 11. We **were supposed to stand** to attention ◀3 12. He considered **himself to have been** lucky beyond reason. ◀4

Erklärungen und Lernhinweise

▶1 **To want** steht immer mit dem Infinitiv + **to** und einem vorausgehenden Objekt (z.B. **you**), es kann keinen Nebensatz mit **that** anschließen.

▶2 Das Subjekt des that-Satzes (z.B. **I**) wird zum Objekt (z.B. **me**), das Verb des that-Satzes wird, und dies ist zu beachten, im Infinitiv mit **to** angeschlossen, **that** entfällt.

▶3 Das Subjekt des that-Satzes (z.B. **she**) wird zum Subjekt des Passivsatzes, die Verbform des Hauptsatzes (z.B. **believed**) wird in die entsprechende Verbform ins Passiv gesetzt (d.h. steht das Verb z.B. im past tense wird im Passiv ebenfalls das past tense verwendet). Das Verb des that-Satzes wird im Infinitiv + **to** angeschlossen. Im Deutschen werden solche Konstruktionen oft mit *man* übersetzt (z.B.: *man glaubte, dass sie log*).

▶4 Das Subjekt des that-Satzes bezeichnet dieselbe Person wie das Subjekt des Hauptsatzes, daher wird hier das Reflexivpronomen verwendet. Der perfect infinitive wird verwendet, da es sich hier, wie das past perfect zeigt, um einen vergangenen Vorgang handelt.

3 Ersetzen Sie die folgenden Sätze durch einen und formulieren Sie die Sätze mit einer Infinitivkonstruktion neu.

1. The suitcase is too heavy **(for me) to carry**. ◀1 2. The coffee is too hot **(for me) to drink**. ◀1 3. He was quick **to follow** their advice. ◀1 4. I think you were right **to tell** us. ◀1 5. You are very kind **not to say** that. ◀2 6. She was naughty **to pull** the kitten's tail. ◀1 7. The opportunity was too favourable **(for us) to miss**. ◀1 8. He is sure **to succeed**. ◀1 9. He racked his brain **for something sensible to say**. ◀1

Erklärungen und Lernhinweise

▶1 Das Verb des zweiten Satzes wird an das Adjektiv des ersten Satzes mit **to** angeschlossen. Das Verb steht dann im Infinitiv. Das Subjekt des zweiten Satzes kann als Objekt + **for** hinzugefügt werden.

▶2 Das Verb des zweiten Satzes ist verneint, es wird daher durch **not + to** + Infinitiv des Verbs ersetzt.

4 Ersetzen Sie die fett gedruckten Nebensätze durch eine Infinitivkonstruktion und formulieren Sie die Sätze neu.

1. She bought a small camera **to take snapshots with**. ◀1 2. He hasn't got a chair **to sit on**. ◀1 3. There's a table **to write on**. ◀1 4. This is a depressing message **to send to you** and I regret it. ◀1 5. Apparently Mrs Miller was the first **to discover the broken window**. ◀1 6. There was no broom **to sweep with**. ◀1 7. I don't know **who to speak to**. ◀1 8. He was the very last **to leave the office**. ◀1 9. Peter was **the next to arrive** at the bottom of the hill. ◀1 10. Peter was the only one **to return** to the hotel. ◀1 11. It was the best thing **to do**. ◀1 12. She didn't really mind having no friend **to play with**. ◀1 13. He is not an easy man **to get along with**. ◀1 14. You think that it's the easiest way **to get rid of us** if you give us what we want. ◀1 15. In New York I have nine channels **to choose from**, and most times I can find nothing. ◀1 16. Carol was the most likely person **to come to** Rome. ◀1 17. In 1964, the millionth guestworker **to enter** the country was given an honorary welcome before the press. ◀1 18. For most women without young children **to look after**, life at home and shopping are unsatisfying. ◀1 19. To the American, who has to travel five days and four nights by railroad to get across the continent, a few hundred miles are just no impediment **to speak of**. ◀1 20. He would have been the first **to resent** the imputation that he was a snob. ◀1

Erklärungen und Lernhinweise

▶1 Der Nebensatz ist ein Relativsatz (er wird eingeleitet durch Relativpronomen wie **which, who, that** etc.), er wird ersetzt durch das Hauptverb des Relativsatzes (z.B. **take**), das im Infinitiv + **to** angeschlossen wird, das Objekt des Relativsatzes (z.B. **snapshots**) wird hinzugefügt. Präpositionen, mit denen der Nebensatz eingeleitet wird, müssen erhalten bleiben, sie stehen nach dem Infinitiv.

5 Ersetzen Sie die fett gedruckten indirekten Fragesätze durch eine Infinitivkonstruktion und formulieren Sie die Sätze neu.

1. Without TV people would not know **what to do** in their spare time. ◀1 2. Peter and Mike could not make up their minds **where to go** for a holiday. ◀1 3. I have so many questions to ask that I don't know **where to start**.◀1 4. Charles halted, stood for several seconds wondering vaguely **what to do**, then turned round and began to retrace his steps. ◀1

Erklärungen und Lernhinweise

▶1 Der Nebensatz ist ein indirekter Fragesatz und wird durch ein Fragewort wie **what, where** etc. eingeleitet. Er wird ersetzt durch das Hauptverb des Nebensatzes, das im Infinitiv + **to** angeschlossen wird.

Der Present Infinitive Passive

1 Setzen Sie die Verben in Klammern in den present infinitive passive.

1. to be handled ◀1 2. to be kept ◀1 3. to be impressed ◀1 4. to be divided ◀1 5. to be trusted ◀1 6. to be seen ◀1 7. to be put off ◀1 8. to be taken account of ◀1 9. to be doubted ◀1 10. to be called ◀1 11. to be given ◀1 12. to be seen ◀1 13. to be settled ◀1 14. to be sent ◀2 15. to be settled ◀1 16. to be seen ◀1 17. to be persuaded ◀1 18. to be killed ◀1 19. to be studied ◀1 20. to be pulled ◀1 21. to be taught, to be carried out ◀1 22. to be considered ◀1 23. to be married to ◀1

Erklärungen und Lernhinweise

▶1 Der present infinitive active wird aus **to be** + 3. Stammform des Verbs gebildet. Dabei sind die Besonderheiten bei der Bildung der 3. Stammform zu beachten (z.B. **-y** kann sich beim Anhängen von **-ed** in **-ie** ändern etc.).

▶2 **Send** gehört zu den Verben, die in der 2. und 3. Stammform die Endung **-d** in **-t** ändern.

2 Setzen Sie den present infinitive active oder den present infinitive passive ein.

1. to be disturbed ◀1 2. to have ◀2 3. to notice ◀2 4. to make ◀2 5. to be found ◀1 6. to be watered ◀1 7. to come ◀2 8. to be blamed ◀1 9. to get ◀2 10. to go ◀2 11. to be addressed ◀1 12. to suspect ◀2 13. to be built up ◀3, to be exploited ◀1 14. to be turned ◀1 15. to live ◀2 16. dismiss ◀4 17. to lose ◀2 18. to be asked ◀1 19. to collect ◀2 20. to be sung ◀1

Erklärungen und Lernhinweise

▶1 Es wird nicht erwähnt, wer die Handlung ausführt, daher steht der passive infinitive (z.B.: in **he didn't want to be disturbed** wird nicht gesagt wer stört).

▶2 Die Person, die die Handlung ausführt, wird genannt, daher steht der active infinitive (z.B.: in **I propose to have a conversation with you** ist "I" die Person, die die Handlung ausführt).

▶3 **Build** gehört zu den Verben, die in der 2. und 3. Stammform die Endung **-d** in **-t** ändern. Es wird der passive infinitive verwendet, da der Ausführende der Handlung nicht genannt wird.

Erklärungen und Lernhinweise

Nach **had better** steht der Infinitiv ohne **to**. Es steht der active infinitive, da der Ausführende der Handlung genannt ist (**you**).

Der Perfect Infinitive Active

1 Setzen Sie die Verben in Klammern in den perfect infinitive active.

1. to have crossed 2. to have got 3. to have known 4. to have left 5. to have lost 6. To have made 7. to have seen 8. to have done 9. to have lost 10. to have gone 11. to have heard 12. to have done 13. to have lost 14. to have met 15. to have passed 16. to have rejoiced 17. to have risen

Erklärungen und Lernhinweise

Der perfect infinitive active wird aus **to have** + 3. Stammform des Verbs gebildet. Dabei sind die Besonderheiten bei der Bildung der 3. Stammform zu beachten (z.B. Endung **-e** entfällt beim Anhängen von **-ed** etc.).

Der Perfect Infinitive Passive

1 Setzen Sie die Verben in Klammern in den perfect infinitive passive.

1. to have been deprived 2. to have been disarranged 3. To have been educated 4. to have been founded 5. to have been served

Erklärungen und Lernhinweise

Der perfect infinitive passive wird aus **to have been** + 3. Stammform des Verbs gebildet. Dabei sind die Besonderheiten bei der Bildung der 3. Stammform zu beachten (z.B. Endung **-e** entfällt beim Anhängen von **-ed** etc.).

Found (gründen) wird regelmäßig durch Anhängen von **-ed** gebildet und ist nicht zu verwechseln mit der 2. bzw. 3. Stammform von **find** (finden).

2 Setzen Sie die Verben in Klammern sowohl in den present infinitive active als auch in den perfect infinitive active und übersetzen Sie jeden Satz.

1. **to change;** Eltern scheinen sich nicht sehr zu ändern, **to have changed;** Eltern scheinen sich nicht sehr geändert zu haben. 2. **to displease**; ich bedaure, Sie zu kränken, mein Herr, **to have displeased**; ich bedaure, Sie gekränkt zu haben, mein Herr. 3. **to grow**; die Sonne schien heißer zu werden, **to have grown**; die Sonne schien heißer geworden zu sein. 4. **to keep**; Ich bedaure, Sie warten zu lassen, **to have kept**; ich bedaure, Sie warten gelassen zu haben. 5. **to lose**; Wir scheinen etwas zu verlieren, **to have lost**; wir scheinen et-

was verloren zu haben. ❷ 6. **to say**; sie sollte das nicht sagen, ❶ **to have said**; sie hätte das nicht sagen sollen. ❷ 7. **to see;** ich würde es gern sehen, ❶ **to have seen**; ich hätte es gern gesehen. ❷ 8. **to trust**; wir sollten ihm vertrauen, ❶ **to have trusted**; wir hätten ihm vertrauen sollen. ❷ 9. **to understand**; ich gab vor sie nicht zu verstehen, ❶ **to have understood**; ich gab vor, sie nicht verstanden zu haben. ❷ 10. **to commit**; man nimmt an, dass sie das Verbrechen begehen, ❶ **to have committed**; man nimmt an, dass sie das Verbrechen begangen haben. ❷ 11. **to do**; sie scheinen die Arbeit ziemlich gut zu machen, ❶ **to have done**; sie scheinen die Arbeit ziemlich gut gemacht zu haben. ❷ 12. **to make**; Scotland Yard scheint noch wenig Fortschritte zu machen ... ❶ **to have made**; Scotland Yard scheint noch wenig Forschritte gemacht zu haben... ❷

Erklärungen und Lernhinweise

1. Der Vorgang bezieht sich auf die Gegenwart, daher steht der present infinitive. Häufig kann in einem Satz sowohl der present als auch der perfect infinitive verwendet werden, je nachdem, ob man sich auf die Gegenwart oder auf die Vergangenheit bezieht.

2. Der Vorgang bezieht sich auf die Vergangenheit, daher steht der perfect infinitive. Zu beachten sind die Besonderheiten bei der Bildung der 3. Stammform (z.B. Endung **-e** entfällt beim Anhängen von **-ed** etc.).
Häufig kann in einem Satz sowohl der present als auch der perfect infinitive verwendet werden, je nachdem, ob man sich auf die Gegenwart oder auf die Vergangenheit bezieht.

Das Gerund (The Gerund)

Das Present Gerund Active

1 Setzen Sie die Verben in Klammern ins gerund.

1. going ◀1 2. doing ◀1 3. laughing ◀1 4. washing up ◀1 5. travelling ◀2, flying ◀3 6. going ◀1 7. being ◀1 8. asking ◀1 9. seeing ◀1 10. laughing ◀1 11. seeing ◀1 12. increasing ◀4 13. spending ◀1 14. polishing ◀1 15. staring ◀4

Erklärungen und Lernhinweise

Das gerund ist ein Verb, das auf **-ing** endet. Es ist nicht zu verwechseln mit der continuous form, die ebenfalls auf **-ing** endet. Vor der continuous form steht immer ein Hilfsverb (z.B. ***are* going, *have been* going** etc.).

▶1 Das Verb bildet das gerund regelmäßig, d.h. die Endung **-ing** wird am Verbende angehängt.

▶2 Verben auf **-l**, verdoppeln dieses beim Anhängen von **-ing.**

▶3 Verben auf **-y** erhalten dieses beim Anhängen von **-ing** (es wird nicht in **-ie** geändert).

▶4 Verben auf **-e** verlieren dieses beim Anhängen von **-ing.**

2 Setzen Sie die folgenden Substantive, die gerunds sind, in den entsprechenden Satz.

1. beginning 2. building 3. crossing 4. dinging-room 5. feeling 6. meaning, meaning 7. meeting 8. shopping 9. being 10. blessing 11. freezing point, drinking water 12. driving test 13. living 14. opening 15. planning 16. saying 17. landing 18. liking 19. training 20. misunderstanding

3 Setzen Sie die Verben in Klammern ins gerund.

1. going ◀1 2. reading ◀1 3. expressing ◀1 4. eating ◀1 5. tossing, catching ◀1 6. trying ◀2 7. jumping ◀1 8. breaking ◀1 9. getting ◀3 10. reading ◀1 11. being ◀1 12. getting ◀3 13. entering ◀4 14. settling ◀5 15. propelling ◀3 16. convincing ◀5 17. working, working ◀1 18. being ◀1 19. being ◀1, solving ◀5 20. saying ◀2 21. driving ◀5, reading ◀1 22. caving ◀5 23. learning ◀1

Erklärungen und Lernhinweise

Das gerund steht nach Präpositionen, die mit Substantiven, Verben oder Adjektiven verbunden sind.

▶1 Das Verb bildet das gerund regelmäßig, d.h. die Endung **-ing** wird am Verbende angehängt.

▶2 Verben auf **-y** erhalten dieses beim Anhängen von **-ing** (es wird nicht in **-ie** geändert).

▶3 Das Verb endet auf Konsonant, dem ein kurzer, betonter Vokal vorausgeht, daher verdoppelt sich der Endkonsonant beim Anhängen von **-ing**. Der betonte Vokal ist unterstrichen.

Erklärungen und Lernhinweise

▶4 Das Verb endet auf Konsonant, dem ein unbetonter Vokal vorausgeht, daher verdoppelt sich der Endkonsonant beim Anhängen von **-ing** nicht. Der betonte Vokal ist unterstrichen.

▶5 Verben auf **-e** verlieren dieses beim Anhängen von **-ing.**

4 Ersetzen Sie die folgenden fett gedruckten Sätze unter Verwendung des gerunds und schreiben Sie die Sätze neu.

1. After defeating the Norwegians at Stamford Bridge ◀1 2. before going to court ◀1 3. In spite of feeling bad ◀2 4. before replying ◀1 5. from sitting in the sun ◀3 6. In spite of having a cold ◀2 7. In spite of trusting you ◀2 8. for stealing ◀3 9. for being disobedient ◀3 10. instead of standing there criticising ◀4 11. without making friends again ◀4 12. when instead of turning green (they) went out ◀4 13. Since finishing college ◀1 14. without meeting anybody ◀4 15. without appearing to do so ◀4

Erklärungen und Lernhinweise

▶1 Der Nebensatz gibt die Zeit an, er wird daher durch **after** oder **before +** gerund, das aus dem Verb des Nebensatzes gebildet wird, ersetzt. Das Subjekt des Nebensatzes entfällt.

▶2 Der Nebensatz, drückt eine Einräumung aus, er wird daher durch **in spite of** + gerund, das aus dem Verb des Nebensatzes gebildet wird, ersetzt. Das Subjekt des Nebensatzes entfällt.

▶3 Der Nebensatz gibt den Grund an, er wird daher durch **from** oder **for** + gerund, das aus dem Verb des Nebensatzes gebildet wird, ersetzt. Das Subjekt des Nebensatzes entfällt.

▶4 Der Nebensatz gibt die Art und Weise, den Umstand an, er wird daher durch **instead of** oder **without** + gerund, das aus dem Verb des Nebensatzes gebildet wird, ersetzt. Das Subjekt des Nebensatzes entfällt.

5 Verwenden Sie das gerund oder den Infinitiv oder beide.

1. began **knitting/to knit** ◀1 2. started **learning/to learn** ◀1 3. hate **interfering/to interfere** ◀1 4. like **working/to work** ◀1 5. prefer **staying/to stay** ◀1 6. proposed **leaving/to leave** ◀1 7. remember **to post** ◀2 8. remembered **going** ◀3 9. want me **to say** ◀4 10. didn't mind **climbing** ◀5 11. couldn't help **crying** ◀5 12. continued **reading/to read** ◀1 13. prefer **watching, attending** ◀5 14. want **watering** ◀5 15. stopped **asking** ◀3 16. stopped **to rest** ◀2 17. It's no use **objecting** ◀5

Erklärungen und Lernhinweise

▶1 Das Verb kann sowohl mit dem gerund als auch mit dem Infinitiv stehen.

▶2 **Remember** und **stop** stehen hier in der übertragenen Bedeutung *nicht vergessen* und *anhalten,* daher steht der Infinitiv.

▶3 **Remember** und **stop** stehen hier in ihrer Grundbedeutung *sich erinnern* und *aufhören,* daher steht das gerund.

Erklärungen und Lernhinweise

▶4 Das Verb verlangt stets den Infinitiv.

▶5 Das Verb verlangt stets das gerund.

6 Setzen Sie die Verben in Klammern ins gerund und die Personalpronomen in den Objektfall oder verwenden Sie das entsprechende Possessivpronomen.

1. you/your coming ◀1 2. me/my eating ◀1 3. you/your going ◀1 4. me/my leaving ◀1 5. her friend reading ◀1 6. you/your returning ◀1 7. her mother being ◀1 8. you/your coming ◀1 9. you/your interrupting ◀1 10. him/his posting ◀1 11. you/your smoking ◀1 12. you/your being ◀1 13. you/your having ◀1 14. you/your knowing ◀1 15. him/his leaving ◀1 16. them/their supporting ◀1 17. you/your talking ◀1

Erklärungen und Lernhinweise

▶1 Das Subjekt des Hauptsatzes (z.B.: **I**) bezeichnet eine andere Person, als das mit dem gerund verbundene (z.B. **you**). Dieses wird daher dem gerund als attributives Possessivpronomen, als Personalpronomen (im Objektfall) oder als Substantiv, wenn kein Pronomen vorhanden ist, vorangestellt (Subjekt des gerunds). Das Personalpronomen ist zur besseren Unterscheidung hier zuerst genannt.
Im Deutschen wird diese Konstruktion meist mit einem Nebensatz übersetzt (z.B.: *ich kann es nicht ausstehen, wenn du zu spät kommst*).

Das Present Gerund Passive

1 Setzen Sie die Verben in Klammern ins present gerund passive.

1. being fired ◀1 2. being misunderstood ◀1 3. being seen ◀1 4. being stared at ◀1 5. being treated ◀1 6. being discovered ◀1 7. being welcomed ◀1 8. being captured , being recaptured ◀1 9. being followed ◀1 10. being known ◀1 11. being laughed at ◀1 12. being obliged ◀1 13. being told ◀1

Erklärungen und Lernhinweise

▶1 Das present gerund passive wird aus **being** + 3. Stammform des Verbs gebildet. Dabei sind die Besonderheiten bei der Bildung der 3. Stammform zu beachten (z.B. Endung **-e** entfällt beim Anhängen von -**ed** etc.).
Das present gerund active wird häufig nur als gerund bezeichnet, dies ist auch in den Übungen vor dieser Übung der Fall.

2 Verwenden Sie das present gerund active (gerund) oder das present gerund passive.

1. answering ◀1 2. laughing ◀1 3. swimming ◀1 4. being deceived ◀2 5. speaking ◀1 6. being

appointed 7. being chosen, being elected 8. seeing 9. being bound 10. being copied 11. being erased 12. being overheard

Erklärungen und Lernhinweise

- Die Person, die die Handlung ausführt, wird genannt, daher steht das active gerund (z.B.: in **He avoided answering** ist "**he**" die Person, die die Handlung ausführt).
- Die Person, die die Handlung ausführt, wird nicht genannt, daher steht das passive gerund (z.B.: in **he was not a man who would forgive being deceived** wird nicht gesagt wer betrügt).

Das Perfect Gerund Active

1 Setzen Sie die Verben in Klammern ins perfect gerund active.

1. having accepted 2. having done 3. having eaten 4. having left 5. having saved 6. having seen 7. having studied 8. having failed 9. having given up 10. having grown 11. having appointed 12. having done 13. having heard 14. having known 15. having received

Erklärungen und Lernhinweise

- Das perfect gerund active wird aus **having** + 3. Stammform des Verbs gebildet. Dabei sind die Besonderheiten bei der Bildung der 3. Stammform zu beachten (z.B. Endung **-e** entfällt beim Anhängen von -**ed** etc.).

Das Perfect Gerund Passive

1 Setzen Sie die Verben in Klammern ins perfect gerund passive.

1. having been elected 2. having been recognized 3. having been robbed 4. having been told 5. having been sentenced

Erklärungen und Lernhinweise

- Das perfect gerund passive wird aus **having been** + 3. Stammform des Verbs gebildet. Dabei sind die Besonderheiten bei der Bildung der 3. Stammform zu beachten (z.B. Endung **-e** entfällt beim Anhängen von -**ed** etc.).

2 Setzen Sie die Verben in Klammern ins present gerund active oder ins perfect gerund active oder beides.

1. **troubling**; ich bedaure, Sie zu stören **having troubled**; ich bedaure, Sie gestört zu haben
2. **reading** /**having read**; bitte geben Sie den beigefügten Brief zurück, nachdem Sie ihn gelesen haben.

3. **having seen** [2]; er erinnerte sich den Mann gesehen zu haben
4. **finding, buying**[1]**;** nachdem er diesen Artikel nicht gefunden hatte, verließ er den Laden ohne etwas zu kaufen **having found, having bought**[2]**;** nachdem er diesen Artikel nicht gefunden hatte, verließ er den Laden, ohne etwas gekauft zu haben
5. **reaching** [1]**/having reached** [2]; Nachdem er die Themsemündung erreicht hatte, schloss sich Roger einer Schmugglerbande an.
6. **trying** [1]**/having tried** [2]; nachdem er vergeblich versucht hatte in einem Restaurant eine Arbeit zu finden, wollte er einen Schlafplatz in einem Park finden.
7. **having** [1]; als der Junge vom Schulleiter zu dem Verschwinden eines Fahrrades aus dem Fahrradkeller der Schule vor zwei Tagen befragt wurde, leugnete der Junge rundweg irgendetwas damit zu tun zu haben
8. **accepting** [1]**/having accepted** [2]; da er den Abend außerordentlich langweilig fand, verfluchte sich Herr Burton, die Einladung angenommen zu haben
9. **leaving** [1]**/having left** [2]; nachdem er den Bus verlassen hatte, wurde er von einer so großen Unruhe erfasst, dass er kaum wagte, sich dem einsamen Haus zu nähern.

Erklärungen und Lernhinweise

[1] Der Vorgang bezieht sich auf die Gegenwart, daher steht das present gerund. Häufig kann in einem Satz sowohl das present als auch das perfect gerund verwendet werden, je nachdem, ob man sich auf die Gegenwart oder auf die Vergangenheit bezieht. Dies ist besonders bei der Konjunktion **after** der Fall, das present gerund wird in der modernen Sprache immer mehr bevorzugt.

[2] Der Vorgang bezieht sich auf die Vergangenheit, daher steht das perfect gerund. Häufig kann in einem Satz sowohl das present als auch das perfect gerund verwendet werden, je nachdem, ob man sich auf die Gegenwart oder auf die Vergangenheit bezieht.
Das perfect gerund wird in der modernen Sprache immer mehr vom present gerund verdrängt.

Die Partizipien (The Participles)

Das Present Participle Active

1 Setzen Sie die Verben in Klammern ins present participle.

1. whistling ◀1 2. sitting ◀2 3. running down ◀2 4. encouraging ◀1 5. lying ◀3 6. saying ◀4 7. listening ◀5 8. twisting ◀6 9. watching ◀6 10. starving ◀1 11. frightening ◀5

Erklärungen und Lernhinweise

▶1 Das Verb endet auf **-e,** es verliert das **-e** beim Anhängen von **-ing**.

▶2 Das Verb endet auf Konsonant, dem ein kurzer, betonter Vokal vorausgeht, daher wird der Endkonsonant beim Anhängen von **-ing** verdoppelt. Der betonte Vokal ist unterstrichen.

▶3 Das Verb endet auf **-ie**, dieses wird beim Anhängen von **-ing** zu **-y**.

▶4 Auf **-y** endende Verben erhalten dieses beim Anhängen von **-ing** (es wird nicht in **-ie** geändert).

▶5 Das Verb endet auf Konsonant, dem ein unbetonter Vokal vorausgeht, daher wird der Endkonsonant beim Anhängen von **-ing** nicht verdoppelt. Der betonte Vokal ist unterstrichen.

▶6 Das Verb bildet das present participle regelmäßig, d.h. es wird **-ing** am Verbende angehängt.

2 Setzen Sie die folgenden present participles, die als Adjektive verwendet werden, in den entsprechenden Satz ein.

1. exciting 2. existing 3. fascinating 4. interesting 5. following 6. developing 7. frightening 8. growing 9. increasing 10. surrounding

3 Verkürzen Sie die folgenden fett gedruckten Nebensätze unter Verwendung des present participles.

1. while watching television ◀1 2. Although being rich ◀2 3. coming to Europe ◀3 4. hurrying along ◀3 5. interrupting a programme every now and again ◀3 6. Falling downstairs ◀1 7. while attending a theatre in Washington ◀1 8. While going about their normal work ◀1 9. When entering the house ◀1 10. Lying there in the darkness ◀1 11. Turning quickly ◀1 12. Persons entering or leaving the train ◀3 13. living in the fifty biggest metropolitan areas ◀3 14. Coming home ◀1 15. when talking to people from elsewhere ◀1 16. While packing a suitcase ◀1 17. Looking up ◀1 18. While waiting bareheaded in the rain ◀1 19. entering higher education ◀3 20. holding a life peerage ◀3 21. waiting for her ◀3

Erklärungen und Lernhinweise

▶1 Der Nebensatz gibt die Zeit an und wird durch die Konjunktionen **while, when, as** eingeleitet, er wird daher durch das present participle, das aus dem Verb des Nebensatzes gebildet wird, ersetzt. Das Subjekt des Nebensatzes entfällt.

Erklärungen und Lernhinweise

▶2 Der Nebensatz drückt eine Einräumung aus und wird durch die Konjunktion **although** eingeleitet, er wird daher durch das present participle, das aus dem Verb des Nebensatzes gebildet wird, ersetzt. Das Subjekt des Nebensatzes entfällt.

▶3 Der Nebensatz ist ein Relativsatz, er wird durch die Relativpronomen **who, which, that** eingeleitet, er wird daher durch das present participle, das aus dem Verb des Nebensatzes gebildet wird, ersetzt. Die Relativpronomen entfallen dabei.

Das Past Participle

1 Setzen Sie die Verben in Klammern ins past participle.

1. depressed ◀1 2. injured ◀2 3. lost ◀3 4. relieved ◀2 5. occupied ◀4 6. petrified ◀4 7. seated ◀1 8. discouraged ◀2 9. pleased ◀2 10. rejected ◀1

Erklärungen und Lernhinweise

▶1 Dieses Verb bildet das past participle regelmäßig, d.h. es wird **-ed** am Verbende angehängt.

▶2 Das Verb endet auf **-e,** es verliert das **-e** beim Amhängen von **-ed**.

▶3 Das Verb bildet das past participle unregelmäßig.

▶4 Das Verb endet auf **-y,** dem ein Konsonant vorausgeht, dieses wird beim Anhängen von **-ed** in **-ie** geändert.

2 Setzen Sie die folgenden past participles, die in der Funktion eines Adjektivs stehen, in den entsprechenden Satz ein.

1. broken 2. excited 3. injured 4. satisfied 5. fallen 6. surprised 7. trained 8. complicated 9. increased 10. learned

3 Verkürzen Sie die folgenden fett gedruckten Nebensätze unter Verwendung des past participles.

1. Questioned ◀1 2. as practised in England today ◀2 3. If posted at once ◀3 4. Unless forced to return ◀3 5. when compared with the other dangers ◀1 6. When focused to a sharp point at very close range ◀1 7. as if turned to stone ◀2 8. Determined to earn her own living ◀5 9. Provided with thousands of solar cells ◀5 10. when compelled ◀1 11. Accompanied by his friend ◀1 12. Founded by William the Conqueror, Windsor Castle ◀6 13. Bought for 25 dollars from the Indians in 1626 Manhattan Island is now ◀6

Erklärungen und Lernhinweise

▶1 Der Nebensatz gibt die Zeit an und wird durch die Konjunktionen **while, when, as** eingeleitet, er wird daher durch das past participle, das aus dem Verb des Nebensatzes gebildet wird, ersetzt. Das Subjekt des Nebensatzes entfällt.

Erklärungen und Lernhinweise

▶2 Der Nebensatz drückt den Vergleich aus und wird durch die Konjunktionen **as, as if** eingeleitet, er wird daher durch das past participle, das aus dem Verb des Nebensatzes gebildet wird, ersetzt. Das Subjekt des Nebensatzes entfällt.

▶3 Der Nebensatz drückt die Bedingung aus und wird durch die Konjunktionen **if, unless** eingeleitet, er wird daher durch das past participle, das aus dem Verb des Nebensatzes gebildet wird, ersetzt. Das Subjekt des Nebensatzes entfällt.

▶4 Der Nebensatz ist ein Relativsatz, er wird durch die Relativpronomen **who, which, that** eingeleitet, er wird daher durch das past participle, das aus dem Verb des Nebensatzes gebildet wird, ersetzt. Das Subjekt des Nebensatzes entfällt und die Relativpronomen entfallen.

▶5 Der Nebensatz gibt den Grund an, er wird durch die Konjunktion **as** eingeleitet und wird daher durch das past participle, das aus dem Verb des Nebensatzes gebildet wird, ersetzt. Das Subjekt des Nebensatzes entfällt.

▶6 Das Subjekt des Hauptsatzes steht vor dem zu ersetzenden Relativsatz, der in den Hauptsatz eingeschoben ist (**Windsor Castle - which was founded by William the Conqueror - stands ...).** Der ersetzte Relativsatz tritt vor den Hauptsatz, es muss das Subjekt daher im folgenden Hauptsatz eingefügt werden, da ein Hauptsatz nicht ohne Subjekt stehen kann.

4 Setzen Sie die Verben in Klammern ins present participle oder past participle.

1. **talking**◀1; Wir können nicht hier sitzen und *uns unterhalten*. 2. **hunched** ◀2, **smoking, thinking** ◀1; er saß nach *vorne gebeugt* in einem Lehnstuhl, und *rauchte* und *dachte nach*. 3. **exciting**◀1; es fing an *aufregend* zu klingen. 4. **pleased**◀2; sie klang *erfreut*. 5. **disappointed**◀2; sie sah *enttäuscht* aus. 6. **inviting**◀1; in dem warmen, schwachen Licht, sah der Platz *einladend* aus. 7. **exciting**◀1; ich hatte das starke Gefühl, dass *aufregende* Zeiten auf mich zukamen. 8. **excited**◀2; I helfe sehr gerne, wenn ich kann, sagte Bob mit ziemlich *aufgeregter* Stimme. 9. **depressed**◀2; eine Weile saßen sie da und schwiegen *bedrückt*. 10. **depressing**◀1; ich bedaure, Ihnen diese *bedrückende* Nachricht zu schicken. 11. **increased, decreased**◀2; In der Natur, werden zu große Tierpopulationen durch eine *erhöhte* Sterblichkeitsrate, eine *verminderte* Geburtenrate oder durch Abwanderung in Grenzen gehalten. 12. **increasing**◀1; eine *steigende* Anzahl von verheirateten Frauen hat Arbeitsstellen in Büros, Läden, Fabriken angenommen. 13. **Left alone**◀2; so *allein gelassen*, hatte Konsul Carrington keinen Appetit auf seine gewohnte Zigarre nach dem Frühstück. 14. **Leaving**◀1; Ich *ließ* sie *allein* mit ihrer Mutter, eilte nach unten und traf Ben, der aus der Küche kam. 15. **waiting**◀1; ich erwartete ihn *wartend* am Bahnhof vorzufinden. 16. **suited**◀2; dies ist ein Leben, das zu ihren Ansprüchen *passt*. 17. **surprising**◀1; in Anbetracht der Tatsache, dass die Verfassung sagt, dass niemand seiner Freiheit ohne ein ordentliches Gerichtsverfahren beraubt werden darf, ist es eigentlich *überraschend*, dass die Sklaverei überhaupt existieren konnte. 18. **focused**◀2; seine Aufmerksamkeit schien auf Donald *konzentriert*.

Erklärungen und Lernhinweise

▶1 Der Satz drückt den Verlauf aus, dass etwas im Gange ist, daher steht das present particple. Der Unterschied zwischen present und past participle wird durch die Übersetzung besonders deutlich. Im Deutschen steht hier häufig das Partizip Präsens in der Funktion eines Adjektivs, was an der Endung -end zu erkennen und hier kursiv dargestellt ist.

Erklärungen und Lernhinweise

▶2 Der Satz drückt den Zustand, das Ergebnis aus, es steht daher das past participle. Der Unterschied zwischen present und past participle wird durch die Übersetzung besonders deutlich. Im Deutschen steht hier häufig das Partizip Perfekt in der Funktion eines Adjektivs, was an der Vorsilbe ge- oder der Endung -t zu erkennen und hier kursiv dargestellt ist.

Das Perfect Participle Active

1 Verkürzen Sie die fett gedruckten Nebensätze unter Verwendung des perfect particple.

1. Having laboured ◀1 2. Having lost ◀1 3. having finished ◀2 4. If having your car repaired ◀3 5. Having been cheated ◀4

Erklärungen und Lernhinweise

▶1 Der Nebensatz drückt den Grund aus und wird durch die Konjunktion **as** eingeleitet, er wird durch das perfect participle ersetzt. Das Subjekt des Nebensatzes entfällt.

▶2 Der Nebensatz gibt die Zeit an und wird durch die Konjunktion **when** eingeleitet, er wird durch das perfect participle ersetzt. Das Subjekt des Nebensatzes entfällt.

▶3 Der Nebensatz drückt die Bedingung aus und wird durch die Konjunktionen **if** eingeleitet, er wird durch das perfect participle ersetzt. Das Subjekt des Nebensatzes entfällt.

▶4 Der Nebensatz drückt den Grund aus und wird durch die Konjunktion **as** eingeleitet. Der Ausführende der Handlung wird nicht genannt (wer der Betrügende ist, wird nicht gesagt), daher wird das perfect participle passive verwendet.

Das Present Participle Passive

1 Setzen Sie die Verben in Klammern ins present participle passive.

1. being done ◀1 2. being looked for ◀1 3. being said ◀1 4. being felt ◀1 5. being waited for ◀1 6. being watched ◀1

Erklärungen und Lernhinweise

▶1 Das present particple passive wird aus **being** + 3. Stammform des Verbs gebildet. Zusammen mit dem Hilfsverb **to be** bildet es die continuous form des Passivs. Es sind die Besonderheiten bei der Bildung der 3. Stammform zu beachten (z.B.: Endung **-e** entfällt beim Anhängen von **-ed**).

2 Setzen Sie die Verben in Klammern ins present participle active oder passive.

1. watching ◀2 2. singing ◀2 3. running ◀2 4. being looked at ◀1 5. having ◀2 6. being done ◀1 7. standing ◀2 8. being asked ◀1

Erklärungen und Lernhinweise

1. Die Person, die die Handlung ausführt, wird nicht genannt, daher steht das present participle passive (z.B.: in **all employers are being asked** wird nicht gesagt wer die Arbeitgeber auffordert).
2. Die Person, die die Handlung ausführt, wird genannt, daher steht das present participle active (z.B.: in **I lay watching** ist "I" die Person, die die Handlung ausführt).

Das Perfect Participle Passive

1 Setzen Sie die Verben in Klammern ins perfect participle passive.

1. having been found 1 2. having been founded 2 3. having been settled 1 4. Having been bitten 1

Erklärungen und Lernhinweise

1. Das perfect particple passive wird aus **having been** + 3. Stammform gebildet. Es sind die Besonderheiten bei der Bildung der 3. Stammform zu beachten (z.B.: Endung **-e** entfällt beim Anhängen von **-ed**).
2. **Found** (gründen) bildet die 3. Stammform regelmäßig durch Anhängen von **-ed** und ist nicht zu verwechseln mit der 3. Stammform von **find, found** (finden).

Das deutsche *lassen*

1 Schreiben Sie die folgenden Sätze neu und verwenden Sie **to have**, um das deutsche *lassen* auszudrücken.

1. **had my hair cut** [1]; ich *ließ* mir die Haare schneiden. 2. **has the windows cleaned** [1]; Frau Stevens *lässt* die Fenster jeden Monat putzen. 3. **am having my car washed** [1]; ich *lasse* meinen Wagen waschen, während ich meine Einkäufe erledige. 4. **had had my car washed**[1]; ich *hatte* meinen Wagen waschen lassen, bevor ich herkam. 5. **will have my car washed** [1]; ich *werde* meinen Wagen waschen lassen, bevor ich ihn in die Inspektion gebe. 6. **has had her hair dyed** [1]; sie *hat* ihre Haare färben lassen 7. **will have our house redecorated** [1]; wir werden unser Haus renovieren lassen 8. **must have another picture taken** [2]; du musst ein anderes Foto machen lassen 9. **have to have your name entered** [2]**;** um in den USA wählen zu können, muss man seinen Namen in eine Wählerliste eintragen lassen. 10. **may have his eyes tested** [2]; Jedermann kann seine Augen bei einem Optiker oder Augenarzt testen lassen, muss jedoch einen Teil der Kosten zu einer Brille dazu bezahlen. 11. **had a son born** [1]; im Juni 1688 wurde James II. ein Sohn geboren. 12. **to have the roof made** [1]**;** der Hausbesitzer rief den Mieter und sagte ihm, dass er das Dach machen lassen soll 13. **has he the boy trained** [3]; warum hat er den Jungen zum Läufer ausbilden lassen?

Erklärungen und Lernhinweise

[1] *Lassen* im Sinne von *veranlassen,* dass jemand etwas tut, wird durch die Formen von **have** + Objekt + 3. Stammform ausgedrückt. Die Zeit, in der der Ausdruck steht wird also durch **to have** bestimmt (z.B. im present perfect steht also **has had** + Objekt + 3. Stammform. Es sind die Besonderheiten bei der Bildung der 3. Stammform zu beachten (z.B. **-y** wird zu **-ie** beim Anhängen von **-ed** etc.). Beachten Sie den Unterschied zu **I have cut my hair** *ich habe mir die Haare geschnitten.*

[2] Es ist ein Modalverb vorhanden, daher steht Modalverb **+ have** + Objekt + 3. Stammform.

[3] Im Fragesatz tritt das Subjekt hinter das Verb, daher steht das Subjekt nach **to have** und vor dem Objekt, also **to have** + Subjekt + Objekt + 3. Stammform.

2 Schreiben Sie die folgenden Sätze neu und verwenden Sie **to let,** um das deutsche *lassen* auszudrücken.

1. let me hear [1] 2. had let her cigarette go out [1] 3. let them approach [1] 4. let me have [1] 5. don't let him get away [2] 6. didn't let me finish [2] 7. won't/will not let you do [2] 8. Has your father ever let you drive [2] 9. would let her know [1] 10. would not have let him go off [2] 11. to let her go [1] 12. let oneself be worried [3] 13. Don't let yourself be trapped in [3]

Erklärungen und Lernhinweise

[1] *Lassen* im Sinne von *zulassen,* wird durch die Formen **let** + Objekt + Infinitiv ohne **to** ausgedrückt. Die Zeit in der der Ausdruck steht wird also durch **let** bestimmt (z.B. im present perfect steht **has let** + Objekt + Infinitiv ohne **to)**.

Erklärungen und Lernhinweise

▶2 Im verneinten und fragenden Satz wird **let** im present und past tense simple mit **to do** umschrieben, da **let** Vollverb ist. In den zusammengesetzten Zeiten ist ein Hilfsverb vorhanden, daher wird die Verneinung bzw. Frage nicht mit **to do** gebildet.

▶3 Das Fragewort ist selbst Subjekt, d.h. es folgt kein weiteres Subjekt, sondern das Verb, daher wird **to do** nicht verwendet, das Vollverb **let** folgt unmittelbar auf **why**. Der Ausführende der Handlung wird nicht genannt, daher wird der passive infinitive (**be worried**) benötigt, der ohne **to** an das Objekt **oneself** angeschlossen wird.

▶4 Der verneinte Imperativ wird mit **to do** gebildet. Der Ausführende der Handlung wird nicht genannt, daher wird der passive infinitive (**be trapped in**) benötigt, der ohne **to** an das Objekt **yourself** angeschlossen wird.

3 Schreiben Sie die folgenden Sätze neu, und verwenden Sie **to make,** um das deutsche *lassen* auszudrücken.

1. made the children get up and wash and dress ◀1 2. make Simon come back ◀1 3. make the students think ◀1 4. made Consul Carrington write ◀1 5. would make you laugh ◀1 6. makes people think ◀1 7. has made Mary forget ◀1 8. made Ben feel ◀1 9. is usually made to compensate ◀2

Erklärungen und Lernhinweise

▶1 *Lassen* im Sinne von jemanden *veranlassen* etwas zu tun*,* wird durch die Formen von **make** + Objekt + Infinitiv ausgedrückt. Der Infinitiv steht ohne **to**, wenn der Satz im Aktiv steht.

▶2 Der Satz steht im Passiv, daher wird der Infinitiv mit **to** an **make** + Objekt angeschlossen.

4 Schreiben Sie die folgenden Sätze neu, und verwenden Sie **to keep** oder **to leave,** um das deutsche *lassen* auszudrücken.

1. leave everything lying about ◀1 2. left me wondering ◀1 3. left them discussing ◀1 4. Leave them playing ◀1 5. Had Ben kept her waiting ◀2

Erklärungen und Lernhinweise

▶1 *Lassen* im Sinne von *zurück-, liegen lassen,* wird durch die Formen von **leave** + Objekt + present participle ausgedrückt. Die Zeit, in der der Ausdruck steht wird also durch **leave** bestimmt. **Leave** drückt eher den Vorgang aus. Es sind die Besonderheiten bei der Bildung des present participle zu beachten (z.B. **-ie** wird zu **-y** beim Anhängen von **-ing** etc.).

▶2 *Lassen,* durch die Formen von **keep** + Objekt + present participle ausgedrückt, bezeichnet eher den Zustand, das Ergebnis aus. Die Zeit, in der der Ausdruck steht wird also durch **keep** bestimmt. Es sind die Besonderheiten bei der Bildung des present participle zu beachten (z.B. **-ie** wird zu **-y** beim Anhängen von **-ing** etc.).

5 Schreiben Sie die folgenden Sätze neu, und verwenden Sie **to allow**, um das deutsche *lassen*, auszudrücken.

1. allow him to go ◀1 2. allow her to lead ◀1 3. would allow him to talk ◀1 4. allow him to ring up ◀1 5. allow local communities to impose ◀1 6. did not allow himself to be intimidated ◀2

Erklärungen und Lernhinweise

▶1 *Lassen* im Sinne von *zulassen, erlauben,* wird durch die Formen von **allow** + Objekt + Infinitiv + **to** ausgedrückt. Die Zeit, in der der Ausdruck steht wird also durch **allow** bestimmt.

▶2 Die Verneinung wird mit **to do** gebildet, da **allow** Vollverb ist. Es ist zu beachten, dass im past tense simple auf **did** der Infinitiv von **allow** folgt (also **did not allow** und nicht **did not allowed**).

6 Verwenden Sie **to have, to let, to make, to keep, to leave** oder **to allow** zum Ausdruck des deutschen *lassen* und schreiben Sie die folgenden Sätze neu.

1. made Mary think ◀1 2. have not had my car washed ◀2 3. was having my car washed ◀2 4. Let me show ◀3 5. leave the wounded soldiers lying about ◀4 6. let our hair grow ◀5 7. had strong castles built ◀2 8. did you have your hair cut ◀6 9. to have a programme organized ◀2 10. will let me know ◀5 11. Don't let the dog run free ◀3 12. Don't let the others see you ◀3 13. to have your passport endorsed ◀2 14. to let Perkins help ◀5 15. to have his house painted ◀2 16. not to let him go ◀7 17. to have kept you waiting ◀8 18. were made to live ◀1 19. to have the sandwiches made ◀2 20. Let's let it go ◀3

Erklärungen und Lernhinweise

▶1 *Lassen* wird hier im Sinne von *jemanden veranlassen* verwendet, daher stehen die Formen von **make** + Objekt + Infinitiv. Der Infinitiv steht ohne **to**, wenn der Satz im Aktiv steht, steht der Satz im Passiv steht der Infinitiv + **to**.

▶2 *Lassen* wird hier im Sinne von *veranlassen,* dass jemand etwas tut verwendet, daher stehen die Formen von **have** + Objekt + 3. Stammform.
Es sind die Besonderheiten bei der Bildung der 3. Stammform zu beachten, insbesondere bei den Verben, die die Endung **-d** in **-t** ändern.

▶3 Der Satz drückt eine Aufforderung aus, daher werden die Formen von **let** + Objekt + Infinitiv ohne **to** verwendet.
Der verneinte Imperativ wird mit **to do** gebildet. Auf **don't** folgt **let** + Objekt + Infinitiv ohne **to**.

▶4 *Lassen* wird hier im Sinne von *zurück-, liegen lassen* verwendet, daher werden die Formen **to leave** + Objekt + present participle verwendet.

▶5 *Lassen* wird hier im Sinne von *zulassen,* dass etwas geschieht verwendet, daher werden die Formen von **let** + Objekt + Infinitiv ohne **to** verwendet.

▶6 *Lassen* wird hier im Sinne von *veranlassen,* dass jemand etwas tut verwendet, daher stehen die Formen von **have**. Das Fragewort (**why**) ist nicht selbst Subjekt, d.h. das Subjekt (**you**) folgt auf das Fragewort und **have** ist Vollverb, daher wird die Frage mit **to do** gebildet.

▶7 *Lassen* wird hier im Sinne von *zulassen,* dass etwas geschieht verwendet, daher werden die Formen von **let** verwendet. Der Infinitiv wird durch **not to** verneint, daher steht **not to** + Infinitiv **let**.

▶8 *Lassen,* durch die Formen von **keep** + Objekt + present participle ausgedrückt, bezeichnet den Zustand, das Ergebnis.

Der bestimmte und unbestimmte Artikel (The Definite and Indefinite Article)

1 Setzen Sie den bestimmten oder unbestimmten Artikel ein, wo notwendig.

1. - ◀1 2. The ◀2, a ◀3 3. -, - ◀1 4. - ◀1 5. an ◀3 6. - ◀1 7. a ◀3 8. -, - ◀1 9. the ◀2 10. - ◀1 11. the ◀2 12. a, a ◀3 13. the ◀2, a ◀3 14. a ◀3 15. a ◀3 16. - ◀1 17. - ◀1 18. the ◀4 19. - ◀5 20. - ◀5 21. the ◀2/ a ◀3 22. a ◀3, - ◀5 23. - ◀1 24. - ◀1 25. the, the ◀2 26. an ◀3

Erklärungen und Lernhinweise

▶1 Das Substantiv wird in allgemeiner Bedeutung verwendet, es sind keine bestimmten Personen oder Sachen gemeint, daher steht kein Artikel.

▶2 Das Substantiv bezeichnet eine oder mehrere bestimmte Personen oder Sachen, daher steht der bestimmte Artikel. Ein Substantiv ist näher bestimmt, wenn es zum Beispiel vor einem Relativsatz, mit einem Adjektiv, einer Beifügung mit **of** steht.

▶3 Das Substantiv bezeichnet eine unbestimmte, irgendeine Person oder Sache ganz allgemein, daher steht der unbestimmte Artikel. Vor Substantiven, die mit Vokal beginnen, steht **an**.

▶4 **Man** wird nicht nur in der Bedeutung *Mann* sondern auch *Mensch* verwendet. **Man** bezeichnet hier einen bestimmten Menschen (z.B. der den Computer benutzt), daher steht hier der bestimmte Artikel.

▶5 **Man** wird nicht nur in der Bedeutung *Mann* sondern auch *Mensch* verwendet. **Man** bezeichnet hier keinen bestimmten Menschen, sondern den Menschen ganz allgemein, daher steht hier kein Artikel. Im Deutschen wird hier der bestimmte Artikel verwendet (z.B. der Mensch muss essen, um zu leben).

2 Fügen Sie den bestimmten oder unbestimmten Artikel zu den folgenden Namen, wo nötig.

1. - ◀1 2. - ◀2 3. an ◀3 4. - - ◀1 5. the ◀4 6. - ◀1 7. - ◀1 8. - ◀1 the ◀4 9. a ◀5 10. - ◀1 11. the ◀4 12. - ◀2 13. the ◀6 14. - ◀1 15. - ◀1 16. - ◀1 17. the ◀4, - ◀1 18. the, the ◀7 19. -, - ◀1 the ◀6 20. the ◀6,- ◀1

Erklärungen und Lernhinweise

▶1 Personen- bzw. Familiennamen im Singular stehen ohne Artikel. Dies gilt auch, wenn dem Personennamen ein Adjektiv vorangeht.

▶2 Verwandtschaftsbezeichnungen + Personenname stehen ohne Artikel.

▶3 Verwandtschaftsbezeichnung ohne Personenname stehen mit unbestimmtem Artikel. Vor Verwandtschaftsbezeichnungen, die mit Vokal beginnen, steht **an**.

▶4 Familiennamen im Plural stehen mit dem bestimmten Artikel. Dies gilt auch, wenn eine bestimmte Familie bezeichnet wird (z.B. the Harrison family).

▶5 Der Personen- bzw. Familienname bezeichnet eine dem Sprecher unbekannte Person, daher steht der unbestimmte Artikel. Vor Namen, die mit Vokal beginnen, steht **an**.

▶6 Das Substantiv bezeichnet eine bestimmte Person, daher steht der bestimmte Artikel.

▶7 Dies ist ein Eigenname, der eine bestimmte, einmalige Person oder Sache bezeichnet, daher steht der bestimmte Artikel.

3 Fügen Sie den bestimmten oder unbestimmten Artikel zu den folgenden Titeln, Berufsbezeichnungen, gesellschaftlichen, politischen und religiösen Begriffen, wo nötig.

1. - ◀1 2. an ◀2 3. the ◀3 4. - ◀4 5. the ◀3, the ◀5 6. - ◀6 7. a ◀2 8. -, - ◀1 9. a ◀2 10. - ◀1 11. The ◀3 12. - ◀4 13. -, -, -, - ◀6 14. - ◀6 15. a ◀2 16. an ◀2 17. -, - ◀4 18. the, the ◀3 19. the ◀3 20. a, a ◀2

Erklärungen und Lernhinweise

▶1 Titel + Namen stehen ohne Artikel.

▶2 Berufs-, religiöse, politische Bezeichnungen stehen mit dem unbestimmten Artikel. Vor Bezeichnungen, die mit Vokal beginnen, steht **an**. Es ist zu beachten, dass im Deutschen hier kein Artikel steht.

▶3 Titel mit einer Beifügung + **of** stehen mit dem bestimmten Artikel.

▶4 Titel mit den Verben **appoint, become, crown, elect, make, turn** oder den Ausdrücken **the rank of, the office of, the post of, the titel of** stehen ohne Artikel. Im Deutschen steht hier *zum*.

▶5 Der Titel bezeichnet eine ganz bestimmte Person (z.B. den Vorsitzenden des House of Commons), daher steht hier der bestimmte Artikel.

▶6 Der Titel wird in ganz allgemeiner Bedeutung verwendet, daher steht hier kein Artikel.

4 Fügen Sie den bestimmten oder unbestimmten Artikel zu den folgenden geografischen Begriffen, wo nötig.

1. - ◀1 2. the ◀2 3. - ◀1 4. - ◀1 5. the ◀3, -,-, - ◀1 6. - ◀1, the ◀4 7. an ◀5 8. -, -, -, -, -, - ◀1 9. -, - ◀1 10. - ◀1 11. The ◀6 12. the ◀6 13. the ◀7, - ◀1 14. the ◀7 15. -, -, -, - ◀1 16. the ◀3, -, -, -, - ◀1, the ◀6 17. -, -, -, -, -, - ◀1 18. - ◀1 19. - ◀1 20. - ◀1, the ◀7 21. the ◀2, the ◀8, - ◀1 22. the ◀2 23. the ◀6 24. -,-,- ◀1, the ◀2 25. an, an ◀5 26. - ◀1 27. -, - ◀1 28. - ◀1 29. the ◀6 30. -, - ◀1, the ◀6 31. -, - ◀1 32. -, - ◀1, the ◀7

Erklärungen und Lernhinweise

▶1 Die Namen von Erdteilen, Städten, Ländern, Meeren und Seen (vor allem in Verbindung mit **Bay, Cape, Harbour, Gulf, Sea, Strait, Lake, Loch)**, Bergen (vor allem in Verbindung mit **Mount**), Himmelsrichtungen (vor allem in **from north to south, east of**) stehen ohne Artikel.

▶2 Geografische Namen mit einer Beifügung + **of** stehen mit dem bestimmten Artikel. Hierzu gehören auch fremdsprachliche Bezeichnungen mit einer Beifügung (z.B.: **Côte *d'* Azur**).
Beachten Sie: **the city of New York** und **New York City**.

▶3 Spezielle Bezeichnungen für bestimmte Länder (z.B. **the Continent, the United Kingdom**) stehen mit dem bestimmten Artikel.

▶4 Das Substantiv bezeichnet eine Person, die stellvertretend für eine gesamte, bestimmte Nation steht, daher steht der bestimmte Artikel.

▶5 Bezeichnungen der Nationalität stehen mit dem unbestimmten Artikel.

▶6 Die Namen der Berge nicht englischsprachiger Länder und die Namen von Bergen und Ländern im Plural stehen mit dem bestimmten Artikel.

▶7 Die Namen der Flüsse stehen generell mit dem bestimmten Artikel.

DER ARTIKEL Der bestimmte und unbestimmte Artikel

Erklärungen und Lernhinweise

▶3 Die Namen der Himmelrichtungen, die nicht in der Wendung **from north to south** und **from east to west** stehen mit dem bestimmten Artikel.

5 Fügen Sie den bestimmten oder unbestimmten Artikel zu den folgenden Straßennamen, Namen von Plätzen, Brücken und Gebäuden, wo nötig.

1. -, -, - ◀1 2. The, the ◀2 3. - ◀2 4. - ◀1, - ◀3 5. - ◀1 6. The ◀4 7. - ◀3 8. the ◀5 9. - ◀6 10. The ◀5 11. - ◀6 12. the ◀5 13. - ◀6 14. - ◀6 15. - ◀6 16. the ◀5 17. the ◀7 18. the ◀7 19. The ◀5 20. - ◀6 21. -, -, - ◀1 22. - ◀6 23. -, - ◀3 24. - ◀6 25. the ◀4 26. The ◀5 27. the ◀5 28. - ◀6 29. - ◀6 30. the ◀5 31. - ◀1 32. - ◀3 33. - ◀6 34. the ◀5 35. the ◀7 36. The ◀5

Erklärungen und Lernhinweise

▶1 Die Namen von Straßen und Plätzen in Verbindung mit **Street, Road, Avenue, Square, Circus, Park, Gardens, Station, Bridge** stehen ohne Artikel.

▶2 Die Namen von Straßen und Plätzen stehen, außer **Broadway**, generell mit dem bestimmten Artikel.

▶3 Gebäudenamen ohne nähere Bestimmung (z.B. eine Beifügung mit **of**, ein Adjektiv) stehen ohne Artikel.

▶4 Gebäudenamen mit einer Beifügung + **of** oder einem Adjektiv, oder solche, die ein bestimmtes Gebäude bezeichnen, stehen mit dem bestimmten Artikel.

▶5 Der Gebäudename bezeichnet nur das Gebäude, den Ort an sich, daher steht der bestimmte Artikel.

▶6 Der Gebäudename bezeichnet die Funktion des Gebäudes (z.B. Gottesdienst, Unterricht etc.), daher steht kein Artikel.

▶7 Gebäudenamen wie **cathedral** (wenn kein Name vorausgeht) **office, cinema** und **theatre** stehen generell mit dem bestimmten Artikel.

6 Fügen Sie den bestimmten oder unbestimmten Artikel zu den folgenden Monatsnamen, Namen von Wochentagen, Feiertagen, wo nötig.

1. - ◀1 2. - ◀1 3. The ◀2 4. the/- ◀3 5. the/- ◀3 6. - ◀4/the ◀5 7. the ◀5 8. - ◀6 9. - ◀4 10. - ◀4 11. - ◀4/the ◀5 12. the ◀2 13. - ◀4/the ◀5 14. the, the ◀5 15. the ◀5 16. the ◀2 17. -/the, -/the ◀3 18. - ◀6 19. the ◀2 20. - ◀4 21. - ◀4/the ◀5 22. the ◀2 23. the ◀5, the ◀1 24. the, the ◀5 25. - ◀4/the ◀5, - ◀4/the ◀5 26. - ◀4/the ◀5 27. - ◀4 28. - ◀4

Erklärungen und Lernhinweise

▶1 **Next** bzw. **last** weisen von der Gegenwart aus gesehen in die Zukunft bzw. Vergangenheit, daher steht kein Artikel.

▶2 Es ist eine bestimmte Jahreszeit, Tageszeit gemeint, daher steht der bestimmte Artikel.

▶3 Nach der Präposition **in**, kann der bestimmte Artikel bei Jahreszeiten stehen oder entfallen.

▶4 Es ist keine bestimmte Jahreszeit, kein bestimmter Monatsname, Wochentag, Feiertag gemeint, daher steht kein Artikel.

Erklärungen und Lernhinweise

▶5 Hier wird ein Zeitraum bezeichnet, daher steht der bestimmte Artikel. Zeiträume werden besonders durch die Präpositionen **during, through, in** bezeichnet.

▶6 Das Tagesdatum steht nach dem Monatsnamen, daher entfällt der Artikel.

7 Fügen Sie den bestimmten Artikel oder das entsprechende Possessivpronomen zu den folgenden Kleidungsstücken oder Körperteilen.

1. the ◀1 2. her ◀2 3. the ◀1 4. the ◀1 5. my ◀2 6. your ◀2 7. your ◀2 8. the ◀3 9. their ◀2 10. the ◀1 11. the ◀1 12. the ◀1 13. its ◀2 14. his, his ◀2 15. his ◀2 16. the ◀1 17. her, her ◀2 18. his ◀2 19. the ◀1 20. the ◀1

Erklärungen und Lernhinweise

▶1 Der Körperteil, das Kleidungsstück gehört nicht zum Subjekt, sondern zum Objekt, daher steht der bestimmte Artikel (z.B.: bei **look me in the eyes** gehören die "Augen" zum Objekt **me** und nicht zum das durch den Imperativ **look** bezeichnete Subjekt **you).**

▶2 Der Körperteil, das Kleidungsstück gehört zum Subjekt, daher steht das zum Subjekt gehörende Possessivpronomen (z.B.: in **Caroline put her arm** gehört der "Arm" zum Subjekt **Caroline**).

▶3 Dies ist ein Passivsatz, daher steht der bestimmte Artikel.

Die Stellung des Artikels (The Position of the Article)

1 Fügen Sie den bestimmten oder unbestimmten Artikel zu den folgenden Adjektiven und Substantiven in Klammern und setzen Sie ihn an die richtige Position.

1. close a friend ◀1 2. good a dish ◀1 3. half an hour ◀1 4. important a question ◀1 5. quite a relief ◀1 6. terrible a prospect ◀1 7. twice a week ◀1 8. half the women ◀2 9. many a man ◀1 10. quite a possibility ◀1 11. small a reward ◀1 12. twice the acreage ◀2 13. both the degree ◀2 14. good a chance ◀1 15. great a proportion ◀1 16. half a million ◀1 17. twice the average rate ◀2 18. unpleasant a climate ◀1 19. quite an opinion ◀1

Erklärungen und Lernhinweise

▶1 Nach **how, as, so, too** oder **quite, many, rather** oder **half, twice, both, double** steht der Artikel zwischen dem vorhandenen Adjektiv und dem folgenden Substantiv. Im Deutschen steht der Artikel vor dem Adjektiv und dem folgenden Substantiv (z.B. was für *ein* enger Freund).
Das Substantiv bezeichnet eine unbestimmte, dem Sprecher nicht bekannte Person oder Sache, daher steht der unbestimmte Artikel. Vor Substantiven, die mit Vokal beginnen, steht **an**.

▶2 Das Substantiv bezeichnet eine bestimmte Person oder Sache, daher steht der bestimmte Artikel. Er steht ebenfalls zwischen dem vorhandenen Adjektiv und dem folgenden Substantiv.

Das Geschlecht des Substantivs (The Gender of the Noun)

1 Setzen Sie die entsprechenden Personal- oder Possessivpronomen ein.

1. its/her ◄1 2. its/her ◄1 3. it ◄2 4. his ◄3 5. her ◄4 6. He ◄5 7. it, it ◄2 8. he ◄6 9. she ◄4 10. its/her ◄1 11. its/her ◄1 12. its ◄2 13. it ◄2 14. its ◄7 15. his ◄6 16. its/her ◄1 17. its/her ◄1

Erklärungen und Lernhinweise

►1 Länder gelten als Sache, daher werden sie durch das sächliche Pronomen **it** ersetzt. Sie können jedoch auch durch das weibliche Pronomen **she** ersetzt werden, wenn nicht die rein geografische Bedeutung im Vordergrund steht. Wenn es sich um ein Besitzverhältnis handelt steht **its** bzw. **her**.

►2 Das Geschlecht des Tieres ist unbekannt, daher steht das sächliche Pronomen **it** bzw., wenn es sich um ein Besitzverhältnis handelt, **its**.

►3 Das Geschlecht des Tieres ist bekannt, da sein Name genannt wird, daher steht hier das männliche Pronomen **he** bzw., wenn es sich um ein Besitzverhältnis handelt **his**.

►4 Das Geschlecht der Person ist bekannt und es ist weiblich (es wird der Name, die Bezeichnung des Geschlechts **girl, woman** etc. genannt), daher steht das weibliche Pronomen **she** bzw., wenn es sich um ein Besitzverhältnis handelt **her**.

►5 Das Geschlecht der Person ist bekannt und es ist männlich (es wird der Name, die Bezeichnung des Geschlechts **boy, man** etc. genannt), daher steht das männliche Pronomen **he** bzw., wenn es sich um ein Besitzverhältnis handelt **his**.

►6 Das Geschlecht der Person ist nicht bekannt, das Substantiv wird jedoch in allgemeiner Bedeutung verwendet, daher steht stellvertretend für männliche und weibliche Personen das Pronomen **he** bzw., wenn es sich um ein Besitzverhältnis handelt, **his.**

►7 Das Geschlecht ist nicht bekannt, daher steht für Kinder das sächliche Pronomen **it** bzw., wenn es sich um ein Besitzverhältnis handelt, **its**.

Der Numerus des Substantivs (The Number of the Noun)

Die Bildung des Plurals

1 Setzen Sie die folgenden Substantive in den Plural und setzen Sie sie in die entsprechende Spalte der folgenden Tabelle ein.

1. **-y → -ies:** difficulty - difficulties, sky - skies, inquiry - inquiries, butterfly - butterflies, facility - facilities; ❶
   -y → -ys: journey - journeys, key - keys, guy - guys, toy - toys, delay - delays, chimney - chimneys; ❶
   -ie → -ies: tie - ties ❷
2. **-ch + -es:** church - churches, speech - speeches, witch - witches; ❸
   -sh + -es: wish - wishes, bush - bushes, flash - flashes; ❸
   -ss + -es: success - successes, progress - progresses, witness - witnesses ❸
   -x + -es: box - boxes, tax - taxes, ax - axes ❸
3. **-sis → -ses:** crisis - crises, basis - bases, hypothesis - hypotheses ❹
4. **-f(e) → -v(e)s:** life - lives, thief - thieves, loaf - loaves; ❺
   -f(e) → -f(e)s: roof - roofs, proof - proofs, motif - motifs ❺
5. **-o → -oes:** buffalo - buffaloes, hero - heroes, echo - echoes; ❻
   -o → -os: studio - studios, ghetto - ghettos, casino - casinos ❻

Erklärungen und Lernhinweise

❶ Dem **-y** geht ein Konsonant voraus, daher wird das **-y** beim Anhängen des Plural-s zu **-ie,** dem **-y** geht ein Vokal voraus, daher bleibt das **-y** beim Anhängen des Plural-s erhalten.

❷ Die Endung **-ie** bleibt beim Anhängen des Plural-s erhalten.

❸ Substantive auf **-ch, -sh, -ss** und **-x** hängen im Plural **-es** an.

❹ Substantive auf **-sis** ändern die Endung im Plural in **-ses**.

❺ Substantive auf **-f(e)** ändern die Endung im Plural in **-v(e)s,** wenn sie germanischer Herkunft sind, Substantive auf **-f(e)** behalten im Plural die Endung **-f(e),** wenn sie romanischer Herkunft sind.

❻ Substantive auf **-o** hängen im Plural **-es** an, wenn dem **-o** ein Konsonant vorausgeht, Substantive auf **-o** hängen im Plural **-s** an, wenn sie als Fremdwörter gelten.

Substantive, die nur im Singular oder Plural vorkommen

1 Setzen Sie die entsprechende Verbform von **to be** im present tense simple ein.

1. is ❶ 2. is ❹ 3. are ❺ 4. are ❺ 5. is ❶ 6. is ❶ 7. is ❶ 8. is ❶ 9. are ❷ 10. is ❶ 11. are ❸ 12. is ❶ 13. are ❸ 14. are ❷ 15. is ❶ 16. are ❷ 17. are ❺/is ❻ 18. are ❺ 19. are ❺ 20. is ❻ 21. is ❻ 22. are ❺ 23. is ❻ 24. are ❺ 25. are ❸ 26. is ❶ 27. are ❸ 28. is ❶ 29. are ❷ 30. are ❺/is ❻ 31. is ❶ 32. are ❺ 33. is ❶

Erklärungen und Lernhinweise

1 Das Substantiv gilt trotz des Plural-s als Substantiv im Singular, es wird daher auch mit einem Verb im Singular verbunden.

2 Das Substantiv gilt trotz des fehlenden Plural-s als Substantiv im Plural, es wird daher auch mit einem Verb im Plural verbunden.

3 Das Substantiv kommt nur im Plural vor, es wird daher auch mit einem Verb im Plural verbunden. Im Deutschen sind diese Substantive meist Substantive im Singular und stehen daher auch mit einem Verb im Singular (z.B. **the stairs are steep** *die Treppe ist steil*).

4 Das Substantiv kommt nur im Plural vor, wird jedoch, wenn es mit Ausdrücken wie **a pair of** verbunden ist, zur Verdeutlichung, dass es sich um ein Stück handelt, mit einem Verb im Singular verbunden.

5 Das Substantiv hat im Singular und Plural dieselbe Form. Es bezeichnet hier jede einzelne Person der Gruppe, daher wird es mit einem Verb im Plural verbunden.

6 Das Substantiv hat im Singular und Plural dieselbe Form. Es bezeichnet hier die Gesamtheit, eine Gruppe, daher wird es mit einem Verb im Singular verbunden.

7 Die Mengenangabe **dozen** ist nicht mit einem Zahlwort verbunden, daher wird sie mit einem Verb im Plural verbunden. Dies gilt auch für die Mengenangaben **hundred, thousand, million.**

Common und Possessive Case

Die Bildung des Possessive Case

1 Setzen Sie die folgenden fett gedruckten Substantive in den possessive case.

1. children's ◀1 2. Jenny's ◀2 3. father's ◀2 4. James's ◀3 5. Fools' ◀4 6. parents' ◀4 7. Scotts' ◀4 8. boys' ◀4 9. women's ◀1 10. Mrs Stevens's ◀3 11. one's ◀2 12. gentlemen's ◀1 13. Indians' ◀4 14. Smith's ◀2 15. bees' ◀4 16. people's ◀1 17. stewardess's ◀3 18. Nicholas's ◀3 19. Columbus's ◀3 20. colonists' ◀4 21. men's ◀1 22. Columbus's ◀3 23. Congress's ◀3

Erklärungen und Lernhinweise

▶1 Das Substantiv steht zwar im Plural, endet jedoch nicht auf Plural-s, es erhält daher **'s.**

▶2 Das Substantiv steht im Singular, es erhält daher, auch wenn es auf -th endet, **'s.**

▶3 Das Substantiv steht im Singular und endet bereits auf **-s**, es erhält dennoch **'s**.

▶4 Das Substantiv steht im Plural und endet demnach auf **-s**, es erhält daher nur **'**.

Die Verwendung von Common und Possessive Case und der Beifügung mit of

1 Verwenden Sie den possessive oder common case oder eine Beifügung mit **of**.

1. bottle of wine ◀1 2. a hundred pounds ◀2 3. Ben Robinson's wife, Mrs Stevens's husband ◀4 4. chairman of the House of Commons ◀5 5. Duke of Parma ◀5 6. Britain's universities ◀4 7. city of Boston ◀6 8. St Paul's ◀7 9. River Thine, River Thames ◀8 10. father's ◀7 11. baker's ◀7 12. Woolworth's ◀7 13. five-year plans ◀2 14. piece of baggage ◀1 15. a hundred years ◀2, Australia's chief customer ◀4 16. United Kingdom of Great Britain and Ireland ◀5 17. River Thames ◀8 18. everybody's family secrets ◀4 19. Empress of India ◀5 20. five-year period ◀2 21. three months' period ◀3 22. 10 years' time ◀3 23. Canada's prosperity ◀4 24. majority of the jobless ◀1 25. pride of the British ◀5 26. Scout's honour ◀4 27. rank of Consul ◀5 28. a few hundred miles ◀2 29. four-year terms ◀2 30. dozens of new office and apartment buildings ◀1

Erklärungen und Lernhinweise

▶1 Dies ist eine Mengenangabe (**a cup, a glass, a bottle** etc.) oder ein Zahlwort, dem keine Grundzahl vorausgeht, daher steht die Beifügung + **of**.

▶2 Dem Zahlwort **hundred, thousand, million** oder **dozen** geht eine Grundzahl oder **a** voraus, daher steht der common case.
Dies gilt auch für Zahlwörter, denen eine Zeitbestimmung folgt, die einen Zeitraum bezeichnen, Zahlwort und Zeitbestimmung sind durch Bindestrich verbunden (z.B. **five-year plans**).

▶3 Dem Zahlwort folgt eine Zeitbestimmung im Plural, daher steht diese im possessive case.

Erklärungen und Lernhinweise

4 Der Besitzer, Urheber, die Ursache ist ein Lebewesen (z.B.: ***Ben Robinson's*** **wife**), daher steht der possessive case. Dies gilt auch bei personifizierten Substantiven (z.B. Länder).

5 Der Besitzer, Urheber, die Ursache ist eine Sache (z.B.: ***the pride*** **of the British**), daher steht eine Beifügung + **of**. Dies gilt auch bei Titeln (z.B. **Duke of Parma**).

6 Dem Eigennamen (z.B. **Boston**) geht ein geografischer Begriff wie **city** voraus, daher wird der Eigenname mit **of** angeschlossen.

7 Öffentliche Gebäude, Geschäfte, Häuser oder Wohnungen stehen im possessive case. Es wäre die Gebäudebezeichnung zu ergänzen (z.B. **St Paul's** ***Cathedral***).

8 Dem Eigennamen geht **mount, number, river, year, world** voraus, daher steht der common case.

Die Steigerung des Adjektivs (The Comparison of the Adjective)

Die Bildung der Steigerungsformen

1 Setzen Sie die Adjektive in Klammern in den Komparativ oder Superlativ durch Hinzufügen von **-er** oder **-est** und setzen Sie diese Formen in die Tabelle auf der rechten Seite ein.

1. **closest** ◀1, close - closer - closest ◀3 2. **busiest** ◀1, busy - busier - busiest ◀4 3. **fatter** ◀2, fat - fatter - fattest ◀5, **stronger** ◀2, strong - stronger - strongest 4. **better** ◀2, good - better - best 5. **worse** ◀2, bad - worse - worst 6. **less** ◀2, little - less - least 7. **larger** ◀2, large - larger - largest, **fewer** ◀2, few - fewer - fewest 8. **heavier** ◀2, heavy - heavier - heaviest ◀4, **faster** ◀2, fast - faster - fastest 9. **fittest** ◀1, fit - fitter - fittest ◀5 10. **best** ◀1, good - better - best 11. **worst** ◀1, bad - worse - worst 12. **less** ◀2, little - less - least 13. **elder** ◀2, old - elder - eldest ◀6 14. **older** ◀2 old - older - oldest ◀7 15. **earliest** ◀1, early - earlier - earliest ◀4 16. **hottest** ◀1, hot - hotter - hottest ◀5, **sleepiest** ◀1, sleepy - sleepier - sleepiest ◀4 17. **most** ◀1, much - more - most 18. **farther** ◀2, far - farther - farthest 19. **latter** ◀2, late - latter - latest ◀8 20. **nearer** ◀2, near - nearer - nearest ◀8 21. next ◀1, near - nearer - next ◀8 22. **least** ◀1, little - less - least

Erklärungen und Lernhinweise

▶1 Es wird der höchste Grad ausgedrückt, daher steht der Superlativ, der durch Anhängen der Endung **-est** an das Adjektiv gebildet wird. Ein Indiz für die Verwendung des Superlativs ist der bestimmte Artikel vor dem Substantiv. Diese Art der Steigerung nennt man germanische Steigerung.

▶2 Es wird ein höherer Grad ausgedrückt, daher steht der Komparativ, der durch Anhängen der Endung **-er** an das Adjektiv gebildet wird. Ein Indiz für die Verwendung des Komparativs ist **than** zum Ausdruck des Vergleichs. Diese Art der Steigerung nennt man germanische Steigerung.

▶3 Auf **-e** endende Adjektive verlieren dieses beim Anhängen von **-er** und **-est.**

▶4 Auf **-y** endende Adjektive ändern das **-y** beim Anhängen von **-er** und **-est** in -**ie**.

▶5 Auf Konsonant endende Adjektive verdoppeln diesen beim Anhängen von **-er** und **-est**, wenn dem Endkonsonant ein kurzer, betonter Vokal vorausgeht. Der betonte Vokal ist unterstrichen.

▶6 Das Substantiv bezeichnet ein Familienmitglied, daher lauten die Steigerungsformen von **old, elder** und **eldest**.

▶7 Das Adjektiv bezeichnet das tatsächliche Alter, daher wird **old** regelmäßig gesteigert (**older, oldest**).

▶8 Das Adjektiv bezeichnet die Reihenfolge, daher werden **late** bzw. **near** unregelmäßig **(the) latter** (letzterer), **(the) last** (letzter) bzw. **nearer** (nächster) - **next** (am nächsten) gesteigert. Die regelmäßigen Steigerungsformen von **late** bzw. **near, later - latest** bzw. **nearer - nearest** bezeichnen die Zeit bzw. die Entfernung (später - am spätesten bzw. näher - am nächsten).

Bei den nicht markierten Adjektiven sind keine Besonderheiten zu beachten oder sie werden unregelmäßig gesteigert.

2 Setzen Sie die Adjektive in Klammern in den Komparativ oder Superlativ durch Hinzufügen von **more** oder **most** und setzen Sie diese Formen in die Tabelle auf der rechten Seite ein.

1. **more dangerous** ◀1, dangerous - more dangerous - most dangerous 2. **more lovely** ◀1, lovely - more lovely - most lovely 3. **most fantastic** ◀2, fantastic - more fantastic - most fantastic 4. **most famous** ◀2, famous - more famous - most famous 5. **more important** ◀1 **/most important** ◀2, important - more important - most important 6. **more conscious** ◀1, conscious - more conscious - most conscious 7. **most distinctive** ◀2, distinctive - more distinctive - most distinctive 8. **most modern** ◀2, modern - more modern - most modern 9. **more disagreeable** ◀1, disagreeable - more disagreeable - most disagreeable 10. **more distant** ◀1, distant - more distant - most distant 11. **most influential** ◀2, influential - more influential - most influential 12. **most frequent** ◀2, frequent - more frequent - most frequent

Erklärungen und Lernhinweise

▶1 Es wird ein höherer Grad ausgerückt, daher steht der Komparativ, d.h. dem Adjektiv wird **more** vorangestellt. Ein Indiz für die Verwendung des Komparativs ist **than** zum Ausdruck des Vergleichs. Diese Art der Steigerung nennt man romanische Steigerung.

▶2 Es wird der höchste Grad ausgedrückt, daher steht der Superlativ, d.h. dem Adjektiv wird **most** vorangestellt. Ein Indiz für die Verwendung des Superlativs ist der bestimmte Artikel vor dem Substantiv. Diese Art der Steigerung nennt man romanische Steigerung.

Bei den mit **more** und **most** gesteigerten Adjektiven (romanische Steigerung) sind nicht wie bei den mit **-er** und **-est** gesteigerten Adjektiven (germanische Steigerung) orthografische Besonderheiten zu beachten, da das Adjektiv selbst unverändert bleibt.

Die Verwendung der Steigerungsformen

1 Setzen Sie die Adjektive in Klammern in den Komparativ oder Superlativ durch Hinzufügen von **-er** oder **-est** oder **more** oder **most.**

1. cheaper ◀1, easier ◀2 2. paler ◀1 3. more difficult ◀3 4. bigger ◀1, larger ◀1, noisier ◀2, madder ◀1, more fascinating ◀3 5. more clever or more stupid ◀4 6. more massive ◀4, bigger ◀1 7. more stupid ◀4 8. most civilised ◀3, least ◀5 9. earlier ◀2 10. more varied ◀4 11. quieter ◀6 12. simplest ◀2 13. best ◀5, fewest ◀1 14. fullest ◀1 15. most learned ◀4 16. more efficient ◀3

Erklärungen und Lernhinweise

▶1 Das Adjektiv ist einsilbig, es wird daher auf germanische Art gesteigert.

▶2 Das Adjektiv ist zweisilbig und endet auf **-y, -le, -er** oder **-ow**, es wird daher auf germanische Art gesteigert.

▶3 Das Adjektiv ist drei- oder mehrsilbig, es wird daher auf romanische Art gesteigert.

▶4 Das Adjektiv ist zweisilbig und wird auf der 1. Silbe betont, es wird daher auf romanische Art gesteigert.

▶5 Das Adjektiv wird unregelmäßig gesteigert.

▶6 **Quiet** steht vor einem Substantiv, es wird daher auf germanische Art gesteigert.

Das Adjektiv mit dem Stützwort one (The Adjective with the Prop-Word **one**)

1 Setzen Sie das Stützwort **one, ones** hinter die folgenden, fett gedruckten Adjektive wo nötig.

1. one ◀1 2. one, one ◀1 3. one ◀1 4. - ◀3 5. - ◀3 6. - ◀4 7. -, -, - ◀5 8. - ◀4 9. - ◀6 10. - ◀7 11. ones ◀2 12. ones ◀2 13. one ◀1 14. - ◀3 15. - ◀3 16. - ◀4 17. - ◀4 18. - ◀7 19. - ◀5 20. - ◀6 21. ones ◀2 22. one ◀1 23. one ◀1 24. - ◀3 25. - ◀5 26. - ◀4

Erklärungen und Lernhinweise

▶1 Das Substantiv (z.B. **eggs**) steht nicht unmittelbar nach dem Adjektiv (z.B. **bad**), es steht daher das Stützwort **one, ones**. Es handelt sich um eine Sache, daher steht **one**.

▶2 Das Substantiv (z.B. **rules**) steht nicht unmittelbar nach dem Adjektiv (z.B. **big**), es steht daher das Stützwort **one, ones**. Es handelt sich um mehrere Sachen, daher steht **ones**.

▶3 Der Superlativ bzw. Komparativ ist mit dem bestimmten Artikel verbunden, es entfällt daher **one, ones**.

▶4 Die Adjektive **few** und **many** stehen immer ohne **one, ones**.

▶5 Die Ordnungszahlen bezeichnen keine bestimmte Person oder Sache aus einer Gruppe, es entfällt daher **one**, **ones**.

▶6 Die Possessivpronomen + **own** stehen immer ohne **one, ones**.

▶7 Die Grundzahl bezieht sich auf das zuvor erwähnte Substantiv (z.B. **teenagers**), daher entfällt **one, ones**.

Der Vergleich (The Comparison)

1 Setzen Sie **than, like** oder **as** ein.

1. than ◀1 2. as ◀2 3. as ◀2 4. as ◀3 5. as ◀3 6. like ◀4 7. like ◀4 8. than ◀1 9. than ◀1 10. like ◀4 11. like ◀4 12. as ◀3 13. as ◀3 14. as ◀2 15. as ◀2 16. than ◀1 17. as ◀3 18. as ◀2 19. like ◀4 20. as, as ◀3 21. than ◀1 22. like ◀4 23. as ◀3 24. than ◀1

Erklärungen und Lernhinweise

▶1 Das Adjektiv steht im Komparativ, daher wird der Vergleich durch **than** ausgedrückt. Im Deutschen steht nach Komparativen *als* und nicht *wie*.

▶2 Vor Substantiven oder Pronomen steht **as,** wenn ein ganzer Satz folgt. Im Deutschen steht *wie*.

▶3 Nach Adjektiven oder Adverbien steht bezüglich Substantiven **as**. Vor dem Adjektiv steht häufig **as** oder **so**, im Deutschen wird dies durch *so ... wie* übersetzt.

▶4 Vor Substantiven oder Pronomen, auf die kein ganzer Satz folgt, sondern die einzeln stehen, steht **like**. Häufig geht **like** ein Verb voraus.

Die Bildung des Adverbs (The Forms of the Adverb)

1 Ändern Sie die folgenden Adjektive in Adverbien und setzen Sie diese in die entsprechende Spalte der folgenden Tabelle.

1. **-y → -i:** angry - angrily, gay - gaily, lucky - luckily 1
   Ausnahmen: dry - dryly, shy - shyly
2. **Endung -e nach Konsonant bleibt**: attentive - attentively, extreme - extremely, sure - surely, unique - uniquely, vague - vaguely 2
   Endung -e nach Vokal entfällt: due - duly, true - truly 2
3. **-le nach Konsonant entfällt:** gentle - gently, idle -idly, terrible - terribly 3
   Ausnahme: whole - wholly
   -le nach Vokal bleibt: pale - palely, sole - solely, vile - vilely 3
4. **-l bleibt:** careful - carefully, cool - coolly, cruel - cruelly 4
   -ll → -l: dull -dully, full - fully, shrill - shrilly 5
5. **-ic → -ically:** heroic - heroically, practical - practically, radical - radically, 6

Erklärungen und Lernhinweise

1 Auf **-y** endende Adjektive ändern das **-y** in **-i** beim Anhängen von **-ly**.

2 Die Endung **-e** bleibt beim Anhängen von **-ly** erhalten, wenn dem **-e** ein Konsonant vorausgeht. **-gu** und **-qu** gelten als ein Buchstabe.
Die Endung **-e** entfällt beim Anhängen von **-ly**, wenn dem **-e** ein Vokal vorausgeht.

3 Die Endung **-le** entfällt beim Anhängen von **-ly**, wenn dem **-le** ein Konsonant vorausgeht.
Die Endung **-le** bleibt beim Anhängen von **-ly** erhalten, wenn dem **-le** ein Vokal vorausgeht.

4 Die Endung **-l** bleibt beim Anhängen von **-ly** erhalten, dadurch verdoppelt sich das **-l**.

5 Die Endung **-ll** wird zu **-l** beim Anhängen von **-ly**.

6 Ajektive auf **-ic** hängen **-ally** an.

Die Steigerung des Adverbs (The Comparison of the Adverb)

Die Bildung der Steigerungsformen

1 Setzen Sie die Adverbien in Klammern in den Komparativ oder Superlativ durch Hinzufügen von **-er** oder **-est.**

1. earlier ◀1 2. better ◀3 3. best ◀4/better ◀3 4. less ◀3 5. better ◀3 6. less ◀3 7. least ◀4 8. best ◀4/ better ◀3 9. farther ◀6 10. further ◀7 11. less ◀3 12. deeper ◀5 13. higher ◀5 14. most, least ◀4

Erklärungen und Lernhinweise

▶1 Es wird ein höherer Grad ausgedrückt, daher steht der Komparativ, der durch Anhängen der Endung **-er** an das Adverb gebildet wird. Diese Art der Steigerung nennt man germanische Steigerung. Ein Indiz für die Verwendung des Komparativs ist **than** zum Ausdruck des Vergleichs.
Auf **-y** endende Adverbien ändern dieses in **-i** beim Anhängen von **-er**.

▶2 Es wird der höchste Grad ausgedrückt, daher steht der Superlativ, der durch Anhängen der Endung **-est** an das Adverb gebildet wird. Diese Art der Steigerung nennt man germanische Steigerung. Ein Indiz für die Verwendung des Superlativs ist der bestimmte Artikel.

▶3 Es wird ein höherer Grad ausgedrückt, daher steht der Komparativ. Das Adverb wird unregelmäßig gesteigert.

▶4 Es wird der höchste Grad ausgedrückt, daher steht der Superlativ. Das Adverb wird unregelmäßig gesteigert.

▶5 Es wird ein höherer Grad ausgedrückt, daher steht der Komparativ. Das Adverb wird regelmäßig gesteigert.

▶6 Es wird ein höherer Grad ausgedrückt, daher steht der Komparativ. **Far** wird in seiner ursprünglichen, die Entfernung betreffenden Bedeutung verwendet, es wird daher regelmäßig gesteigert: **far - farther - farthest.**

▶7 Es wird ein höherer Grad ausgedrückt, daher steht der Komparativ. **Far** wird in übertragener Bedeutung verwendet, es wird daher unregelmäßig gesteigert: **far - further - furthest.**

2 Setzen Sie die Adverbien in Klammern in den Komparativ oder Superlativ durch Hinzufügen von **more** oder **most.**

1. more carefully ◀1 2. more coolly ◀1 3. more easily ◀1 4. more heavily ◀1 5. more loudly ◀1 6. more neatly, more distinctly ◀1 7. more closely ◀1 8. more easily ◀1 9. more favourably ◀1 10. more genially ◀1 11. more cheaply ◀1 12. more darkly ◀1 13. more deeply, more intricately, more learnedly ◀1 14. most frequently ◀2 15. more fully ◀1

Erklärungen und Lernhinweise

▶1 Es wird ein höherer Grad ausgedrückt, daher steht der Komparativ, d.h. dem Adverb wird **more** vorangestellt. Diese Art der Steigerung nennt man romanische Steigerung. Ein Indiz für die Verwendung des Komparativs ist **than** zum Ausdruck des Vergleichs.

Erklärungen und Lernhinweise

▶2 Es wird der höchste Grad ausgedrückt, daher steht der Superlativ, d.h. dem Adverb wird **most** vorangestellt. Diese Art der Steigerung nennt man romanische Steigerung. Ein Indiz für die Verwendung des Superlativs ist der bestimmte Artikel.

Bei den mit **more** und **most** gesteigerten Adverbien sind keine orthografischen Besonderheiten zu beachten, da das Adverb selbst nicht verändert wird.

Die Verwendung der Steigerungsformen

1 Setzen Sie die Adverbien in Klammern in den Komparativ oder Superlativ durch Hinzufügen von **-er** oder **-est** oder **more** oder **most**.

1. more precisely ◀1 2. later ◀2 3. closer, closer ◀2 4. faster ◀2 5. lower ◀2 6. more often ◀1 7. more efficiently, more accurately ◀1 8. longer ◀2 9. harder ◀2 10. louder ◀2 11. higher ◀2 12. sooner ◀2 13. more acutely ◀1

Erklärungen und Lernhinweise

▶1 Das Adverb ist zwei- oder mehrsilbig, es wird daher auf romanische Art gesteigert.

▶2 Das Adverb ist einsilbig oder es hat dieselbe Form wie das entsprechende Adjektiv, es wird daher auf germanische Art gesteigert.

Die Stellung des Adverbs (The Position of the Adverb)

1 Setzen Sie die Adverbien in Klammern vor oder hinter das Verb.

1. spoke **absently** ◀1 2. **apparently** wants to spend *the winter* ◀2 3. answered **calmly** ◀1 4. **cautiously** followed *the trace* ◀2 5. can **certainly** be ◀3 6. are not **directly** concerned ◀3 7. was **just** breaking ◀3 8. **calmly** took off *his tie* ◀2 9. is to be handled **carefully** ◀1 10. was **thoroughly and carefully** worked out ◀3 11. were **desperately** wanted ◀3 12. wish **heartily** ◀1 13. has **just** been brought ◀4 14. might **easily** become ◀3 15. had narrowed **enormously** ◀5 16. was **exactly** aimed at ◀3 17. was **firmly** fixed upon, must **inevitably** come to pass ◀3 18. **just** do not think ◀6 19. You **just** watch ◀6 20. cannot **legally** spend ◀3

Erklärungen und Lernhinweise

▶1 Es ist nur ein Vollverb vorhanden, auf das kein Objekt folgt, daher steht das Adverb nach dem Vollverb.

▶2 Es ist nur ein Vollverb vorhanden, auf das ein Objekt (kursiv dargestellt) folgt, daher steht das Adverb vor dem Vollverb.

▶3 Es ist ein Hilfs- bzw. Modalverb + Vollverb vorhanden, daher steht das Adverb zwischen dem Hilfs- bzw. Modalverb und dem Vollverb.

▶4 Es sind zwei Hilfsverben + Vollverb (Passiv) vorhanden, daher steht das Adverb nach dem ersten Hilfsverb.

▶5 Hilfsverb + Vollverb stehen am Satzende, daher tritt das Adverb hinter das Verb ans Satzende.

▶6 **Just** steht häufig vor dem Verb.

2 Setzen Sie die Adverbien in Klammern vor oder hinter das Adjektiv oder Adverb.

1. **only** to the doctor ◀1 2. **clearly** just ◀2 3. **here** just ◀3 4. clearly **enough** ◀4 5. here **last night** ◀3 6. big **enough** ◀4 7. **only** on January sixth ◀1 8. **carefully** horizontal ◀5 9. an **awfully** bad ◀5 10. **absolutely** unreasonable ◀5 11. here **last night** ◀3 12. wide **enough** ◀4 13. **there** just ◀3 14. **only** 50 cents left ◀1 15. **really astoundingly** well done ◀6 16. adequately **enough** ◀4 17. **only** Mr Robinson ◀1 18. **there** often ◀3 19. **certainly extraordinarily** beautiful ◀6 20. **comparatively** small ◀5

Erklärungen und Lernhinweise

▶1 **Only** tritt vor sein Bezugswort (z.B. ein Substantiv).

▶2 Das Adverb tritt vor ein anderes Adverb.

▶3 Das Adverb des Ortes tritt vor das Adverb der Zeit.

▶4 **Enough** steht hinter anderen Adverbien oder Adjektiven.

▶5 Das Adverb tritt vor das Adjektiv. Vor Adverbien, die mit Vokal beginnen, wird der unbestimmte Artikel zu **an.**

Erklärungen und Lernhinweise

▶6 Das Adverb tritt vor ein anderes Adverb, beide zusammen treten dann vor das Adjektiv oder ein anderes Adverb.

3 Setzen Sie die Adverbien in Klammern an den Satzanfang oder an das Satzende.

1. **Apparently** no one... ◀1 2. **Carefully** he folded... ◀1 3. **Eventually** they reached... ◀1 4. **Finally** a little girl... ◀1 5. **Generally** the British people... ◀1 6. **Indeed**, segregation and discrimination... ◀1 7. **Instantly** a warm wave... ◀1 8. **Calmly** he let them approach... ◀1 9. **Curiously** people... ◀1

Erklärungen und Lernhinweise

▶1 Das Adverb kann zur besonderen Hervorhebung an den Satzanfang oder an das Satzende treten. Es tritt hier an den Satzanfang, da es den Satz einleitet.

4 Setzen Sie die Adverbien in Klammern an die richtige Position.

1. listening **attentively** ◀1 2. will **eventually** drop ◀2 3. **frequently** merge *into big trusts* ◀4 4. **certainly** nice ◀3 5. **badly** injured ◀3 6. **Abruptly** he turned ◀7/**abruptly** away ◀3 7. **drastically** reduced *others* ◀4 8. washed **hurriedly** ◀1, **hurriedly** brushed *his teeth* ◀4, and **hurriedly** changed *his shirt* ◀4 9. **just** saved *himself* ◀4 10. had **actually** met ◀2/ **Actually** it was ◀7 11. do not hope **greatly** ◀1, **still** we hope ◀7 12. **Completely** alone ◀7 13. have **completely** become ◀2 14. **here** long before ◀5 15. **there** never ◀5 16. has **seriously and extensively** been adopted ◀8, **only** in the Commonwealth ◀6

Erklärungen und Lernhinweise

▶1 Es ist nur ein Vollverb vorhanden, auf das kein Objekt folgt, daher steht das Adverb nach dem Vollverb.

▶2 Es ist ein Hilfs- bzw. Modalverb + Vollverb vorhanden, daher steht das Adverb zwischen dem Hilfs- bzw. Modalverb und dem Vollverb.

▶3 Es ist ein Adjektiv bzw. Adverb vorhanden, daher steht das Adverb vor diesem.

▶4 Es ist ein Vollverb vorhanden, auf das ein Objekt (kursiv gedruckt) folgt, daher steht das Adverb vor dem Vollverb.

▶5 Das Adverb des Ortes tritt vor das Adverb der Zeit.

▶6 **Only** tritt vor das Wort, auf das es sich bezieht.

▶7 Das Adverb wird hier besonders betont, es tritt daher an den Satzanfang (auch bei einem Teilsatz).

▶8 Es sind zwei Hilfsverben + Vollverb (Passiv) vorhanden, daher steht das Adverb nach dem ersten Hilfsverb.

Adverb oder Adjektiv (Adverb or Adjective)

1 Ändern Sie die Wörter in Klammern in Adverbien oder Adjektive.

1. quiet ◀1 2. close ◀1 3. early ◀2 4. attentive ◀1 5. angrily ◀3 6. close ◀1 7. badly ◀4 8. least ◀2 9. little ◀2 10. completely ◀4 11. less ◀2 12. much ◀2 13. best ◀2 14. independent ◀1 15. silent, scornful ◀1 16. better ◀2 17. worst ◀2 18. attentive ◀1 attentively ◀3 19. last ◀2 20. abruptly ◀3 21. clear ◀1 22. much ◀2 23. fast ◀1 24. enough ◀2 25. straight ◀1 26. little ◀2 27. constantly ◀3 28. short ◀1 29. less ◀2 30. worst ◀2 31. completely ◀5 32. calm, cheerful ◀1 33. much ◀2 34. less ◀2 35. old, stiff, spiteful ◀1 36. well ◀3, truly ◀6, correctly ◀3 37. possible ◀1 38. little ◀2 39. worst ◀2 40. barely ◀3

Erklärungen und Lernhinweise

▶1 Dieses Verb wird mit dem Adjektiv verbunden, sonst werden Verben durch Adverbien näher bestimmt.

▶2 Das näher zu bestimmende Wort ist ein Substantiv, daher steht das Adjektiv. **Early, little, much, good, bad** und ihre Steigerungsformen können sowohl Adjektiv als auch Adverb sein, hier sind sie Adjektiv.

▶3 Das näher zu bestimmende Wort ist ein Verb, daher steht das Adverb (z.B. in **Arthur stopped abruptly** ist das Innehalten abrupt und nicht Arthur).

▶4 Das näher zu bestimmende Wort ist ein Adjektiv, daher steht das Adverb (z.B. in **her face seems badly hurt** ist die Verletzung schlimm, nicht ihr Gesicht).

▶5 **Completely** bezieht sich hier auf das Adjektiv **unscrutable**, daher steht das Adverb **completely** und nicht das Adjektiv **complete** trotz des vorausgehenden Verbs **remain**.

▶6 **True** verliert die Endung **-e** beim Anhängen von **-ly.**

2 Ändern Sie die Wörter in Klammern in Adverbien oder Adjektive.

1. **lately**; kürzlich ◀1 2. **late**; spät ◀2 3. **clear**; klar ◀2 4. **clearly**; deutlich ◀1 5. **pretty;** hübsch ◀3 6. **pretty**; ziemlich ◀4 7. **hard**; hart ◀2 8. **hard;** hart ◀2 9. **hardly**; kaum ◀1 10. **hard**; hart ◀2 11. **high**; hoch ◀2 12. **highly**; äußerst ◀1 13. **high**; hoch ◀2 14. **high**; hoch ◀2 15. **only**; einzig ◀3 16. **only**; nur ◀4 17. **fairly**; ziemlich ◀1 18. **fair**; fair ◀2 19. **justly**; zurecht ◀1 20. **justly**; zurecht ◀1 21. **just**; gerecht ◀2 22. **deeply**; zutiefst ◀1 23. **deep**; tief ◀2 24. **nearest**; kürzesten ◀2 25. **nearly**; beinahe, fast ◀1

Erklärungen und Lernhinweise

▶1 Das näher zu bestimmende Wort ist ein Verb, Adjektiv oder Adverb (das Verb, Adjektiv, Adverb steht meist unmittelbar nach dem Adverb), daher steht das Adverb auf **-ly**. Das Adjektiv (ohne **-ly**) steht zur näheren Bestimmung von Substantiven. Häufig liegt zwischen Adjektiv und Adverb ein Bedeutungsunterschied vor, dies wird durch die Übersetzung deutlich.

▶2 Das näher zu bestimmende Wort ist ein Substantiv, daher steht hier das Adjektiv (ohne **-ly**).

▶3 Dieses Adjektiv kann auch Adverb sein, es hat dieselbe Form. Hier ist es Adjektiv, da es zur näheren Bestimmung von Substantiven dient (das Substantiv steht unmittelbar nach dem Adjektiv). Meist liegt zwischen Adjektiv und Adverb ein Bedeutungsunterschied vor, dies wird durch die Übersetzung deutlich.

▶4 Dieses Adverb kann auch Adjektiv sein, es hat dieselbe Form. Hier ist es Adverb, da es zur näheren Bestimmung von Verben, Adjektiven oder Adverbien dient (das Verb, Adjektiv, Adverb steht meist unmittelbar nach dem Adverb). Meist liegt zwischen Adjektiv und Adverb ein Bedeutungsunterschied vor, dies wird durch die Übersetzung deutlich.

Das Personalpronomen (The Personal Pronoun)

Das deutsche *es*

1 Setzen Sie **it** + die entsprechende Verbform von **to be** im past tense simple ein, um das deutsche *es* auszudrücken.

1. It was 2. it was 3. It was 4. it was 5. It was 6. It was 7. It was 8. It was 9. it was 10. It is

Erklärungen und Lernhinweise

1 Zur Hervorhebung der Person bzw. Sache steht **it +** die entsprechende Form von **be** (z.B. **it is, it was**).

2 Auf **it** folgendes **be** steht immer im Singular, selbst wenn die folgende, hervorzuhebende Person oder Sache im Plural steht (also z.B. **it was two Americans** und nicht **it were**).

2 Setzen Sie **there** + die entsprechende Form der Verben in Klammern im past tense simple oder verwenden Sie die in Klammern angegebene Zeit.

1. there came 2. there was 3. there had been 4. There were 5. there was 6. There was 7. There was 8. There was 9. There was 10. There appeared 11. There remained 12. There were 13. There were 14. there seems 15. there emerged 16. there sat 17. There stepped 18. there sprang 19. there was 20. there is

Erklärungen und Lernhinweise

1 Zur Hervorhebung der Person bzw. Sache steht **there + Verb.** Das hervorzuhebende Satzglied (Subjekt) tritt hinter **there** + Verb. Es ist zu beachten, dass sich das Verb nach dem folgenden Subjekt richtet.

2 Vor **be** tritt **there** als sogenanntes Vorsubjekt, das Subjekt des Satzes folgt nach. Es ist zu beachten, dass sich **be** nach dem folgenden Subjekt richtet, d.h. steht das folgende Subjekt z.B. in der 3. Person Plural (z.B. **no sausages**) steht **be** ebenfalls in der 3. Person Plural (**were**, da hier das past tense verlangt wird).
Im Deutschen wird diese Konstruktion mit *es gibt* übersetzt oder es bleibt unübersetzt.

3 **Fish** bezeichnet trotz des fehlenden Plural-s mehrere Tiere, daher steht das Verb **be** im Plural.

3 Setzen Sie **so** ein, um das deutsche *es* auszudrücken.

1. hope **so** 2. said **so** 3. suppose **so** 4. think **so** 5. **So** am I 6. hope **so** 7. said **so** 8. suppose **so** 9. think **so** 10. **So** I've heard 11. do **so**

Erklärungen und Lernhinweise

1 Das Verb ist ein Verb des Sagens und Denkens bzw. der Sinneswahrnehmung, daher steht **so** zum Ausdruck des deutschen *es*.

Erklärungen und Lernhinweise

2 **So** steht im Sinne von *auch*. Das Subjekt tritt hinter das Verb. (z.B.: **he is a really poor guy so am I** *bedeutet also er ist ein wirlich armer Kerl, das bin ich auch*).

4 Setzen Sie **it** oder **there** oder **so** + die entsprechende Form des Verbs in Klammern im past tense simple ein, um das deutsche *es* auszudrücken.

1. It was 1 2. there came 3 3. it was 1 4. so 4 5. It was 2 6. there was, there were 3 7. there was 3 8. It was 1 9. so 4 10. There were 3 11. It was 2 12. There remained 3 13. so 4 14. There seemed 3 15. There was 3 16. There was 3

Erklärungen und Lernhinweise

1 Es ist eine bestimmte Person bzw. Sache hervorzuheben und das Verb ist **be**, daher steht **it**.

2 Auf **it** folgendes **be** steht immer im Singular, selbst wenn die folgende, hervorzuhebende Person oder Sache im Plural steht.

3 Es ist keine bestimmte Person bzw. Sache hervorzuheben und das Verb ist **be** oder ein anderes Verb, daher steht **there**. Das hervorzuhebende Satzglied (Subjekt) tritt hinter **there** + Verb. Es ist zu beachten, dass sich das Verb nach dem folgenden Subjekt richtet.

4 Das Verb ist ein Verb des Sagens und Denkens bzw. der Sinneswahrnehmung, daher steht **so** zum Ausdruck des deutschen *es*.

Das Reflexivpronomen (The Reflexive Pronoun)

1 Setzen Sie das entsprechende Reflexivpronomen ein.

1. myself ◀1 2. yourself/yourselves ◀2 3. himself ◀3 4. themselves ◀5 5. ourselves ◀4 6. itself ◀6 7. oneself ◀8 8. yourself ◀2 9. himself ◀3 10. yourself/yourselves ◀2 11. yourself/ yourselves ◀2 12. herself ◀3 13. himself ◀3 14. myself ◀1 15. yourself/yourselves ◀2 16. himself ◀7 17. himself ◀3 18. himself ◀7 19. himself ◀7 20. itself ◀6

Erklärungen und Lernhinweise

▶1 Das Subjekt bezeichnet die 1. Person Singular, daher lautet das Reflexivpronomen **myself.** Das Subjekt kann auch nach dem Reflexivpronomen stehen.

▶2 Das Subjekt bezeichnet die 2. Person Singular bzw. Plural, daher lautet das Reflexivpronomen **yourself** bzw. **yourselves.** Das Subjekt kann auch nach dem Reflexivpronomen stehen.
Yourself, yourselves steht auch beim Imperativ, da der Imperativ die 2. Person bezeichnet (z.B. in **if you doubt me, ask her yourself**).

▶3 Das Subjekt bezeichnet die 3. Person Singular, daher lautet das Reflexivpronomen für männliche Personen **himself** bzw. für weibliche Personen **herself**. Das Subjekt kann auch nach dem Reflexivpronomen stehen.

▶4 Das Subjekt bezeichnet die 1. Person Plural, daher lautet das Reflexivpronomen **ourselves.** Das Subjekt kann auch nach dem Reflexivpronomen stehen.

▶5 Das Subjekt bezeichnet die 3. Person Plural, daher lautet das Reflexivpronomen **themselves**. Das Subjekt kann auch nach dem Reflexivpronomen stehen.

▶6 Das Subjekt bezeichnet eine Sache (**it, this**), daher lautet das Reflexivpronomen **itself**.

▶7 Das Subjekt bezeichnet eine unbestimmte, dritte Person (**everyone, each person's, no one** etc.), daher lautet das Reflexivpronomen **himself**. Das Subjekt kann auch nach dem Reflexivpronomen stehen.

▶8 Das Subjekt ist das Pronomen **one**, daher lautet das Reflexivpronomen **oneself**.

2 Setzen Sie das entsprechende Reflexiv- oder Personalpronomen ein.

1. him ◀1 2. myself ◀2 3. him ◀1 4. him ◀1 5. himself ◀3 6. himself ◀2 7. himself ◀3 8. himself ◀4 9. herself ◀2 10. herself ◀3 11. himself ◀4 12. himself ◀4 13. himself ◀3 14. himself ◀3 15. myself ◀2 16. myself ◀2 17. myself ◀4 18. them ◀1 19. them ◀1 20. us ◀1 21. ourselves ◀4 22. himself ◀3, himself ◀3 23. her ◀1 24. him ◀1, himself ◀3

Erklärungen und Lernhinweise

▶1 Nach Präpositionen steht häufig das Personalpronomen.

▶2 In Aufzählungen (besonders nach **and** und **or**) steht das Reflexivpronomen.

▶3 Es wird das Subjekt hervorgehoben (*selbst*), daher steht das Reflexivpronomen (z.B. in **he swore to himself** wird hervorgehoben, dass er es *sich selbst* schwor und nicht jemand anderem).

▶4 In Vergleichen (besonders nach **as, than, like**) steht das Reflexivpronomen.

Das Reziprokpronomen (The Reciprocal Pronoun)

1 Setzen Sie **each other** oder **one another** ein.

1. one another ◄1 2. each other ◄2 3. one another ◄1 4. each other ◄2 5. each other ◄2 6. one another ◄1 7. one another ◄1 8. each other ◄2 9. one another's ◄3 10. each other ◄2 11. one another ◄1 12. one another ◄1 13. one another ◄1 14. each other's ◄3 15. one another's ◄3 16. each other ◄2 17. one another ◄1

Erklärungen und Lernhinweise

▶1 Es handelt sich um mehrere Personen(gruppen), daher steht **one another**.

▶2 Es handelt sich um zwei Personen, daher steht **each other**. Dies gilt auch für Personengruppen (z.B. **boys** and **girls** sind zwar mehrere Personen, aber zwei Personengruppen).

▶3 Es wird ein Besitzverhältnis (z.B. die Augen von ihnen) ausgedrückt, daher steht der possessive case und zwar **'s**, da **one another** bzw. **each other** nicht auf -s enden oder im Plural stehen.

Das Possessivpronomen (The Possessive Pronoun)

Das attributive Possessivpronomen

1 Setzen Sie das entsprechende attributive Possessivpronomen oder den bestimmten Artikel ein.

1. his ◀1 2. the ◀2 3. the ◀2 4. the ◀2 5. his ◀1, the ◀2 6. his ◀1, his ◀1, his ◀1 7. his ◀1, his ◀1, his ◀1, his ◀1 8. his ◀1 9. your ◀1 10. the ◀2 11. the ◀2, the ◀2 12. his ◀1, his ◀1 13. the ◀1 14. her ◀1 15. his/its ◀1 16. the ◀2 17. the ◀2 18. his ◀1, his ◀1 19. his ◀1, his ◀1 20. the ◀2 21. his ◀1

Erklärungen und Lernhinweise

▶1 Der Körperteil, das Kleidungsstück gehört zum Subjekt, daher steht das zum Subjekt gehörende Possessivpronomen (z.B.: in **He tucked them under his arm** gehört der "Arm" zum Subjekt **he**).

▶2 Der Körperteil, das Kleidungsstück gehört zum Objekt, daher steht der bestimmte Artikel (z.B.: bei **the shot hit the king in the breast** gehört die "Brust" zum Objekt **the king** und nicht zum Subjekt **the shot**).

Das substantivische Possessivpronomen

1 Setzen Sie das substantivische oder attributive Possessivpronomen ein.

1. his *work* ◀1 2. mine/yours/his/hers/ours/theirs ◀2 3. mine/his/hers/ours/theirs ◀2 4. her *friends* ◀1 5. his ◀2 6. mine/yours/his/hers/ours/theirs ◀2 7. my *eye* ◀1 8. their *marriage* ◀1 9. her ◀3 10. mine/yours/his/hers/ours/theirs ◀2 11. my *classmates* ◀1 12. mine/yours/his/hers/ours/theirs ◀2 13. hers ◀2 14. your *time* ◀1 15. mine/yours/his/hers/ours/theirs ◀2 16. My/your/his/her/our/their *time* ◀1 17. mine/yours/his/ hers/ours/theirs ◀2 18. His *Royal Highness* ◀1

Erklärungen und Lernhinweise

▶1 Auf das Pronomen folgt ein Substantiv, daher wird das attributive Possessivpronomen verwendet, denn dieses steht immer bei einem Substantiv (kursiv dargestellt). Welches Pronomen gewählt wird, hängt davon ab, wer der Besitzer ist (z.B. in **does a scientist have to think about possible consequences of his work** gehört das "Besitzobjekt" **work** zum "Besitzer" **a scientist**, daher steht **his**).

▶2 Auf das Pronomen folgt kein Substantiv, daher steht das substantivische Possessivpronomen, denn dieses steht immer alleine. Welches Pronomen gewählt wird, hängt davon ab, wer der Besitzer ist (z.B. in **he is no true friend of mine** etc. gehört das "Besitzobjekt" **friend** zu *mir* etc., daher steht **mine** etc.).

▶3 In Verbindung mit **own** steht das attributive Possessivpronomen.

2 Ändern Sie die folgenden fett gedruckten attributiven Possessivpronomen in substantivische Possessivpronomen und schreiben Sie die Sätze neu.

1. that car of his ◀1 2. other village acquaintances of his ◀1 3. that visit of mine ◀1 4. friends of yours ◀1 5. a friend of yours ◀1 6. mine ◀2 7. yours ◀2 8. his ◀2 9. this interest of yours ◀1 10. all voices of theirs ◀1

Erklärungen und Lernhinweise

▶1 Das Substantiv wird dem substantivischen Possessivpronomen vorangestellt und mit **of** angeschlossen.

▶2 Dem attributiven Possessivpronomen geht **be** voraus, es wird nur durch das substantivische Possessivpronomen ersetzt. Beide Konstruktionen bedeuten *gehören*.

Das Demonstrativpronomen (The Demonstrative Pronoun)

1 Setzen Sie **this, these** oder **that, those** ein.

1. this ◀1 2. those ◀2 3. these ◀1 4. these ◀1 5. those ◀2 6. that ◀2 7. that ◀2 8. those ◀3 9. this ◀4 10. That ◀2 11. those ◀2 12. that ◀3 13. these ◀1 14. those ◀2 15. that ◀2 16. this ◀1 17. these ◀1 18. this ◀1 19. this ◀1 20. these ◀1 21. this ◀1 22. this ◀1 23. that ◀2 24. those ◀2 25. those ◀2

Erklärungen und Lernhinweise

▶1 Die Person bzw. Sache befindet sich nahe beim Sprecher, daher steht **this** für eine, **these** für mehrere. Im Deutschen werden diese Pronomen durch *dieser, diese, dieses* übersetzt.

▶2 Die Person bzw. Sache befindet sich vom Sprecher entfernt, daher steht **that** für eine und **those** für mehrere. Dass es sich um Fernerliegendes handelt, ist z.B. zu erkennen an Ortsangaben wie **over there**. Im Deutschen werden diese Pronomen durch *jener, jene, jenes* übersetzt.

▶3 Es wird auf das zuvor Genannte hingewiesen, daher steht **that** für eines, **those** für mehrere (z.B. in **there were only very few roads and even those roads...** weist **those roads** auf die zuvor genannten).

▶4 Es wird auf das Folgende hingewiesen, daher steht **this** für eines, **these** für mehrere (z.B. in **... sent this radio message** weist **this radio message** auf die anschließend folgende Nachricht).

2 Setzen Sie **this, these** oder **that, those** ein.

1. those ◀1 2. that ◀1 3. this ◀2 4. this ◀2 5. this ◀2 6. this ◀2 7. these ◀2 8. these ◀2 9. that ◀1 10. this ◀2 11. those ◀1 12. that ◀1 13. that ◀1 14. these ◀2 15. this ◀2 16. that ◀1 17. that ◀1 18. that ◀1 19. These ◀2 20. those ◀1

Erklärungen und Lernhinweise

▶1 Der Vorgang bezieht sich auf die Vergangenheit, daher steht **that** bezüglich eines Substantivs, **those** bezüglich mehrerer. Ein Indiz hierfür ist das Verb in einer Zeit der Vergangenheit.

▶2 Der Vorgang bezieht sich auf die Gegenwart, daher steht **this** bezüglich eines Substantivs, **these** bezüglich mehrerer. Ein Indiz hierfür ist das Verb in einer Zeit der Gegenwart.

3 Setzen Sie **this, that** oder **these, those** ein und fügen Sie **one** hinzu wo nötig.

1. this one ◀1 2. that one ◀1 3. That ◀2 4. this ◀2 5. this one ◀1 6. this one ◀1 7. This ◀2 8. these ◀3 9. that one ◀1 10. That ◀2 11. That one ◀1 12. this one ◀1 13. that one ◀1 14. this one ◀1, that one ◀1 15. this one ◀1 16. those ◀3 17. That ◀2 18. This ◀2 19. these ◀3

Erklärungen und Lernhinweise

▶1 Die Person bzw. Sache wird zuvor erwähnt, daher wird **one** hinzugefügt (z.B. in **don't ask for another book until you've finished this one** wird **book** vorher genannt).

▶2 Auf **this** bzw. **that** folgt **be**, daher entfällt **one**.

▶3 **These** und **those** stehen immer ohne **one**.

Das Determinativpronomen (The Determinative Pronoun)

Das substantivische Determinativpronomen

1 Setzen Sie **that of, those of** oder **the one, the ones** ein.

1. that of ◀1 2. the one ◀2 3. the one ◀2 4. the ones ◀2 5. the one ◀2 6. those of ◀1 7. that of ◀1 8. that of ◀1, that of ◀1 9. that of ◀1 10. the one ◀2 11. those of ◀1 12. that of ◀1 13. that of ◀1 14. those of ◀1 15. those of ◀1

Erklärungen und Lernhinweise

▶1 Es wird eine Person bzw. Sache ganz allgemein, nicht aus einer Gruppe bezeichnet, daher steht **that of** für eine, **those of** für mehrere.

▶2 Es wird eine Person bzw. Sache aus einer Gruppe bezeichnet, daher steht **the one** für eine, **the ones** für mehrere (z.B. in **Would you like a cappuccino or an espresso? Which is the one with milk** wird der **cappuccino** aus der Gruppe mehrerer Kaffees (**cappuccino** und **espresso**) bezeichnet.

2 Setzen Sie **he who, those who** oder **that which, those which** oder **the one who, the ones who** ein.

1. the one who ◀1 2. He who ◀2 3. he who ◀2 4. he who ◀2 5. those who ◀2 6. the ones who ◀1 7. those who ◀2 8. the one who ◀1 9. The one who ◀1 10. those which ◀3 11. those which ◀3 12. those which ◀3 13. He who ◀2 14. those who ◀2 15. those who ◀2 16. the one who ◀1 17. those who ◀2 18. He who ◀2 19. he who ◀2 20. that which ◀3

Erklärungen und Lernhinweise

▶1 Es ist eine bestimmte Person aus einer Gruppe gemeint, daher steht **the one who** für eine, **the ones who** für mehrere (z.B. in **he is the one who showed me** ist **he** die bestimmte, zuvor genannte Person).

▶2 Es ist keine bestimmte Person gemeint, daher steht **he who** für eine männliche Person oder wenn das Geschlecht unbekannt ist, für mehrere Personen steht **they** oder **those who** (z.B. in **many settlers died and those who ...** sind keine bestimmten Siedler aus der Gruppe der vielen Siedler gemeint).

▶3 Es ist eine Sache, aber keine bestimmte gemeint, daher steht **that which** für eine, **those which** für mehrere.

Das attributive Determinativpronomen

1 Setzen Sie **those who, the who** oder **the which** ein.

1. those ... who ◀1 2. The ... which ◀2 3. The ... which ◀2 4. The ... who ◀2 5. The ... which ◀2 6. The ... who ◀2 7. the ... who ◀2 8. the ... who ◀2 9. those ... who ◀1 10. the ... which ◀2 11. the ... which ◀2 12. the ... who ◀2 13. the ... which ◀2 14. the ... which ◀2 15. the ... who ◀2

Erklärungen und Lernhinweise

▶1 Es ist eine Person aus einer Gruppe näher zu bestimmen, daher steht **that who** für eine Person, **those who** für mehrere (z.B. **she was one of those people who** ... weist **one of** auf die Gruppe).

▶2 Es ist eine Sache bzw. Person ganz allgemein näher zu bestimmen, daher steht **the which** für eine und mehrere Sachen bzw. **the who** für eine und mehrere Personen.

Das Relativpronomen (The Relative Pronoun)

1 Setzen Sie **who** oder **whom** ein.

1. whom ◀1 2. whom ◀1 3. whom ◀1 4. who ◀2 5. whom ◀1 6. whom ◀1 7. who ◀2 8. whom ◀1 9. whom ◀1 10. who ◀2 11. whom ◀1 12. who ◀2 13. whom ◀1 14. who ◀2 15. who ◀2 16. whom ◀1 17. who ◀2

Erklärungen und Lernhinweise

▶1 Die Person, auf die sich das Pronomen bezieht ist Objekt, daher steht **whom**. Dass die Person Objekt ist, ist z.B. daran zu erkennen, dass auf **whom** das Subjekt folgt (z.B. in **the wounded whom she found** folgt auf **whom** das Subjekt **she, the wounded** ist Objekt).

▶2 Die Person, auf die sich das Pronomen bezieht ist Subjekt, daher steht **who**. Dass die Person Subjekt ist, ist z.B. daran zu erkennen, dass auf **who** das Verb folgt (z.B. in **it was the Millers who called us** folgt auf **who** das Verb **called**).

2 Setzen Sie **which** oder **that, who** oder **whom** ein.

1. who ◀1 2. which ◀2 3. that ◀3 4. that ◀3 5. who ◀1 6. whom ◀4 7. whom ◀4 8. who ◀1 9. that ◀3 10. who ◀1 11. who ◀1 12. whom ◀4 13. whom ◀4 14. which ◀2 15. that ◀3 16. that ◀3 17. which ◀2 18. which ◀2 19. that ◀3 20. who ◀1 21. which ◀2 22. that ◀3 23. that ◀3

Erklärungen und Lernhinweise

▶1 Das Pronomen bezieht sich auf eine Person und die ist Subjekt, daher steht **who**. Dass die Person Subjekt ist, ist z.B. daran zu erkennen, dass auf **who** das Verb folgt.

▶2 Das Pronomen bezieht sich auf eine bestimmte Sache aus einer Gruppe, die Subjekt oder Objekt ist, daher steht **which**. Dass es sich um eine Sache aus einer Gruppe handelt ist z.B. an **one of, among** zu erkennen.

▶3 Das Pronomen bezieht sich auf eine Sache oder Person ganz allgemein, die Subjekt oder Objekt ist, daher steht **that**. In der modernen Sprache wird bezüglich Personen **who** bzw. **whom** bevorzugt.

▶4 Das Pronomen bezieht sich auf eine Person und die ist Objekt, daher steht **whom**. Dass die Person Objekt ist, ist daran zu erkennen, dass auf **whom** das Subjekt folgt.

3 Setzen Sie **whose** oder **of which** ein.

1. of which ◀1 2. of which ◀1 3. of which ◀1 4. whose ◀2 5. whose ◀2 6. whose ◀2 7. whose ◀2 8. whose ◀2 9. whose ◀2 10. whose ◀2 11. whose ◀2 12. whose ◀2 13. whose ◀2 14. whose ◀2 15. whose ◀2 16. of which ◀1 17. of which ◀1 18. whose ◀2 19. whose ◀2

Erklärungen und Lernhinweise

▶1 Das Pronomen bezieht sich auf eine Sache und drückt ein Besitzverhältnis aus, daher steht **of which**. **Of which** wird häufig durch **whose** ersetzt, jedoch ist dies nur möglich, wenn das "Besitzobjekt" nach dem Pronomen steht (z.B. in **he looked into the hotel bar whose door...** steht das "Besitzobjekt" **door** nach **whose**), steht das "Besitzobjekt" vor dem Pronomen, ist nur **of which** möglich (z.B. **he looked into the hotel bar the door of which...**).

▶2 Das Pronomen bezieht sich auf eine Person und drückt ein Besitzverhältnis aus, daher steht **whose**. Bezüglich Sachen kann **whose** ebenfalls stehen, allerdings muss das "Besitzobjekt" nach dem Pronomen stehen (z.B. in **he looked into the hotel bar whose door...** steht das "Besitzobjekt" **door** nach **whose**).

4 Setzen Sie **whoever, whichever** oder **whatever** ein.

1. Whatever ◀1 2. Whichever ◀2/whatever ◀1 3. Whatever ◀1 4. whoever ◀3 5. Whatever ◀1 6. whatever ◀1 7. Whoever ◀3 8. whatever ◀1 9. whichever ◀2 10. Whatever ◀1 11. whatever ◀1/ whichever ◀2 12. whoever ◀3 13. whatever ◀1

Erklärungen und Lernhinweise

▶1 Das Pronomen bezeichnet einen allgemeinen, folgenden Sachverhalt oder eine unbestimmte Sache ganz allgemein, daher steht **whatever**.

▶2 Das Pronomen bezeichnet eine unbestimmte Sache aus einer Gruppe, daher steht **whichever**.

▶3 Das Pronomen bezeichnet eine unbestimmte Person, daher steht **whoever** (z.B. in **... whoever wants Philip not to be chief** bezieht sich **whoever** auf irgendeine Person, die nicht möchte, dass Philip Chef wird).

5 Setzen Sie **that, when, whenever, where** oder **wherever** ein.

1. whenever ◀1 2. when ◀2 3. whenever ◀1 4. when ◀2/that ◀3 5. where ◀4 6. where ◀4 7. when ◀2 8. that ◀3/when ◀2 9. wherever ◀5 10. where ◀4 11. when ◀2 12. when ◀2 13. that ◀3/when ◀2 14. that ◀3/when ◀2 15. where ◀4 16. that ◀3/when ◀2 17. where ◀4 18. when ◀2 19. wherever ◀5

Erklärungen und Lernhinweise

▶1 Das Pronomen bezeichnet einen unbestimmten Zeitpunkt, -raum, daher steht **whenever** (z.B. in **...their travel plans whenever they discussed them** wird der Zeitpunkt der Diskussion nicht genannt (wann auch immer)).

▶2 Das Pronomen bezeichnet einen bestimmten Zeitpunkt, -raum, daher steht **when** (z.B. in **he was walking back to his car when a sports car ...** ist der bestimmte Zeitpunkt als der Sportwagen erscheint).

▶3 Das Pronomen bezeichnet einen bestimmten Zeitpunkt, -raum und es leitet einen notwendigen Relativsatz (der zum Verständnis des Satzes notwendig ist und daher nicht weggelassen werden kann), daher steht **that**.

▶4 Das Pronomen bezeichnet einen bestimmten Ort, daher steht **where** (z.B. in ... **provide canteens where ...** ist der bestimmte Ort die Kantinen).

▶5 Das Pronomen bezeichnet einen unbestimmten Ort, daher steht **wherever** (z.B. in **... to detect discrimination wherever it can be identified** wird der Ort der Entdeckung nicht genannt (wo auch immer)).

Das Interrogativpronomen (The Interrogative Pronoun)

1 Ersetzen Sie die fett gedruckten Wörter durch **who, whom** oder **whose** und schreiben Sie die Sätze neu.

1. Who told you that ◀1 2. Who/whom are you calling? ◀2 3. Whom/who do you believe? ◀3 4. Whom/who do you blame? ◀3 5. Whose hat do you want? ◀4 6. Who are you going to share your room with?/With whom are you going to share your room? ◀2 7. Whose job is it to make plans for houses? ◀5 8. Who is going to look after my children? ◀1 9. Who helps you with your homework? ◀1 10. Who/whom did she marry? ◀3 11. Who was she talking to?/To whom was she talking? ◀2 12. Who does this black bag belong to?/To whom does this black bag belong? ◀3 13. Who might have asked the following question? ◀1 14. Who/whom does the inspector suspect? ◀3 15. Whose socks are these? ◀5 16. Who/whom did they begin to help ◀3 17. Whose fault was this? ◀5 18. Who were you making fun of?/Of whom were you making fun? ◀2 19. Who/whom was he shield-ing? ◀2 20. Who/whom would you call the father of railroading? ◀2 21. Who/whom did Mr Burton suspect of being the thief? ◀3 22. Who is to be blamed for Jack's failure to get the job? ◀1 23. Who would have thought you had so much courage? ◀1

Erklärungen und Lernhinweise

▶1 Es wird das Subjekt erfragt, daher steht **who**. Da **who** damit Subjekt ist, wird die Frage ohne **to do** gebildet. **I** bzw. **me** werden sinnvollerweise in **you** bzw. **your** umgewandelt.

▶2 Es wird das Objekt erfragt, daher steht **whom** oder **who**. Das Subjekt tritt hinter das Verb, das auf **whom** bzw. **who** folgt. Das Verb ist ein Hilfs- bzw. Modalverb, daher wird die Frage nicht mit **to do** gebildet. Präpositionen treten bei **who** ans Satzende oder vor **whom**.

▶3 Es wird das Objekt erfragt, daher steht **whom** oder **who**. Das Verb ist ein Vollverb und das Fragewort ist nicht Subjekt (z.B. in **I believe Bob** bleibt das Subjekt **I** des Aussagesatzes ja erhalten), daher wird die Frage mit **do** gebildet. Im present tense simple steht **do** bzw. **does** in der 3. Person Singular, im past tense simple steht **did**. Es ist zu beachten, dass auf **did** stets der Infinitiv des Vollverbs folgt (also **who did they begin** und nicht **who did they began**).
Das Subjekt tritt hinter **do**. Ist das Subjekt **I** wird es sinnvollerweise in **you** umgewandelt.

▶4 Es wird der Besitzer erfragt, daher steht **whose**. Das Verb ist ein Vollverb und das Fragewort ist nicht Subjekt, daher wird die Frage mit **to do** gebildet. Das Subjekt tritt hinter **do**. Ist das Subjekt **I** wird es sinnvollerweise in **you** umgewandelt.

▶5 Es wird der Besitzer erfragt (possessive case), daher steht **whose**. Das Verb ist ein Hilfsverb, daher wird die Frage nicht mit **to do** gebildet. Das Subjekt tritt hinter das Verb.

2 Setzen Sie **which** oder **what** ein.

1. What ◀1 2. What ◀1 3. What ◀1 4. Which ◀2 5. What ◀1 6. What ◀1 7. Which ◀2 8. Which ◀2 9. What ◀1 10. What ◀1 11. Which ◀2 12. What ◀1 13. Which ◀2 14. Which ◀2 15. What ◀1 16. What ◀1 17. What ◀1 18. What ◀1 19. What ◀1 20. Which ◀2 21. What ◀1 22. What ◀1 23. Which ◀2

Erklärungen und Lernhinweise

▶1 Es wird eine unbestimmte (irgendeine) Person oder Sache erfragt oder, daher steht **what**.

▶2 Es wird eine bestimmte Person oder Sache aus einer Gruppe erfragt, daher steht **which** (z.B. in **which key is this one** wird nach einem bestimmten Schlüssel aus mehreren gefragt).

3 Setzen Sie **how** oder **what** ein.

1. How *is* ◀1 2. How *long* ◀2 3. How/what *was* ◀1 4. What/how *is* ◀1 5. How *much* ◀2 6. What *sort* ◀3 7. What/how about ◀5 8. How *does* ◀4 9. How *many* ◀2 10. How/what *was* ◀1 11. What/how *is* ◀1 12. How *old* ◀2 13. What *kind* ◀3 14. How *well* ◀2 15. How/what *is* ◀1 16. What *colour* ◀3 17. What *size* ◀3 18. How *could* ◀4 19. What ◀1 20. How *far* ◀2 21. How *much* ◀2 22. How *was* ◀1

Erklärungen und Lernhinweise

▶1 Das Pronomen bezieht sich auf **be**, daher steht **how** oder **what.** Es ist zu beachten, dass die Frage nach dem Befinden einer Person nur mit **how** gebildet werden kann (z.B. **How is your Uncle Edward** *wie geht es deinem Onkel Edward*).

▶2 Das Pronomen bezieht sich auf ein Adjektiv oder Adverb, daher steht **how**.

▶3 Das Pronomen bezieht sich auf ein Substantiv, daher steht **what**.

▶4 Das Pronomen bezieht sich auf ein Verb (nicht **to be**), daher steht **how**.

▶5 In der festen Redewendung **how/what about** (wie war's mit) sind beide Pronomen möglich.

4 Setzen Sie **when, where** oder **why** ein.

1. When ◀1 2. Why ◀2 3. Where ◀3/when ◀1 4. Why ◀2 5. When ◀1 6. When ◀1/where ◀3 7. Why ◀2 8. Why ◀2

Erklärungen und Lernhinweise

▶1 Es wird die Zeit erfragt, daher steht **when**.

▶2 Es wird nach dem Grund gefragt, daher steht **why**.

▶3 Es wird nach dem Ort gefragt, daher steht **where**.

Das Indefinitpronomen (The Indefinite Pronouns)

Some und any

1 Setzen Sie **some** oder **any** ein.

1. some ◀1 2. any ◀2 3. any ◀2 4. anything ◀2 5. any ◀2 6. any ◀2 7. some ◀1 8. any ◀2 9. Some ◀1 10. some ◀1 11. any ◀2 12. some ◀1 13. any ◀2 14. any ◀2 15. any ◀3 16. any ◀3 17. some ◀1 18. some ◀1 19. any ◀2 20. some ◀1 21. any ◀2 22. any ◀2 23. some ◀1 24. someone ◀1, anything ◀2 25. anyone ◀2 26. any ◀2 27. any ◀2 28. any ◀2 29. Some ◀1

Erklärungen und Lernhinweise

▶1 Der Satz ist bejaht, daher steht **some**. Dies gilt auch für die Zusammensetzungen mit **some** (**something, someone, somebody** etc.)

▶2 Der Satz ist verneint oder er ist ein Fragesatz oder Bedingungssatz (if-clause), daher steht **any**. Dies gilt auch für die Zusammensetzungen mit **any** (**anything, anyone, anybody** etc.)

▶3 **Hardly** (kaum) ist ein einschränkender Ausdruck, daher steht **any** auch im bejahten Satz.

2 Setzen Sie **some** oder **any** ein.

1. some ◀1 2. Any ◀2 3. some ◀3 4. some ◀4 5. some ◀4 6. someone ◀5 7. something ◀5 8. some ◀5 9. any ◀2 10. any ◀2 11. some ◀4 12. something ◀3 13. some ◀3 14. some ◀3 15. some ◀4 16. Any ◀2 17. any ◀2 18. some ◀5 19. any ◀2, any ◀2 20. some ◀3 21. some ◀3 22. Some ◀1 23. some ◀4 24. some ◀3 25. any ◀2

Erklärungen und Lernhinweise

▶1 Es wird die unbestimmte Anzahl (einige, manche) bezeichnet, daher steht **some** auch im verneinten Satz.

▶2 Es wird eine beliebige Person oder Sache (irgendjemand, -etwas) bezeichnet, daher steht **any** auch im bejahten Satz.

▶3 Es wird etwas tatsächlich Vorhandenes bezeichnet, daher steht **some** auch im verneinten Satz oder im Frage- oder Bedingungssatz (z.B. in ... **it might be a wiser decision not to make use of some of these machines** sind die Maschinen ja tatsächlich vorhanden).

▶4 Es wird eine höfliche Frage, auf die eine bejahte Antwort erwartet wird, gestellt, daher steht **some** auch im Fragesatz.

▶5 Es wird ein Wunsch ausgedrückt bzw. die gestellte Bedingung ist erfüllbar, daher steht **some** auch im Bedingungssatz.

Every und each

1 Setzen Sie **every** oder **each** ein.

1. each ◀1 2. every ◀2 3. each ◀1 4. Every ◀2 5. each ◀1 6. every ◀2 7. every ◀2 8. each ◀1 9. each ◀1, every ◀2 10. each ◀1 11. every ◀2 12. Every ◀2 13. Every ◀2 14. each ◀1, each ◀1 15. every ◀2 16. each ◀1 17. each ◀1, each ◀1 18. each ◀1 19. each ◀1 20. every ◀2 21. each ◀1, every ◀2

Erklärungen und Lernhinweise

▶1 Es ist jede einzelne Person oder Sache aus der Gruppe gemeint, daher steht **each** (z.B. in **Simon Atkinson had two banks with five thousand dollars in each account** ist jedes einzelne der Konten in den beiden Banken gemeint).

▶2 Es ist jede Person oder Sache ganz allgemein, nicht aus einer Gruppe gemeint, daher steht **every** (z.B. in **Do you have to get up early every day** ist jeder Tag ganz allgemein, nicht aus einer bestimmten Gruppe von Tagen gemeint).

All und whole

1 Setzen Sie **all** oder **the whole** oder **a whole** ein.

1. the whole ◀1 2. the whole ◀1 3. all ◀2 4. all ◀2 5. all ◀2 6. all ◀2 7. all ◀2 8. all/the whole ◀3 9. the whole ◀1/a whole ◀4 10. all ◀2 11. all ◀2 12. all ◀2 13. all ◀2 14. the whole ◀1 15. all ◀2 16. a whole ◀4 17. a whole ◀5 18. the whole ◀1 19. all/the whole ◀3 20. all/the whole ◀3 21. a whole ◀4 22. the whole ◀6 23. the whole ◀1

Erklärungen und Lernhinweise

Da beide Pronomen die Gesamtheit bezeichnen ist die Unterscheidung zwischen **all** und **the whole** häufig schwierig, es empfiehlt sich daher, wie hier dargestellt, zusätzliche Auswahlkriterien zu beachten.

▶1 Es ist eine bestimmte Sache gemeint, daher steht **the whole.**

▶2 Auf das Pronomen folgt eine Präposition (z.B. **about, over, by**) oder ein Demonstrativpronomen (z.B. **this**) oder ein Substantiv + Adjektiv (z.B. **day long**) oder der bestimmte Artikel, daher steht **all.**

▶3 Es ist das Ganze, die Gesamtheit als solche gemeint, in dieser Funktion sind **all** und **the whole** oft austauschbar. Dies ist häufig bei Zeitbestimmungen der Fall.

▶4 Es ist eine unbestimmte, irgendeine Sache gemeint, daher steht **a whole** (z.B. in **she said a whole lot more** ist **lot** die unbestimmte Sache (Menge), *sie sagte eine ganze Menge mehr*).

▶5 In bestimmten Redewendungen wie **as a whole** ist nur **whole** möglich.

▶6 Auf das Pronomen folgt eine Beifügung + **of**, daher steht **the whole.**

Much und many

1 Setzen Sie **much** oder **many** ein.

1. many ◀1 2. much ◀2 3. much ◀3 4. much ◀3 5. many ◀1 6. much ◀3 7. Many ◀1 8. Many ◀1, much ◀3 9. Much ◀3 10. many ◀1 11. much ◀3 12. much ◀2 13. many ◀1 14. much ◀3 15. many ◀1 16. much ◀3 17. many ◀1 18. Much ◀3 19. much ◀3 20. much ◀3 21. many ◀1 22. much ◀3 23. many ◀1 24. many ◀1 25. much ◀3

Erklärungen und Lernhinweise

▶1 Das Substantiv ist zählbar, daher steht **many**. Es ist zu beachten, dass das Substantiv auch fehlen kann, in diesem Fall steht **many** stellvertretend für das Substantiv (z.B. in **Although many pay lip service ...** bezeichnet **many** die vielen Personen, die Lippenbekenntnisse abgeben).

▶2 **Money** und **hair** sind zwar zählbar, werden jedoch trotzdem mit **much** verbunden, da die Gesamtheit und nicht jede Münze oder jedes einzelne Haar gemeint ist.

▶3 Das Substantiv ist nicht zählbar, daher steht **much**. Es ist zu beachten, dass das Substantiv auch fehlen kann, in diesem Fall steht **much** stellvertretend für das Substantiv (z.B. in **Much remains to be done**... bezeichnet **much** die Menge, die erledigt werden muss).

Little und few

1 Setzen Sie **little** oder **few** ein.

1. few ◀1 2. few ◀1 3. little ◀2 4. few ◀1 5. little ◀2 6. little ◀3 7. Few ◀1 8. few ◀1 9. little ◀3 10. little ◀3 11. few ◀1 12. few ◀1 13. few ◀1 14. little ◀3 15. few ◀1 16. little ◀3 17. few ◀1 18. little ◀3 19. little ◀3

Erklärungen und Lernhinweise

▶1 Das Substantiv ist zählbar, daher steht **few**. Es ist zu beachten, dass das Substantiv auch fehlen kann, in diesem Fall steht **few** stellvertretend für das Substantiv (z.B. in **... few still live a primitive life** bezeichnet **few** die Personen, die noch ein primitives Leben führen).

▶2 **Money** ist zwar zählbar, wird jedoch trotzdem mit **little** verbunden, da die Gesamtheit und nicht jede Münze gemeint ist. **Information** gehört zu den Substantiven, die nur im Singular vorkommen.

▶3 Das Substantiv ist nicht zählbar, daher steht **little**. Es ist zu beachten, dass das Substantiv auch fehlen kann, in diesem Fall steht **little** stellvertretend für das Substantiv.

No, none und nobody

1 Setzen Sie **no, none** oder **nobody** ein.

1. none ◀1 2. no ◀2 3. none ◀1 4. nobody ◀3 5. no, no ◀2 6. Nobody ◀3 7. Nobody ◀3 8. none ◀1 9. no ◀2 10. Nobody ◀3 11. Nobody ◀3 12. no ◀2 13. none ◀1 14. no ◀2 15. none ◀1 16. no, no ◀2 17. no ◀2 18. none ◀1 19. None ◀1 20. nobody ◀3 21. nobody ◀3

Erklärungen und Lernhinweise

▶1 Es ist jede einzelne Person oder Sache aus der Gruppe von mehr als zweien gemeint, daher steht **none** (keiner). **None** steht nicht wie **no** vor einem Substantiv.

▶2 Auf das Pronomen folgt das Substantiv, daher steht **no** (kein).

▶3 Es wird eine Person bezeichnet, daher steht **nobody** (niemand).

Either und neither

1 Setzen Sie **either** oder **neither** ein.

1. Neither ◀1 2. Either ◀2 3. Either ◀2 4. neither ◀1 5. Neither ◀1 6. either ◀2 7. Neither ◀3 8. Neither ◀3 9. either ◀4 10. either ◀2 11. either ◀4 12. either, either ◀2 13. either ◀2 14. either ◀5 15. neither ◀3 16. either ◀2 17. neither ◀3 18. either ◀2 19. either ◀5 20. either ◀5 21. either ◀2

Erklärungen und Lernhinweise

▶1 Zum Ausdruck von *auch nicht* steht **neither**, wenn das folgende Verb bejaht ist.

▶2 Es ist entweder die eine Person oder Sache oder die andere gemeint, daher steht **either**. Zwischen beiden Ausdrücken steht **or**.

▶3 Es ist weder die eine Person oder Sache noch die andere gemeint (keiner von beiden), daher steht **neither**.

▶4 Zum Ausdruck von *auch nicht* steht **either**, wenn das vorausgehende Verb verneint ist.

▶5 Es sind beide Seiten, sowohl die eine als auch die andere, gleichgültig welche gemeint, daher steht **either** (z.B. in **Either side may object to ...** kann sowohl die eine als auch die andere der beiden Seiten Einwände erheben).

Die Präposition (The Preposition)

1 Setzen Sie die richtige Präposition ein.

1. **at;** in ◀1 2. **at**; um ◀2 3. **at/after/before**; zum/nach/vor ◀2 4. **in**; in ◀2 5. **in/out**; herein/heraus ◀1 6. **from**; von 7. **in**; in ◀1 8. **into**; in (hinein) ◀1 9. **with**; mit ◀3 10. **on**; am ◀2 11. **on**; auf ◀1 12. **for**; für ◀4 13. **up**; hinauf ◀1 14. **down**; hinunter ◀1 15. **before/after;** vor/nach ◀2 16. **behind/before/to**; hinter/vor/ bei ◀1

Erklärungen und Lernhinweise

▶1 Es wird der Ort bezeichnet. In räumlicher Bedeutung können verwendet werden: **at, out, from, in, into, on, up, down behind**.

▶2 Es wird die Zeit bezeichnet. In zeitlicher Bedeutung können verwendet werden: **at** (Zeitpunkt), **after, in, on, before.**

▶3 Es wird die Art und Weise, das Mittel bezeichnet. In diesem Zusammenhang können verwendet werden: **with**

▶4 Zum Ausdruck, dass für jemanden etwas getan wird, steht **for**.

Für die Verwendung der Präpositionen gibt es keine allgemein gültigen Regeln. In dieser Übung sind einige wichtige Präpositionen und deren wichtigste Verwendung dargestellt.

2 Setzen Sie die richtige Präposition nach den folgenden Verben ein.

1. agree **with;** Ich *stimme* dir nicht *zu.* ◀1 2. **on;** Bob und Mary können sich niemals *über* irgendetwas *einigen.* ◀1 3. ask **for;** Der Fahrer hielt an und *fragte nach* dem Weg. ◀1 4. believed **in;** Sein Sohn *glaubte an* ihn. ◀1 5. call **for;** Unmöglich *nach* Hilfe zu *rufen.* ◀1 6. **congratulated on;** Ihnen wurde *zu* ihrem Erfolg *gratuliert.* ◀1 7. look **after;** Du solltest dich *um* deinen kleinen Bruder *kümmern.* ◀1 8. looking **for;** Wo*nach suchst* du? ◀1 9. put **in;** Das ist einfach, *bemerkte* Harry. ◀1 10. Put **up;** Hände *hoch*! ◀1 11. put **up;** Ich werde mich einfach da*mit abfinden* müssen. ◀1 12. put **on;** Ich *ziehe/zog* meine Socken *an* ◀1 13. put **off;** Wir müssen den Urlaub *verschieben.* ◀1 14. Send **for;** *Schicke nach* dem Arzt. ◀1 15. Speak **up;** Sprich lauter! ◀1 16. succeeded **in;** Ich bestand meine Prüfung (es *gelang* mir). ◀1 17. wait **for;** Er *wartete* nicht *auf* eine Antwort. ◀1 18. account **for;** Du wirst diesen Fehler *erklären* müssen. ◀1 19. account **of;** Sein Alter muss *berücksichtigt* werden. ◀1 20. burst **into;** Die Kinder *brachen/brechen* alle in Gelächter *aus.* ◀1 21. burst **out;** Mac und Henry *brechen/brachen* in Gelächter *aus.* ◀1 22. die **of;** Wor*an starb* er? ◀1 23. gave **in;** Sie *gab* lächelnd *nach.* ◀1 24. gave **up;** Wir *gaben* es *auf* ihn aufzuziehen. ◀1 25. live **on;** Wo*von lebten* die Bischöfe und Barone? ◀1 26. arrived **at;** Man *kam* zufällig *auf* die Lösung. ◀1 27. bearing **with;** Danke, dass Sie so *geduldig mit* uns sind. ◀1 28. discriminated **against;** Sie wurden bei der Arbeit nicht *diskriminiert.* ◀1 29. mock **at;** Wenn du nur gehört hättest, wie er sich *über* dich *lustig gemacht hat*! ◀1 30. wondered **at;** Dar*über* muss man *sich* nicht *wundern.* ◀1

Erklärungen und Lernhinweise

Die Präpositionen können mit Verben verbunden werden. Es gibt keine allgemein gültigen Regeln dafür, welche Präposition beim Verb steht, es empfiehlt sich daher, jedes Verb mit seinen möglichen Präpositionen zu lernen. Zum besseren Verständnis ist die deutsche Übersetzung angegeben.

3 Setzen Sie die richtigen Präpositionen nach den folgenden Substantiven ein.

1. difference **in;** Beachte den *Unterschied in* der Bedeutung. 2. difficulty **in;** Wir hatten große *Schwierigkeiten bei* der Übersetzung des Textes. ◀ 3. doubt **about;** Es gibt *keinen Zweifel darüber.* ◀ 4. impression **on;** Es machte keinen großen *Eindruck auf* sie. ◀ 5. interest **in;** Er hat keinerlei *Interesse am* Lesen. ◀ 6. opinion **on/about;** Wie ist deine *Meinung zu* diesen Fragen? ◀ 7. opportunity **of;** Er hatte keine *Gelegenheit* mit ihm *zu* sprechen. ◀ 8. possibility **of;** Sie sprachen nicht über die *Möglichkeit zu* heiraten. ◀ 9. chance **of;** Die *Chance* ihn *zu* treffen, war gering. ◀ 10. chances **for;** Meine *Chancen* befördert *zu* werden sind nicht so berauschend. ◀ 11. **congratulations on;** Meine *Gratulation zu* ihrer Rehabilitation. ◀ 12. fear **of;** Sie sagte nichts aus Angst gefeuert zu werden. ◀ 13. faith **in;** Der *Glaube* der ersten Amerikaner *an* die Verfassung war groß. ◀ 14. improvement **in;** Die Verbesserung ihres Äußeren war verblüffend. ◀ 15. loss **for;** ich war *um* eine Antwort *verlegen.* ◀ 16. proof **against;** Alter *schützt vor* Torheit nicht. ◀

Erklärungen und Lernhinweise

Die Präpositionen können mit Substantiven verbunden werden. Es gibt keine allgemein gültigen Regeln, welche Präposition beim Substantiv stehen kann, es empfiehlt sich daher, jedes Substantiv mit seinen möglichen Präpositionen zu lernen. Zum besseren Verständnis ist die deutsche Übersetzung angegeben.

4 Setzen Sie die richtige Präposition nach den folgenden Adjektiven ein.

1. angry **with;** Bob's Mutter ist *böse auf* ihn. ◀ 2. **angry over/about;** Er wird *über* nichts *ärgerlich.* ◀ 3. concerned **with;** Wir sind nicht direkt *davon betroffen.* ◀ 4. crazy **with;** Er war *verrückt vor* Durst. ◀ 5. crazy **for;** Ich war *verrückt nach* einem guten Agatha Christie Krimi oder etwas ähnlichem. ◀ 6. delighted **with;** Als ich diese Arbeit beendet hatte, war ich sehr *damit zufrieden.* ◀ 7. different **from;** Schottische Städte sehen ganz *anders* aus *als* Englische. ◀ 8. good **at;** Kannst du *gut* Pferde zeichnen. ◀ 9. interested **in;** Es wird erwartet, dass Sie sich *für* die Ihnen angebotene Arbeit *interessieren.* ◀ 10. late **for;** Das Schlimmste was ich mir vorstellen kann, ist zu *spät zur* Schule zu kommen. ◀ 11. prepared **for;** Wir sind *auf* das Schlimmste *gefasst.* ◀ 12. proud **of;** Ich bin *stolz auf* dich. ◀ 13. sorry **for;** Ich habe *Mitleid mit* ihr. ◀ 14. surprised **at;** Ich war *über* die Nachricht *überrascht.* ◀ 15. ashamed **of;** Er *schämte sich* ein bisschen *über* sich und setzte sich am Kopfende des Bettes auf. ◀ 16. bored **with;** Simon *war* es *satt* allein zu leben. ◀ 17. anxious **for;** Harry's Eltern sind *darauf bedacht,* dass er eine gute Ausbildung erhält. ◀ 18. equal **in;** Alle Menschen sind frei geboren und haben die gleiche Würde und die gleichen Rechten. ◀

Erklärungen und Lernhinweise

Die Präpositionen können mit Adjektiven verbunden werden. Es gibt keine allgemein gültigen Regeln, welche Präposition beim Adjektiv stehen kann, es empfiehlt sich daher, jedes Adjektiv mit seinen möglichen Präpositionen zu lernen. Zum besseren Verständnis ist die deutsche Übersetzung angegeben.

Die Wortstellung (The Word Order)

1 Setzen Sie die beiden Objekte in Klammern in die richtige Position.

1. *you* some nosedrops ◀1 2. *him* a form ◀1 3. *her* the flag ◀1 4. *her sister*, the sugar ◀1 5. *him* a shell ◀1 6. *him* the passport ◀1 7. *him* the leisure ◀1 8. *him* a long, smiling answer ◀1 9. *him* the number of his reserved room, *a bellboy* the key ◀1 10. *him* the higher honour ◀1 11. *him* the sheet ◀1 12. *me* some money ◀1 13. *me*, some ship models ◀1 14. *me* all kinds of things ◀1 15. *us* these blessings ◀1

Erklärungen und Lernhinweise

▶1 Das indirekte Objekt (meist eine Person), hier kursiv gedruckt steht vor dem direkten Objekt (meist eine Sache), nicht kursiv gedruckt.

2 Setzen Sie die beiden Objekte in Klammern in die korrekte Position und fügen Sie **to** ein wo nötig.

1. it to *me* ◀1 2. *the cat* some milk/some milk to *the cat* ◀2 3. *the Maxwell family* a postcard/a postcard to *the Maxwell family* ◀2 4. it to *me* ◀1 5. the name to *himself* ◀3 6. *me* her photo ◀2, it to *your brother* ◀1, it to *me* ◀1 7. it to *me* ◀1 8. it to *her* ◀1 9. seats to the parties ◀3 10. it to *him* ◀1 11. money to the universities ◀3 12. it to *me* ◀1 13. it to *me* ◀1 14. it to *her* ◀1 15. it to *me* ◀1 16. it to *him* ◀1

Erklärungen und Lernhinweise

▶1 Das direkte Objekt ist **it** bzw. **them**, daher tritt es vor das indirekte Objekt (kursiv gedruckt).

▶2 Das indirekte Objekt (meist eine Person, Lebewesen), hier kursiv gedruckt steht in der Regel vor dem direkten Objekt (meist eine Sache), nicht kursiv gedruckt, daher entfällt **to**.
Das indirekte Objekt kann nach dem direkten Objekt stehen, wenn es besonders betont wird oder wenn es länger ist als das direkte Objekt, dann wird **to** benötigt.

▶3 Das indirekte Objekt ist besonders betont bzw. ist länger als das direkte Objekt, daher tritt es mit **to** hinter das direkte Objekt.

3 Setzen Sie die Verben vor das Subjekt und schreiben Sie die Sätze neu.

1. There is **my mother**, he called out. ◀1 2. First went **gentlemen, barons, earls, knights of the Garter**, all richly dressed and bareheaded. ◀1 3. Next came **the Queen**, in the 65th year of her age, very majestic. ◀1 4. Then came **the day** when Sitting Bull, the chief of the Sioux, lay in his wigwam dying. ◀1 5. Then comes **the keynote speech**. ◀1 6. There were **commercial interests** involved. ◀1 7. There were **people** sitting all over the stone-flagged floor. ◀1

Erklärungen und Lernhinweise

▶1 Das Subjekt (fett gedruckt) tritt hinter das Verb (Inversion des Subjekts). Dies ist besonders nach **there, first, second** etc., **next, then** der Fall.

Kurzfragen (Question Tags)

1 Setzen Sie den richtigen question tag ein.

1. does he ◄1 2. did he ◄1 3. was he ◄2 4. will he ◄2 5. isn't he ◄3 6. can I ◄2, didn't we ◄4 7. do I ◄1 8. didn't I ◄4 9. will I ◄2 10. aren't I ◄5 11. does he ◄1 12. aren't I ◄5 13. couldn't they ◄6 14. don't they ◄4 15. did they ◄1 16. do they ◄1 17. didn't he ◄4 18. doesn't he ◄4 19. don't you ◄4 20. haven't they ◄3 21. hasn't he ◄7 22. does he ◄1 23. has he ◄7 24. isn't he ◄7 25. is he ◄7 26. hadn't we ◄3 27. have we ◄2 28. won't we ◄3 29. won't we ◄3 30. are we ◄7 31. aren't we ◄3 32. can't you ◄3 33. do you ◄1 34. didn't you ◄4 35. don't you ◄4 36. weren't you ◄7 37. were you ◄7 38. were you ◄2 39. won't you ◄3 40. aren't you ◄3 41. won't you ◄8 42. shall we ◄8 43. shall we ◄8

Erklärungen und Lernhinweise

▶1 Der Vordersatz ist verneint, daher ist der question tag bejaht. Das Verb des Vordersatzes ist ein Vollverb, es wird daher durch **do** wieder aufgenommen. **Do** steht in der gleichen Zeit wie das Vollverb, d.h. steht dieses z.B. im past tense wird **did** verwendet. Das Subjekt tritt hinter **do.** Ist das Subjekt kein Pronomen (z.B. **your uncle**) wird es durch das entsprechende Personalpronomen wieder aufgenommen (z.B. **he**).

▶2 Der Vordersatz ist verneint, daher ist der question tag bejaht. Das Verb des Vordersatzes enthält ein Hilfs- oder Modalverb, daher wird dieses wieder aufgenommen, das Subjekt tritt hinter das Hilfsverb. Ist das Subjekt kein Pronomen (z.B. **your uncle**) wird es durch das entsprechende Personalpronomen wieder aufgenommen (z.B. **he**).

▶3 Der Vordersatz ist bejaht, daher ist der question tag verneint. Das Verb des Vordersatzes enthält ein Hilfs- oder Modalverb, daher wird dieses wieder aufgenommen und zwar verneint. Es ist zu beachten, dass das verneinte Verb im question tag immer in der Kurzform **n't** steht. Das Subjekt tritt hinter das Hilfsverb. Ist das Subjekt kein Pronomen (z.B. **your uncle**) wird es durch das entsprechende Personalpronomen wieder aufgenommen (z.B. **he**).

▶4 Der Vordersatz ist bejaht, daher ist der question tag verneint. Das Verb des Vordersatzes ist ein Vollverb, es wird daher durch verneintes **do** wieder aufgenommen**. Do** steht in der gleichen Zeit wie das Vollverb, d.h. steht dieses z.B. im past tense wird **didn't** verwendet. Das Subjekt tritt hinter **do.** Ist das Subjekt kein Pronomen (z.B. **your uncle**) wird es durch das entsprechende Personalpronomen wieder aufgenommen (z.B. **he**).

▶5 Der verneinte question tag von **I am** lautet **aren't I.**

▶6 Das Subjekt ist ein Indefinitpronomen, es wird daher durch ein Personalpronomen wie **they** ersetzt.

▶7 **Have** ist Vollverb, es wird dennoch nicht durch **to do** wieder aufgenommen. Dies gilt auch für **be**.

▶8 Der Imperativ wird durch **will** wieder aufgenommen, dabei steht **will** beim verneinten Imperativ und **won't** beim bejahten Imperativ. Wird der Imperativ durch **let's** ausgedrückt, steht **shall.**